9 · 25 · 2013

For Jishō
    In the Spirit and
Light of Ryōkan

            Eido Frances Carney

KAKURENBO

Or the Whereabouts
of Zen Priest Ryokan

by

Eido Frances Carney
with translations by Nobuyuki Yuasa

Temple Ground Press
3248 39th Way NE
Olympia, WA 98506

Cover design and interior by Fletcher Ward. Set in Adobe Garamond Pro 8/18.

ISBN 978-0985565114

Library of Congress Control Number: 2013948691

Temple Ground Press, Olympia, WA

Dedicated to

my teacher
Niho Tetsumei Roshi

and

with gratitude to

Professor Nobuyuki Yuasa
for translations of Ryokan's poetry

Table of Contents

Special Acknowledgement

Professor Nobuyuki Yuasa was professor of English at Hiroshima University until he retired in 1995. He is an eminent translator of the works of Basho and Ryokan, and has received awards for his translation of John Donne's poetry into Japanese.

Professor Yuasa so graciously allowed me to use as many of the poems in *The Zen Poems of Ryokan* as I wished, but it is with the generosity of Princeton University Press that we have such permission. Professor Yuasa told me by telephone that of all the translations he has made in his lifetime, he worked the hardest and was the most proud of the Ryokan poems. Of all the collections we have in English, Professor Yuasa has done the lion's share, translating the very difficult Chinese poems and thereby giving us the more serious, complex, and thoughtful Ryokan. What I appreciate in Professor Yuasa's translations is his bountiful use of vowels that create the music of the English language. I have to think that this comes from Professor Yuasa's original Japanese language which is vowel based, but his superb command of English renders the poems in their abiding sensibility of wisdom, felt humanity and elegance of expression. From Professor Yuasa's selections from the approximately 1800 poems that Ryokan wrote in his lifetime, we realize the nature of Ryokan's daily life, his difficulties, his humanness, his celebrations, his profound spirituality, and the ultimate grace and dignity of his chosen life as priest and poet. Much of my knowledge and insight into Ryokan's life is dependent upon Professor Yuasa's translations and I bow in deepest gratitude for this gift of the Ryokan poems which he made possible for us to read in English. It is only unfortunate that the original press run of *The Zen Poems of Ryokan* was so small that the book has nearly disappeared from circulation. If a copy can be found it is quite costly for many people who love Ryokan. The poems in this book are but a taste of this full body of work.

Acknowledgements

Gratitude is extended to Princeton University Press for the generous permission to reprint the translation of several of Ryokan's poems by Nobuyuki Yuasa from *The Zen Poems of Ryokan*, Princeton, NJ: Princeton University Press, 1981.

We never do anything alone including living the solitary path; there are always others supporting our lives and without whom we could not accomplish very much. My mother, Edith Carney, did not live to see any book realized as a result of my teaching and training in Japan and she was greatly disappointed; nevertheless, she prodded me to not forget to write one day.

I want to thank Niho Tetsumei Roshi and his entire family who opened wide the temple door at Entsuji, and to Watanabe Miyoko Sensei who took me right up to the temple gate.

The following people in Japan also contributed to my health and welfare on the Ryokan pathway: my brush teacher Tokunaga Shoen Sensei; translator for Niho Roshi Miyake Masahiro; colleagues Meredith Engel and Lyn Swierski; Arimichi Kazue Sensei; and the many members of the Entsuji Zazenkai. People in the United States helped me in myriad ways: Dharma heir Jikyo C.J. Wolfer, and novice priests Robert Ryozan Witzl and Allyson Jozen Essen took the helm to give me time to complete this work. Others include: my sister Margaret Steele who took care of my home base, my offspring Laureen, Patrick and Ellen O'Connell, Michael Long, Mickey Olson, June McAfee, Eva Neske, and the many Sangha members of Olympia Zen Center who have generously contributed Dana to my welfare, for work on the grounds to support and beautify our temple, and for the persistence of practice over the years in Olympia.

I express gratitude to Professor Donovan Johnson for manuscript assistance and close reading that gave me new eyes for being present with Ryokan. General reading and valuable suggestions for the manuscript came from Linda Strever, Allyson Jozen Essen, and early on Jeanne Lohmann and Kitty Carlsen for which I am immensely grateful. Any misunderstandings, errors, distortions or inaccuracies in the text or concerning Ryokan's life are purely my own.

The treasure of the book is truly in the translations of Professor Nobuyuki Yuasa who expressed immediate enthusiasm for the use of his work. The book would not be the same without the poems to demonstrate the brilliant complexity of Ryokan and to give us the music and wisdom of his mind.

Very special thanks to Fletcher Ward of Straight Light Studio who designed the book cover and interior. Fletcher took the cover photo during a trip to Ryokan Country in Japan. Various chapter photographs are described and credited in the appendices.

Thank you to author Steven Pressfield for his lifelong teachings on resistance.

Deepest gratitude to those who generously contributed to the building of Gogo-an at Olympia Zen Center in 2006-07. Primarily, Fletcher Ward's mother, Winona Ward, now deceased, was the propelling force and main donor who saw the idea of building Gogo-an as a memorial to her late husband Hugh Ward. Judy Fleming of Olympia designed and built the replica from photographs taken in Japan. Robert Fischer volunteered his vacation to assist at laying in the foundation. Contributors included Niho Tetsumei Roshi and Mrs. Kimiko Niho and Family, The Freas Foundation, Roger Cummings in Memory of Kosho Michael Jay Buckley, Francesca Ritson and Brian Williams in Memory of Caterina Edda Elena Martinez Ritson, Doug and Ann Hutcheson Charitable Fund, Mugaku Kataoka Sensei, Niho Seiju Sensei, Tokunaga Shoen Sensei, Tokunaga Rikio Sensei, Miyake Masahiro, Watanabe Shinpei Sensei, Hashimoto Keiko, Furusawa Yoko, Watanabe Miyoko, Arimichi Kazue, Entsuji Zazenkai Members, Jamini Davies, Bob Fischer, Kate Crowe, Ken Peterson, Dick and Viola Mendenhall, Catherine and Richard Williams, Christine Robbins, Maggie Chula, Barbara Courtney, Betsy Dickes, Scott Whitney, Bronwyn Vincent, Kellie Patton, Judith Bouffiou, Bill Broderick, Taylor Pittman, Reiko Suzuki, Enji Boissevain, Susan McRae, Fumiko Kimura, Jeanne Lohmann, Lynn Meyer, and Eido Frances Carney. Others who assisted with a variety of tasks included Jikyo C.J. Wolfer who nourished the workers every day. And Mickey Olson, Diane Miller, Steve Senna, Robert Ryozan Witzl, Pat Labine, Jane Skinner, Donald Bailly, Michael Podlin, John Robinson, Michael McDonald, Roger Barkley, Pete Snell, Brian Baker, Brad Gibson, Randal Johnson. Gratitude to all whose merit shall not be slight, and I bow with deepest apologies to anyone whose name may have inadvertently been overlooked.

Numerous teachers and bodhisattvas have manifested in my life with new teachers appearing every day. As with all of life, some lessons are straightforward, simple and easy to digest. Others come as if plowing into a wall with a thud and a roar. This is the nature of life and of the bodhisattva path that Ryokan knew well and celebrated for all its challenges and difficulties. I thank each teacher for the billions of moments that have made up this life, and for the teachers who have faced me in the direct honesty of the Dharma. I offer Nine Bows, these few thoughts and this brief journey with Ryokan.

Prelude

Prelude

The little girl leaned her face into her bent arm and pressed against a tree counting to fifty. "*Ichi, ni, san, shi, go...*" The children and Ryokan were playing *Kakurenbo*, Hide-and-Go-Seek, and their feet sprung into action as they rushed to find a hideout not far from home base. Dappled sunlight fell on Ryokan with his robes flying and his lanky legs seeming to dance in crazy steps, undecided as to where to hide. Suddenly, he dashed along the road and entered an old squeaky gate that led to a little storage barn beside a house half a street away where an old lady lived at the edge of the woods. He jumped behind some sheaves of grain stalks stacked in a corner, then crouched down enjoying the sweet smell and burying himself in the softness of the grassy bundles against his back. He fell into a comfortable position to wait for the children to find him.

The late, warm afternoon sun angled across the barn floor. Playful voices floated in the distance as the children squealed when they were discovered in their hideouts one by one. Enjoying the sweet moment, his thoughts becoming dreamy, Ryokan quietly meandered into a deep sleep. The children, traveling now in a small pack, their dark heads bobbing among the trees, looked everywhere and could not discover Ryokan's hiding place. They got a little bored too, "He's making it too hard," said one, and another said, "Oh, that nutty Ryokan, he probably went home and forgot all about us." They were ready to give up the search and go on to a different game when supper hour arrived and their mothers called them home. Ryokan forgotten, they cheerfully skipped past the gate where Ryokan hid in the barn, and ran home to their families.

When night came and the moon was high, the old woman lit a torch and went out to the barn for some grains. When she heard Ryokan's deep snoring, she imagined a burglar or even a wild animal had crept into the barn, and she fell back screaming with her shawl thrown aside and her pitchfork ready.

"Shhh, Shhhh." Ryokan said as he roused himself. "Quiet down, quiet down, don't let the children hear."

"Oh Ryokan, it's you." she answered, "You completely startled me."

"Be quiet, you'll give away my hideout." Ryokan got to his feet covered in grain dust and with rice sprigs clinging to his robe.

"Ryokan, what are you thinking? The children have all gone home to bed." She pointed though the doorway to the sky where a nearly full moon threw a mellow glow on the creaky floor.

Ryokan stood up and looked around. "Oh my goodness, oh my goodness," he said scratching his head. "I must have fallen asleep and forgotten all about Kakurenbo." He burst out laughing at himself, and the old woman laughed too.

Kakurenbo, Hide-and-Go-Seek, was Ryokan's favorite childhood game and serves as a metaphor for his life, and conceivably for all our lives: entering the gate and hiding, then coming out through the gate into moonlight, as it were, we move in and out of experiences trying to find ourselves, to find one another, as we thread in and out of awareness and states of realization. All of this seems to begin with the innocent game of peek-a-boo. What is it that fascinates babies, makes them laugh, and holds their attention? What mythic game do we play in the search for the Self that begins in the cradle? Now you see me; now you don't. Look, I'm here; no, I'm over here. What are we getting ready for in such play? We play along, we listen and learn, coming again and again to new hideouts, new games, new gates. Our parents begin this game, teaching us how to hide, yet the important point for the baby is that at the conclusion of the game, the parent is found, is visible to the child so that the child is reassured.

This is the dynamic in the search for Ryokan except that we can't locate him even when he comes into the light. Not much about him sticks for very long except a collective wisdom that begins to seep into the pores as we spend time with his teaching. Whatever hideouts we find ourselves in, we may feel Ryokan rustle the grains like falling stardust. He never fails to shower the moment with quiet wisdom, and then he disappears in the moonlight, a master of the game.

The story of Ryokan (1758-1831), the beloved priest, poet, and calligrapher of Japan is sometimes embellished in folklore and myth, and sometimes is too sparse and lacking in detail to satisfy our wish for substantive information about his life. Much remains hidden that we just don't know. Ryokan was not concerned about his own fame and whether or not his life story would resonate through history. He had no stomach for celebrity. It bemused him to think that his calligraphy had gained enough notoriety that all the local people wanted were his works of calligraphy. He had no plan to publish his poems, to promote himself in any way or to encourage popularized stories detailing his uniqueness. He simply continued to live day by day, not as a unique figure, but as someone authentic to his vow, living the Dharma somewhat hidden away as a hermit priest. There's not much to tell in his daily life, no drama to speak of as he climbed up and down the slope of his mountain refuge bearing the cold in winter and enduring the mosquitos in summer.

Yet nearly 200 years after his death, Ryokan is known globally and we hold him in high esteem. Our wish to know him might suggest our hunger in these difficult times to touch a rare sainted life that is unabashedly simple. Perhaps we long to live fully in the courageous way that Ryokan did, to help us withstand with some grace the frictions and challenges that beset us. Ryokan is like each of us, standing in the mirror and facing those hard questions that life presents. How do we fully live our Buddhist values? How do we live the First Precept, Not Killing Life, in this age of chemistry, science, nuclear war, technology, self-comfort, and complacency? How do we contend with the mesmerizing influence of technology? How do we have the courage to make choices that are uncomfortable and unpopular? How do we save the world and at the same time honor our obligations? How do we go beyond the deceptions and dishonesties of our culture? I don't believe for a moment that simply looking at Ryokan's life can answer these monumental questions, but perhaps because his life is at such an extreme from our own, his life causes us to ask questions that are about a larger world and must be asked even if they can never be answered. As a practicing Buddhist, Ryokan followed the Four Noble Truths and lived the Buddha's prescription to acknowledge suffering, see its cause, and follow the way to overcome it. Having that prescription before us is still not enough to tame the poisons that cause suffering; the prescription has to be chewed up and swallowed and put into practice. Even after some of us do that, there will still be suffering. Ryokan himself said that no matter how hard he tried, he could not stop suffering in the world; yet he lived in the best way he could as a true mendicant of the Buddha's way. The Bodhisattva continues to try even when it seems impossible.

A civilized society does not run from itself, but addresses the most compelling and difficult questions at stake for its own progress. Most of the questions we ought ask can only be worked with as we stumble forward in the world we have created, aiming to alleviate suffering and develop a healthier future for all sentient beings. The questions teach us and help us toward a deeper look at how and what we are doing in this complex world. With incredibly hard work we might realize the way to ease suffering. Ryokan and the life he chose is a silent presence, a spirit of wisdom, as we bear witness to this surging life and try to propitiate the woes of existence.

Ryokan's influence has touched me and my choices about how I shall live. That influence began with Zen practice in 1971 with a teacher, Kobun Chino Otogawa Roshi, who had come from the area of Niigata and the town of Kamo-shi, not far from Gogo-an, Ryokan san's mountain hut. Kobun had come to America to work with Suzuki Shunryu Roshi to help establish the first Soto Zen Monastery in America. When Suzuki Roshi died, Kobun Roshi was invited to lead the Sangha at Haiku Zendo in Los Altos, where Suzuki Roshi had delivered his famous talks that are preserved in *Zen Mind, Beginner's Mind*. Kobun Roshi told occasional stories of Ryokan over the course of his fifteen or so years at Haiku Zendo that opened the poetic heart and spirit of Zen practice. John Stevens' translation of Ryokan's poetry, *One Robe, One Bowl* had a decided impact on many of us who carried its well-worn pages around in our back pockets. The texture of Ryokan's life challenged us to look at and think about troubling aspects of our own culture: the pursuit of financial success at the sacrifice of the environment, the promotion of corporate growth at the expense of creativity, the fostering of aggressive behaviors in its expression, the exaltation of self-indulgence as a virtue, and the spread of egotistical individuality as a central mantra. Yes, the American culture also demonstrates idealism and heroism in a way that only America can, but the condition of the earth today promoted by the Western lifestyle and culture, our greed, anger, and ignorance that continues war and oppression speaks for how we have lived. The example of Ryokan's life offers a profound contrast.

Nearly twenty years after I began Zen practice, my interest in the life of Ryokan led me to walk into Entsuji garden, in Kurashiki, Okayama Prefecture (about halfway between Kyoto and Hiroshima) with my friend and Japanese teacher Miyoko Watanabe. I had gone to Japan to teach at a women's university and now I stood in a temple garden on a sunny afternoon. I cannot say what led the abbot, Niho Tetsumei Roshi, to step outside the door and invite us in. But he did. I was in the garden and he opened the door. I cannot say what forces circling at Entsuji invited me to practice, directed me to study, or permitted me to stay. One feels completely unworthy in the shadow of this temple's history, and at the same time, one is swept into it because the great equalizer of practice reveals that there is no one who is absent from the Buddha. It would be a grave life mistake to refuse such an invitation.

The influence and draw of the Zen hermit poet began much earlier, but my journey and conversation continue to unfold around the presence and teaching of Ryokan. In his lifetime, Ryokan enjoyed conversation with people. Occasionally someone would make the long trek up to his mountain hut Gogo-an and stay with him for a cup of tea. When he'd hike into town, he'd stop and converse by the roadside, or he'd pause for a game of *Go*. In these exchanges, he transmitted a sense of fellowship that gave light and inspiration to everyone he met. At the same time, Ryokan stands in the shadows because he never preached or offered himself in a public way. He simply encountered people and shared what their lives were in the simplicity and vitality of the moment.

Today, the men and women of the Zazenkai of Entsuji, the community of meditators, carry on the conversation with and about Ryokan and the tradition of meditation practice. They continue to bring honor to Ryokan's name. Every week without fail, they rise at dawn, tired after a long week in the workplace, to sit Zazen with Niho Roshi in the Zendo at Entsuji. They are simple and pure people from the surrounding area. There is no one famous, no one puffed up or arrogant. No one is watching and they are not aggressive or chasing after enlightenment. They have chosen to take up this way of Zazen, meditation practice, transmitted by Dogen Zenji, that Ryokan chose early in his life. When the Zazenkai friends come together for fellowship, they are as plain and comfortable as our own friends, never boastful and always kind. The contrast of this from the flurry and drive of my own culture and the city culture of Japan balances the mind and expands the heart.

At Entsuji, the presence of Ryokan shines out like a glowing fire in January and he is visible in numerous works of art and material evidence. *Hannya Shingyo*, The Heart Sutra, in his own arresting, childlike style hangs above the entry to the Buddha Hall. In the small museum beside the Zendo, some of Ryokan's calligraphies reveal the lean, dancing lines of script that cannot be imitated. Ryokan's true, life treasure, a declaration of mastery of Zen from his teacher, hangs silently on the wall as if suspended in time and space. Ryokan-do, the extant, thatch-roofed building where Ryokan lived with his brother priests, carries a special look and atmosphere that reminds us of him and his training at that temple. What is it—a forlornness, an utter simplicity and modesty of style, a naturalness of design, an unselfconscious embracing of poverty, a contented acceptance of non ownership of things, a promise to live secluded from fame and acknowl-edgement, a vow to live a life on the path of virtue? Perhaps it is all of these.

Ryokan is not dead just as Shakyamuni Buddha, Dogen Zenji, and the long lineage of Zen practitioners are not dead. Of course, the body is no longer visible, but the vow to live life in Zen practice was so strong that today we continue to be influenced by their lives. We take up our practice in their shadow, in their deepest intentions to become the heart- mind of the Buddha. We stand on their shoulders and step out moment by moment into a space we call the future.

Because Ryokan comes alive in my own life, because his voice sings so powerfully in my lineage, because my living teacher Niho Tetsumei Roshi is abbot of Entsuji, Ryokan's training temple, because Ryokan's life shows us how to live, because his poetry touches us so closely, because in him I find solace and acceptance, because he holds no artifice, I can approach him and speak with him and take him as teacher. It may be that I come toward Ryokan because I am in dire need of his influence and need him the most. I am surely the least like him and could never live up to the virtues that he breathed. This should not stop me, or anyone, from drawing near to his teachings so that we can strive, from whatever starting place we begin, to be better persons through that proximity. But I am no expert in the subject of Ryokan, I don't own or claim him for myself, and the Ryokan I sometimes fathom may not be the Ryokan that others see. I cannot read Japanese to gain insight from his many biographical commentators, cannot read his poetry, letters, or essays, or even what the Japanese critics say about his poetry. I tiptoe on the outskirts and live intuitively around him. Any discussion of Ryokan comes up against the cultural differences between Japan and America and between the eighteenth and the twenty-first century. How can we possibly talk about Ryokan from the American cultural perspective? How can we take his lifestyle and apply it to America? What possible meaning could Ryokan's monastic life have for us in America? How can we see the deep meanings of his poetry unless we read it in his language? How can we appreciate his calligraphy if we don't understand Japanese? How can we be with him and take him as a Zen teacher without practicing a form of cultural imperialism?

All these and more questions drift around the sensibilities and issues in turning to Ryokan as a model for practice. But Ryokan and the Way of Zen cannot be held or arrested in any culture. Ryokan is a saint of the world just as Dogen Zenji is, or St. Francis of Assisi, or Gandhi. If Ryokan were not alive in this way I would merely be perpetuating memories, but the example of his life is unparalleled and inspiring for our time. There's hardly a question concerning the dilemmas of practice in today's world for which we cannot find guidance in Ryokan's life. This writing, this exploration in encountering Ryokan in contemporary life is my subject for learning and renewal.

Two statues of Ryokan stand at Ryoko-an, the Olympia Zen Center, in Olympia, Washington. One portrays Ryokan as the robust young monk, standing and looking toward the future, toward the potential of his priestly life. The other is of Ryokan aged and thin and seated in Zazen. Each morning we greet the standing Ryokan and include him in our morning circle as we say hello to one another and continue the day after Zazen. The values that Ryokan lived stand before us as we enter what feels like a rocky beginning to the twenty-first century, but our times and the Tokugawa Era were similarly turbulent, politically, economically and geologically. The stress of his times is revealed in some of Ryokan's poems, which are presented throughout these pages. At the Olympia Zen Center, we lift some of these philosophical poems of Ryokan into our liturgy, reciting one each day in the morning ceremony. As the years go by, the poems deepen in the mind and heart's core, and Ryokan's wisdom flourishes in our midst. The poems have become a body of teachings. Professor Nobuyuki Yuasa has translated all of the poems that are found on these pages.

All that has been given to me has been given as pure gift, and everything has been given. Nothing has been withheld. Everyone has opened the way: my first teacher Kobun Roshi and the Haiku Zendo Sangha, Niho Tetsumei Roshi, his family and the Entsuji Zazenkai, my training master Godo Roshi at Shoboji, many Japanese friends, in particular Miyoko Watanabe my Japanese teacher who first took me to Entsuji, my calligraphy master Tokunaga Shoen Sensei, the translator for Niho Roshi, Masan Miyake, my Sangha and students at the Olympia Zen Center, my children and family. Everyone helped pry the gate open even when I've stayed in hiding and been most resistant. At the threshold, Ryokan is waiting, quiet and smiling, greeting with openness and generosity.

Entering the Gate

Ancient sages left their works behind, not to let us know
About themselves, but to help us understand our own stamp.
Had we wisdom deep enough to know ourselves, single-handed,
No benefits would result from the works of ancient saints.
A wise person learns the mystery of existence in a flash
And climbs in a leap beyond the world of hollow phenomena,
Whereas a foolish person holds willfully to facts and details,
To drown in subtle differences of words and lines,
And being envious of others in their supreme achievements,
Wastes the mind night and day in efforts to exceed.
Truth, if you cleave to it as truth, turns into falsehood.
Falsehood, when you see it as such, becomes at once truth.
Truth and falsehood are the mated edges of a double sword.
None alive can separate with certainty one from the other.
Alas, too many people drift with the skiff to fathom the sea.
From time immemorial they are causes of endless deception.

Sweet saintliness is to be sought as a work of your heart.
The rightful path lies not amid things of constant change.
This plainest truth must be implanted time and time again,
Lest you should fall a witless victim to deceiving voices.
If you turn your shafts northward, hoping to travel south,
Alas, how can you ever arrive at your desired destination?

Entering the Gate

"You have left your home and birthplace.
You depend on clouds and you depend on water."

Dogen Zenji

Shobogenzo, Juundo-Shiki

The temple gate or a gateway has deep meaning as a liminal space in Zen Buddhist practice. There is the great visible gate as an entry that distinguishes a temple from the rest of the landscape, and there are the invisible gates, or the gateless gates, which we pass through for the rest of our lives once we step onto the spiritual path. When we leave one temple to go to another for the purpose of Zen training, we leave our home temple by the grand height of the main gate. We enter again by the large main gate of the training temple with its elaborate scrolled carving and guardian statues on either side. The main gate faces straight out from the center altar where the Buddha resides. The Buddha is the guardian, the patriarch, and the teacher of all the practice and activities of the Sangha, the community, that take place in the temple. Therefore we enter and leave with the Buddha's acknowledgement and protection. Once we take up residence at a temple, we come and go in daily life by a side gate that might not even be clearly marked. Only when we are on official business or pilgrimage do we come and go through the auspicious main gate known also as the Mountain Gate because we are lifting ourselves out of the ordinary and climbing into the atmosphere of the sacred.

In the United States there are many places of training and practice where we do not have the ideally situated gate and altar because the buildings were built for other purposes and converted into places of practice. We accommodate ourselves to this condition, but we still keep aware of the physical and spiritual meaning of the gate. Through this passageway we enter the realization of the Buddha. All practice points in the direction

15

of realization. We cannot say there are an "inside" and an "outside," yet we still acknowledge that a temple is a special place where its special concerns and practices stand out in contrast to what takes place in our general cultural setting, the workplace, or the home.

I'm interested in the various gateways that appear in Ryokan's life where he stands as a gauge against which I examine my own journey and test the wisdom of my choices. No one knows the actual Ryokan. He has meaning to those who have encountered him, yet no one can arrest or own him. We try to interpret him, but it's useless to pin down his life to a single meaning. He is full blown for a moment in the threads of one story and then in the next he has escaped into an invisible hideout. Yet he is present right now in this time and age as a vital teacher to help us so that we can interpret the complexity and range of possibilities in our own lives. He is a teacher whose wisdom never tires.

Ryokan was a hermit priest, poet, calligrapher, philosopher, teacher, student, son, cousin, friend, playmate, confidante, healer, indigenous medicine man, naturalist, beggar, scholar, environmentalist, holy fool, cultural critic, eccentric, rebel… His life functioned around multiple activities and relationships and he was given many labels. He was also Japanese, and trying to see him through the eyes of another culture can make for much supposition, projection, interpretation, or conjecture. As a result, the Ryokan I think I know is of my own design, a projection of the Ryokan I choose to see. That seeing may be roused to experience Ryokan in the light of Buddha Nature, with Prajna, wisdom, where the mind has not been confined to imagination alone. For me, Ryokan can function as a ghost teacher capable of appearing in relation to whatever questions I might happen to entertain at any given moment. He can function as an interior spiritual friend with whom I hold counsel. I can converse with him like any teacher. I can have him be friend and confidante. I can have him as mirror with which to practice seeing my extremes, my foibles, foolishness, and impatience. Ryokan allows the range of the psyche to be exercised. Whatever Ryokan I see or have made up, he is a guiding spirit and resides in me. Yet Ryokan never substitutes for my living teacher or for the many teachers in my life, for it would be a mistake to adopt a teacher who could not respond with a live body to my delusion and who could not speak ongoing truth in the mirror of practice.

It is always problematic to cross cultures and to hold as authentic the interpretation we make of people in the other culture. This is one of the reasons we ought understand the limitations of translation. Language is the deepest part of any culture and when we move ideas into a second language, something is lost while something new is added. In a profound sense, the aesthetics of Japanese culture and language cannot be translated into English. When we consider something that has been translated from Japanese, something of simple beauty for instance, we tend to think in our American minds that we immediately understand it because of its direct simplicity. But, this is deceptive. We fail to take in the layers of the long history of aesthetic development in the Japanese language and art. Our languages function in the mind in different ways. Japanese is visually descriptive: we can look at the language and see the pictures of its meaning, whereas in English, we must go from the words to an imagined picture. Of course, one also invents an imagined picture, but the writing itself in Japanese is a picture in a way that the English alphabet is not. So, in this way, any translation is limited, however fine it may be.

Nevertheless, translation opens us to a field of experience, voice, and learning that we would not have without it. I only know as much as I know about Ryokan because of the art of translation and because numerous people took the trouble to interpret his poetry. I feel profoundly grateful to those who have provided translations of his poetry because I can dip my mind into the river of his art. The spirit of Ryokan comes through the translator and I can imagine the beauty of the original work.

Shortly after I began teaching at a Catholic women's college in Okayama, I was offered the opportunity along with other faculty members to write a literary essay for the college's scholarly magazine. It was an easy choice to select Ryokan as my subject. At this point, I had a meager appreciation of the Japanese language but had been in Japan long enough to begin to feel mildly comfortable. I took on the problem of the nature of suffering I saw in Ryokan and expressed how it resonated in his poetry. It seemed to me that Ryokan was deeply in touch with humanity and his humanness made him a cultural hero. He had the spiritual breadth of St. Francis of Assisi and people responded to him in a loving, universal way. He used the difficulties and joys of his own life as the subject of his poetry in ways that revealed the trials, tribulations, and triumphs of his daily life.

For instance, even as many elements of Ryokan's life have been reconstructed through conjecture, the fact that he lived naturally and simply endears him to many people. There are numerous stories that people use to explain Ryokan's priestly vocation. One interpretation espoused by Iizuka Hisatoshi in 1843, twelve years after Ryokan's death, is based on the idea that Ryokan had been a great lover in his youth. Accordingly, there was one particular woman with whom he had fallen madly in love, and he wanted her to pledge herself to him. She apparently rebuffed him, and in his sadness at the loss, he shaved his head and declared monk's vows. This story has great sentimental value for the Japanese and suggests that Ryokan was imperfect enough that even his vocation was flawed, which shows he was deeply human.

Another interpretation is based on a story in which Ryokan was forced to witness the beheading of one of the poor townsmen who had been accused of stealing. The man was under Ryokan's jurisdiction so Ryokan knew the man well and understood his circumstances. Nevertheless, the man was accused of theft and thrown into jail to await the judgment of the magistrates.

Ryokan went to the jail to see the poor man and asked, "Is it true that you've taken the money? Is there any way I can help you?"

The poor man, dirty and disheveled, answered immediately, "Yes, I did it. My wife is deathly ill and we needed some medicine. It was the only way I could get it for her. We have no money and we have nothing I could sell or trade."

Ryokan went to the magistrate, whose sword gleamed at his side as a reminder of power, knelt and pled for the man's life, but to no avail. The poor weeping man was taken out of his cell stumbling and shoeless into the prison yard and beheaded while Ryokan was forced to watch. The speculation is that Ryokan then became a monk so that he would never again have to see a neighbor meet such a cruel fate.

Such stories were told to me when I lived in Japan but a more recent piece of information has surfaced to add to the complexity of these stories. New definitive proof that Ryokan married before he took his priestly vows might overturn them. The record suggests that there was also a divorce, or an annulment, so the woman, quite possibly abandoned by Ryokan while he went off to Zen training, was given her freedom to remarry or to find another life. We don't know what transpired in this relationship. It is possible that Ryokan was compelled to take a wife, as he would have been expected to do. After all, he was earmarked to be the Head of the Town and marriage would be part of the package. It might even have been an arranged marriage, perhaps something that his father had engineered with the father of another town official. It is possible that Ryokan was deeply in love with his bride. We just don't know, but it adds depth to the situation that Ryokan wrestled with, or perhaps slipped past, by coming to a deep personal truth. The beheading story may be likely and could have occurred after he married. It is possible he was a new husband, witnessed the beheading, and knew in his heart of hearts that he couldn't sustain such a life. The priesthood could have been weighing on him for quite some time and he was reluctant to take vows because it would so deeply disappoint his parents. He may have seen that it was wise to finally declare his truth in the face of such trauma, before he was caught up with his own family.

In Japan, one day before I was ordained, when I was still at the women's college where I had gone to teach English, I was called into the chairwoman's office. She was a Japanese Catholic nun in her sixties who taught English but had risen in the ranks to hold the honored position of chair of the department. Her face seemed rigid in expression, incapable of a smile or softness, her lips small and pursed. She wore a modified dark blue business suit that was a modern day nun's habit, a large silver cross around her neck, and a veil that held back her gray hair. We sat opposite one another with the desk separating us like a wide, brown chasm. Numerous Japanese books, which I was incapable of reading, and knickknacks, dotted the shelves behind her. A little ball with a shake-up snow scene inside it held down a stack of papers at the side of the desk.

"I have a proposal for you," she said, "and I'm going to offer you a choice." I had no idea what she was talking about but I sat patiently to find out what things were awaiting me, given this command to appear before her. "There will be an office change.

We are hiring a male faculty member from Britain who needs his own office in the front part of the building, and we've selected your office for him." As the moments went by I felt my mind receding into an awful Dark Ages and I had an image that I was being dragged away by a Neanderthal holding a club. Then she offered me the choice: "You may share the large office next door with another woman faculty member, or you can have an office to yourself in the back corner of another building." She said all of this with a terrible sweetness, as though I'd just been offered a bonus.

There was no real way to swallow the resonance of this predicament at that moment in the chairwoman's office. I certainly had no leverage. I had been a guest in Japan for only six months and I was feeling my way along in a complicated classroom of students who could not grasp the culture of the language they were studying. I was only beginning to learn not to use idioms in the classroom since when I did I received blank stares from the mass of black haired girls seated before me. Once I used the expression, "Hit the ceiling," and twenty-five heads looked upward and then slowly looked down and at one another, fully perplexed.

I was in a land that had no laws regarding gender discrimination. Ads in the classified newspaper regularly sought women employees who were younger than age twenty-five. The unwritten part of the ads surely meant, "Also expected to serve tea." I was in a land where people simply didn't argue. It was clear to me that I could not fare well by bringing up the gender issue. There was a look in that nun's eye that almost dared me to challenge her so she could put me in my place. But I uncharacteristically submitted. What was the point? I couldn't change this decision, but I could certainly hash this out with my American women colleagues who would hoot and howl with me over this dreadful insult to our gender. We could say all the terrible things we wanted to say in our own private gatherings; we could gnash our teeth against the terrible discrimination and then turn around and go forward with our heads held high.

The private office was an easy choice. I didn't want to intrude on the peace of the other woman faculty member who was used to her private space, even though it was a spacious office. I chose the hidden office in the other building where I was secretly thrilled to have enormous privacy. I had the bad habit of just, just barely being on time, so I would race on my bicycle from my apartment to the school, try frantically to find an empty rack to park the bike, rush up the stairs in my slippers, grab my books for class, and enter the classroom breathless thirty seconds after the bell. Not good. Not good. When your office is front and center, such practices become quite noticeable.

In the course of this uncomfortable conversation, the chairwoman expressed her appreciation for my contribution to the college's literary journal and commented on the essay I'd written on Ryokan. She wondered why I had chosen to write about Ryokan. At that time, she was unaware that I was a Buddhist and tacitly teaching in a Catholic college. She had interviewed me for the teaching position, but she had never asked about my religion. She may have assumed I was Catholic since my given legal name was Mary Frances and all parts of that name suggested Catholic and Celtic upbringing. This seemed to be a sure sign of membership in the right faith. Foreign lay women were hired with the hopes that they would extend the missionary work of the sisters, act as Christian models for the students, and possibly gather in converts from the young Japanese women whose parents had sent them to this college in order to protect their marriageability. The young women had to be home in the dormitory by 9:00 p.m. every evening, thus saving them from a life of sexual exploration with young men, or exploitation with married men, and free-for-all drinking rounds at local bars. The students were also required to awaken when the bell rang at 7:00 a.m., eat breakfast promptly, and dress modestly in a school uniform. Try this in the 21st century with American girls 18 to 21 years of age who have gone away to college!

To take on the study of Ryokan in itself did not signify that I was a Buddhist. Many Japanese see Zen practice as purely cultural, and as they sometimes don't understand it, they acknowledge that in view of its popularity, which they also don't understand, foreigners might investigate it. As a poet myself, I expressed my interest in Ryokan to her and said that I thought that I wanted to write yet another paper in the future and compare him to St. Francis of Assisi. To be sure, this was a bit of politicking as I tried to get to her better side. I spoke for a few moments about what I saw as similarities in their lives. Her eyes seemed dark and skeptical as she listened. To her, the comparison of a Catholic saint to a Buddhist saint seemed mightily presumptuous. "I just wish," she said with a cold retort, "that you could read Japanese. Then you would know exactly what the critics say about Ryokan."

This silenced me. I had told her too much and all I had wanted to do was to find a sympathetic opening for some harmony between us. Her tone suggested that Ryokan was neither her favorite poet nor a saint in the league of the great Francis. In truth, Ryokan's literary critics can hold him close to the fire, and this chairwoman of the English Department had a long background in critical research. She well knew that the Japanese critics were not always favorable to Ryokan. They measured him on purely literary terms, apart from his spiritual life, his lifestyle, or the spiritual power that might come with it. It made me realize that I could never hope to read Japanese at a truly critical level and that therefore I was left out of a whole realm of scholarship and good comparative, academic reading. I was already 52 years old and knew how much it takes to learn a language such as Japanese at that reading level. I struggled for every *kanji* I learned at primary levels of reading and writing and if I didn't study every day, I would forget them in a week. I knew fairly soon that the ability to be competent in Japanese would not be mine in this lifetime. There was no longer time to do everything and I had to choose what my focus would be. I had to rely on the work of scholars generous enough to translate in order to read the poetry of Ryokan. And I had to accept the choices they made of what they would translate. I could only know Ryokan's poetry through them and I would always be aware of them as mediators of his thought. Furthermore,

I had to take Ryokan on my own terms and not in dialogue with what the critics had said.

Yes, my chairwoman had silenced me in that moment and it taught me further not to assume that every Japanese person would be open with excitement to the cultural subjects and study that I looked forward to. Ryokan's life as a monk at Entsuji and his life as a hermit at Gogo-an became my deep interest even though I'd gone to Japan without any plans or specific focus. I would later come to experience in my life at Entsuji an even deeper appreciation of Ryokan's training, his life struggles, the roots of his expression, and the sacred pathway he walked. I would live in his room at Entsuji and feel the particular atmosphere of his space, yet extant, immeasurably still, and visited daily by hundreds of pilgrims from Japan and around the world. I would walk on the same cobblestones, climb the same hills, hear the caw of crows in the zendo at sunrise as he did.

I had been in Japan for just six months when Niho Roshi invited me to stay at Entsuji temple. I packed my bag and traveled from Okayama to Kurashiki, a short train trip across the Takahashi River and a hike up the mountain. The smell of Entsuji had a singular musky flavor, dark and ancient like the lotus pool at the base of its stone stairs. On the hill overlooking the rooftops of the temple, a small teahouse burned incense similar to Entsuji's, and this fragrance that permeated the entire hillside became a familiar primal reminder of my home temple. A hint of it can call me back through the gateways of memory as if my experiences there were like the growth of a tree expanding and widening its field of being. At any moment I can be taken by a sudden wind to an unknown hideout where memory waits to mysteriously reappear when fate calls.

Like Ryokan, I would become ordained and then travel to another temple for training since Entsuji is no longer used for monk's training. In order to receive certification as a Zen priest and teacher, I had to go to an authorized training temple. After I had been teaching in the classroom for over three years, going back and forth on weekends to Entsuji, it was time to decide what to do. A friend, Keido Les Kaye Roshi, the abbot of Kannon-do in Mountain View, California, was visiting in Kyoto, having finished a retreat in Uji. We got together and he said to me, "Don't come back to America until you are a fully trained and certified priest. We need good women teachers." It took some time for this to register with me and for me to accept that I might take this path. I had received ordination from Kobun Roshi in 1976, but I had kept this fact a secret while I raised my children. Now they were on their own and I was in Japan teaching, so I was ready to change my life.

The training temple was Shoboji one of the oldest Soto temples in Japan, built in 1348. It was in Iwate Prefecture, 800 miles north of Entsuji, one of the coldest places in Japan. Shoboji is an important cultural heritage site because it is the largest thatched roofed temple in Japan. There were few training temples for me to choose from because some would not take women, and others presented conditions I did not think I could survive. Every training temple has a *Godo Roshi*, which simply means "Training Master." A Godo Roshi will also have his own Dharma and family name and likely his own family temple too. He is both beloved and feared, for your life will depend upon his goodness, generosity, and his ability to transform you from a barbarian into a being with grace and confidence in the beauty of the Soto Zen Japanese forms of practice and their attendant virtues. For most us, this transformation is not without the difficulties and challenges of the demands of training. Godo Roshi requires that you listen and learn everything that he says. He commands obedience; he is not there to entertain you or to listen to your Western ideas of all that you think should be changed in the Japanese system. He has his methods of training and you either fall into line or you leave or you are dismissed. He expects excellence since he is entrusting you with the 800 years of Soto Zen practice of great masters who have gone before you carrying the transmission of the seeds of Awakening.

Godo Roshi was about my height of 5'2" with bright blue eyes. On first seeing him, I took him to be a stocky, muscular Irishman and not at all a dark-eyed Japanese man in his 70s. This feeling of Western familiarity made me like him immediately, and I thought he might actually be enjoyable to learn from. He had a rich sense of humor and laughed easily with a great resonating burst of breath. His voice was strong and demanding and he did not suffer fools gladly. One ought not make the mistake of toying with him. He scolded directly and immediately without hesitation for whatever infraction may have occurred. You might not know what you had done wrong, but you were immediately corrected. He also delivered compliments when a performance was well executed.

After ordination, one becomes an *unsui*, a novice priest-in-training. The name comes from leaving home, forsaking all worldly belongings, and taking the path of renunciation. "*Un*" means cloud and "*sui*" means water. These elements are all that the renouncer depends upon. In other words, *unsui* move effortlessly and unattached, as open and free as the drifting clouds, going to various temples for further learning and to a training temple to complete the course of study and requirements to be a priest. The *unsui* moves the way water behaves, finding its natural direction without resistance.

—until sometimes there is no water. At Shoboji training temple, a severe drought came with months of hot sun and not a drop of rain. The well that had produced delicious, gushing cold water through winter and spring at Shoboji had dried up and there was no longer enough to wash the dishes, much less fill the tub for baths or take showers. Even visitors were warned not to drink the few trickles that came out of the taps because the little remaining water at the bottom of the well had become contaminated. Full buckets with ladles were placed in the bathrooms to use for flushing toilets. We drove up the mountain every few days to fill large water containers from a bubbling spring. Round trip the journey took about two hours and although the drive was dizzying along twisting roads, once at the water site, you could dip your feet in the cool pool that formed above a gentle waterfall. Icy water quickly cooled the body and a cold, wet cloth on the head made the beating sun tolerable. On the particular trail of the return from the springs there was a local favorite shop that sold sweet rice balls on a stick and if Godo Roshi went on the water run, we inevitably received a treat. We got a small one for eating in the car, and a package for everyone back at the temple.

It was hot summer and with the vast amount of work we did, we needed to keep our bodies clean. Therefore the *unsui* were often driven into town to bathe. After dark, we piled into cars and drove to a hotel where Godo Roshi had made arrangements for us to use the hotel spa. It was a pleasant relief of sorts to have a moment of quiet in the tub in the women's section that was large enough to allow comfortably eight to twelve women. The very first night we went, I burst through the door into the women's changing room not expecting anyone to be in there. Lo and behold, about a dozen naked women all at least 85 years old stood nonplussed looking at me—a baldheaded foreigner who looked like a man. Doubtless I'd made a mistake. Their look said they were sure I was a man, but 85-year-old women are past worrying about modesty and none of them made any attempt to hide. I quickly put my things in a locker and jumped out of my clothes as fast as I could to show that I too was a woman and I was in the right place. There is no doubt about it: the body transcends language.

Bathhouses in Japan have changed over the years. It used to be that everyone used them, but nowadays people do not go to the public bathhouse unless they are poor. Everyone has a bathtub at home and you simply wouldn't be seen doing something that might indicate you were down and out. It might even indicate there was trouble at home and you wouldn't want to create any impression that there was even a ripple of difficulty. In the case of the *unsui*, we went to a hotel which was a cut above the local bathhouse and perfectly acceptable in terms of class etiquette. Godo Roshi had to uphold the good names of his *unsui*. All the locals knew about the training monastery and the difficulty with water, so after a few times, we went in and out without much ado.

Going downtown to a hotel to bathe was strange but it was due to unusual circumstances. We left the atmosphere of the temple and entered the stream of activity with its commercialism and the blinking lights of the city. It was not that any of this was wrong; it was simply a striking contrast from the mountain we had climbed when we stepped through that main gate. It is also true that by leaving, if even for a short while out of necessity, we could reflect on what it was that we were leaving. This helped us sense the way in which the space of the temple was held and cared for. A ring of awakened energy intensified by continuous practice throughout hundreds of years filled the air with a stark peace. Within this peace we could learn to move and understand ourselves as participants in the refinement of Zen Buddhist forms, forms that had been transmitted by a timeless series of masters, those who had lived and taught and given their lives for our Awakening in that very place. Nothing but Zen Buddhist practice had occurred there, and it seemed to me that all such temples, even those whose priests had neglected their Zazen, had something special which could only be received and not exploited. Places such as this had deeper clarity than others.

It was also the case that when the young monks piled into cars to go to the hotel for a bath, there was the urge to lighten up, to break down the demeanor and conduct of the temple, and to find ourselves as the people we had known ourselves to be before we came through the gate. Jokes and amusement over the situation opened everyone to stifled laughter. One of the older monks brought about great hilarity by doing a small dance routine with his towel. He knew he could easily make me laugh and I had a terrible time not responding to his antics. I'd try not to look at him, but he was wonderfully playful and I'd be doubled over with laughter in no time at all. He delighted himself that his clowning could reveal a new side of us; Godo Roshi turned a blind eye to this hilarity but he did expect us to conduct ourselves in a mature way.

One autumn night, the rains had just begun but there was still not enough drain-off to fill up the well. September was nearly over and at sundown the mountain air was getting cold. It was dark when we returned to the temple; a man was hidden in the shadows at the entrance to the *sodo*, the monk's quarters. I lagged behind Roshi and saw him speak to the man, but I couldn't quite understand what was happening. I guessed that the man, by the look of his distress, was asking for help of some kind. As I approached I heard Godo Roshi order him to leave. The man looked forlorn and lonely, as only young Japanese men can with sad, watery eyes. Young Japanese men can manage to express a level of emotion and dejection that is nearly theatrical. Godo Roshi entered the building and I delayed outside. I asked the man what the matter was and he said he had wanted to spend the night in the temple but Godo Roshi turned him away. I asked where he would sleep and he said he would spend the night in his car. I asked if he had any blankets and he said no. "What will you do?" I asked and he just shrugged.

I told him to wait a moment and I'd be right back. I found Godo Roshi settling himself in the *tenzo's* tearoom off the kitchen. I begged for the man to be permitted to spend the night. After all, we had many guests come to the temple and stay for *zazenkai*, a layperson's retreat. It wasn't as if there wasn't room. We had many places to stay and a vast array of bedding, enough to handle 50 people or more. Godo Roshi refused. He began to complain about what might happen and he said I had no idea what I was asking for. "He's running away from something in his own life," he said. It was completely inappropriate for this man to be here, he implied. Roshi's shoulders hunched over like a night heron in a moonless forest.

I couldn't believe this. I could see that perhaps the man had run away from home. Perhaps he was deeply unhappy about something, but it seemed to me that one night at the temple might actually save the man's life. If he were on the verge of suicide, for instance, I reasoned that a night at the temple would help cure him. I had that kind of simple rationale, which is often a mistake outside one's native culture. For the man to be in the atmosphere of such a great training temple and with practicing monks, I reasoned, he surely would be saved.

Again Godo Roshi refused. Again I begged. I pointed to the sky and the cold weather. Godo Roshi began to relent. "Oh, you have no idea what you are asking," he said, "You let one in and fifteen come along behind. He's hiding from something and you don't know what it is." But, at last, he agreed and so he went to the door and took the man in. Godo Roshi growled deeply and made it clear to the man that this was a special case. This kind of thing didn't happen very often. Only because of this foreign woman standing here was it even happening now. Godo Roshi made it explicit that I was to be in charge of him and he was to do what I said. He said his name was Masao. I showed him to the small tearoom where visitors may sit quietly and read material about the temple. During the summer, the windows were open in this room and it overlooked the most beautiful scene of all. It revealed a look at the great thatched roof and the garden beneath, the cherry trees and the lane that winds around the temple grounds.

But now it was cold and rainy and the windows were boarded up. I showed Masao to the room and brought linen and a thick winter comforter to use to sleep. It was already very late and we would be up early. It meant that I had to be up extra early to make sure that he was ready ahead of everyone else and in the Buddha Hall when he was supposed to be there. The man was very grateful and obedient.

Godo Roshi continued his growling. He exhaled air out along his throat in such a way that he sounded like a hungry bear. It made him seem quite fierce, but actually he wasn't that way at all. I had grown used to this sound and found a strange, warm comfort in it. I knew it meant an interior struggle for Godo Roshi, an annoyance of some kind, and even perhaps a critique of what was going on, but it did not mean his complete rejection or disapproval.

We got through the night and early next morning when it was cold and gray and not yet light I woke Masao and told him to be ready to follow me to the Buddha Hall. It was a four or nine day, days on the calendar that have a four or nine in them, and on those days we started later and took time to shave our heads, do laundry, and wash our clothing. We would be in the Buddha Hall for chanting, but not for Zazen. When Godo Roshi entered the Buddha Hall and saw Masao, he was half surprised, half disbelieving that the man would actually be there. Godo Roshi himself had gone to the room to bring him along for ceremony and discovered that the bed linens and futon had already been packed up. Godo Roshi had assumed that the man had run away from the temple.

Masao chanted with us and then followed us to the kitchen to prepare breakfast. Again, he was put in my charge. At breakfast, Godo Roshi told everyone that I had interceded on Masao's behalf and asked permission for him to be admitted for the night. He stayed for breakfast, helped with the dishes and talked with the young monks. We learned that he had run away from his wife and he had no place else to go. Masao said he wanted to become a monk, but he didn't see Godo Roshi roll his eyes as if to say, "You don't know what you are saying." When Masao was leaving, he bowed deeply to all of us, went out the gate, and never returned—at least, not while I was there.

When Ryokan was traveling on one of his pilgrimages to various temples in the nearby prefectures, he went to see a Zen master named Soryu in Echigo on the island of Shikoku. He stayed at the temple where Soryu was teaching, but found that Soryu had retired and was staying at a walled-in hermitage, or a subtemple at the back of the main temple grounds. Master Soryu's attendants would not allow Ryokan to enter the hermitage gate and Ryokan was disappointed to think he had come so far to seek out the presence of this important teacher and yet could not get near him. Ryokan continued to hang around and several times tried to get in the gate, but again and again the monks who were Soryu's attendants turned him away. Ryokan was nonplussed since he was familiar to the surrounding abbots as a principal student of the famous master Kokusen.

Late one night, Ryokan completely ignored the gate and went around to the side wall which was layered on top with dark tiles. He climbed over and into the hermitage grounds where he undid his travel pack and penned a short, quick poem to Zen Master Soryu. Then he set the note under a rock near the wash basin hoping that when Master Soryu came out to wash his face in the morning he would find it. Indeed, Master Soryu saw the note and sent word to the temple guesthouse that Ryokan was invited to visit. The pilgrim Ryokan was welcome any time. Ryokan deeply appreciated Soryu's teachings and later spoke of how much they had benefited him. At any such places of practice, the reputation and the atmosphere of effort carry far and wide and the main gate with its shadow falling onto the temple ground is a continual reminder of what the temple stands for.

There are numerous ways of entering a temple such as Ryokan's climbing over the wall when he felt the need to visit as a Wandering Cloud. In this case, he fought for the right to stand in the temple ground as a true guest of the Dharma. This act was the same as entering through the gate, for he was a priest and his intentions were pure. Most of us would not climb the wall. We might hang around outside until someone invited us in. If that didn't work, we could find our way in or walk in naturally when life directs us as—when we felt the compelling pull to enter a new understanding and to take ourselves beyond our own hiding places. For this we should be prepared for the changing forces that shift as we proceed, leaving our home and birthplace and giving our lives over to all that is larger than we are. Most of the gates we encounter are invisible; they are rites of passage that steer us into spiritual maturity. Entering the gate of deciding to commit to the practice of Zazen is just the first step that has to be undertaken as an initial gesture demonstrating the self in search of Self. Any temple master or community will want to test how serious we are. If we are merely window-shopping, it will be evident quite soon. If we are genuine in our wish to practice, the gate will open wide. But we may be tested just as Ryokan was on his first attempt to enter Master Soryu's hermitage. Almost every phase of life can be seen as another gate, another point for submission and letting go, another entry into the unknown. The very first gateway into the Zendo calls us to give away the security of the known. If we choose the path out of the mystery of the Self that does not truly know what the next step means, trusting ourselves not to have to know in the usual way, we can get an inkling of the myriad gateways stretching out before us as a welcome to endless discovery.

Arriving at the Temple

I sat alone, one dark spring night, already past midnight.
Rain, mixed with some snow, poured onto the garden bamboo.
I found no means to console myself in that solitary gloom.
I reached for the holy book, written at the temple, Eihei.
I lit my candle, and perfumed the air, before I opened it.
I saw in every word and phrase a precious jewel contained.
Now years ago, when I dwelled in Tamashima as a young man,
My former teacher at the temple, Entsu,
Read me the elements of this same book.
Already, I had in my heart deepest respect for the author.
I borrowed the book, and practiced what I learned from it.
Then it dawned on me that my former work had been a waste,
So I obtained my teacher's leave, and roamed far and wide.
Whatever has brought together this sacred book and myself,
I find, wherever I range, its teachings irresistibly true.
Teacher after teacher have I sought in my past wanderings.
Alas, no one gave me a lash, such as I felt from the book.
Laws and doctrines have I had many opportunities to study,
None convinced me so well as this book on my return to it.
We live in the age of mad confusion, steeped in ignorance.
We can hardly separate priceless jewels from false stones.
For five hundred years, this book has lain in sleepy dust,
Because none of us had eyes clear enough to see its value.
For whom, do you think, the author has put down his ideas?
Never take me for a cynic, applauding him at your expense.
That spring night, I sat and wept, with a light before me,
Till the book on my lap was thoroughly soaked in my tears.
The following day, I had a call from an old man next door.
As soon as he saw the book, he asked me why it was so wet.
I groped for an answer, for I sincerely hoped to tell him,
But for once my speech failed me, for I had my heart full.
After a short period of bowed silence, I found this reply.
A leak through the roof flooded my books during the night.

Arriving at the Temple

Kokusen Roshi, a well-known Zen master in the Soto Zen Buddhist lineage, was traveling around the countryside giving lectures when they met. Ryokan had been studying Zen at Koshoji in Amaze under Genjo Haryo Roshi. Kokusen Roshi arrived at the temple to bring the teachings. In one account we learn that Ryokan was in the garden raking leaves when Kokusen Roshi arrived with three of his monks. The travelers stopped in front of a statue of a Bodhisattva and Kokusen Roshi took a moment to test his monks' understanding of the Dharma.

"What do you suppose the Bodhisattva is looking at," he asked his monks. "I think the Bodhisattva is looking at the trees and enjoying the view," said the first monk.

"Hmm. Hmmm" said Kokusen Roshi.

The next monk said that the Bodhisattva was looking out for other Bodhisattvas. Ryokan, who was hidden in the shadows nearby listening to all of this, leaned on his rake and spontaneously said, "The Bodhisattva is looking into his own mind."

With that, the young monks burst out laughing. Kokusen Roshi let out a great roar and the young monks were called to silence. Ryokan stepped out of the shadow and faced Kokusen Roshi who said to him, "You have a clear mind. You see clearly."

This began the first encounter between Kokusen Roshi and Ryokan, and Ryokan was moved enough to shave his head, take monk's vows, pack his bag, and immediately follow the teacher wherever he may go. Kokusen Roshi came from the area around Musashi. He was born in 1718, forty years ahead of Ryokan. He had been a monk from the age of thirteen, living at Seiryoji temple at Hikone. He was a true disciplinarian, a severe teacher who believed that hauling rock and dirt was more to be prized than holding to principles. When they met, Kokusen Roshi was already sixty years old, yet fit enough for a 400-mile trek. Ryokan must have seen in him a powerful father figure who represented values to be admired and an earnestness of heart he could follow.

Ryokan's own mother now age forty-two was at home with a two year old, the last of the Yamamoto children to be born. In leaving with Kokusen Roshi, Ryokan departed from this maternal relationship that he had a deep attachment to. He would leave whatever assistance with the other children that he might have been providing to his mother. He couldn't know then that it would be the last time he would see his mother. She died four years later in 1883, while Ryokan was a monk at Entsuji and her youngest child a mere seven years old. The event must have shaken Ryokan to the core. He had many differences with his father, but with his mother he held a maternal bond and admiration throughout his life. Needless to say, because he had taken the holy robe, Ryokan was bound to remain at Entsuji, so the grief of this time may have provoked a penetrating sense of isolation, perhaps even a sense of remorse that his own choice may have caused a burden for his dear mother. Because as the eldest son, he was to help raise the younger children and to influence their lives as a support to the family, he knew that his absence from home would put much stress on his mother.

In those days, Entsuji was an active training center with perhaps twenty to thirty monks in residence. What led Ryokan to this life? He was the eldest son with three younger brothers and three younger sisters, all born between the years 1758 and 1777. This means that Ryokan was old enough to bear witness to many of his mother's pregnancies. Consider the years: Ryokan, 1758; sister Murako, 1760; brother Shinzaemon, 1762; sister Takako, 1769; brother Encho, 1770; brother Kaoru, 1774; and sister Mikako, 1777. Shinzaemon succeeded his father in administrating the town of Izumozaki. Encho became head priest at Enmeiji temple in Izumozaki. Kaoru became a scholar, somewhat renowned in the area around Kyoto, but died at the young age of 29. The two eldest sisters married. His youngest sister married and later became a nun taking the Dharma name Myogen. All of the brothers and sisters, and the parents too, were interested in poetry, literature, and religion.

One can only imagine how it must have been for Ryokan on that long journey on foot with his teacher Kokusen Roshi, from his family home in Niigata to Entsuji in Tamashima. How did it feel to venture across Japan for the first time at the age of twenty-one? What did Kokusen Roshi say to Ryokan during those days of travel? What was the atmosphere between them? What was Ryokan feeling as he made the determination to go straight ahead with Kokusen Roshi without looking back? For Ryokan to decide so quickly, it was surely an immediate sense of rightness, a decisive recognition between teacher and student, a fated moment without retreat or escape. There was no alternative but to go, to leave behind the earthly concerns of home, and familiarity with the people and the area he knew— the small comforts of the world of 1779 in the snow country of northern Japan.

There were no shortcuts across Lake Biwa to save time, just a long persistent 400 mile walk, goods in hand, on a journey of about thirty days to the Inland Sea, the citrus belt of Japan. This was foreign enough for a shy young man out on his own for the first time. From start to finish, Ryokan's day at Entsuji would have been without rest. He rose at 4:00 a.m. or earlier and sat Zazen for several hours before entering the Dharma Hall for an hour of Morning Ceremony. There would be the preparation of breakfast, eating a simple rice soup with pickles in ceremony and cleaning up. Next might come cleaning of the temple on the inside, perhaps some work on the outside. Mid-morning ceremony would come before lunch. Lunch would be a simple dish of noodles with pickles, perhaps with a dash of tofu and a cup of tea. Afternoons would call for further work in the garden and some heavy lifting of stones to build the retaining walls and secure the grounds from erosion. Then might come further meditation and afternoon ceremony before a short tea break. The monks had to bathe, clothing had to be washed. Then dinner had to be prepared and served with cleaning up afterward. In the evening there would be more Zazen and perhaps some study of ceremony or a lecture. Bedtime wouldn't come until 9:30 p.m. or so.

The climate is fairly moderate in this part of Honshu, but summer heat can be oppressive, with mosquitos that never sleep. It can be cold enough to snow but the snow not remain on the ground for long. Each of these extremes is difficult. Monks wear only three layers of clothing, no socks, and no one in those days had the advantage of Gore-Tex, plasma thermal linings, or laminated hoods to cover their shaved heads. The best way to stay warm in winter was to keep busy moving stones, or in summer to keep moving faster than the mosquitos could land. There are no screens or glass on the window openings of the monks' quarters; only the curlicue designs or the emblems of the temple cover such openings. Ryokan lived this life at Entsuji for thirteen years. Soon after arriving he began his life of begging, a practice that would come to represent one of his deepest teachings.

Nothing prepared me for Entsuji; everything prepared me for Entsuji. "En" means circle, the gateless gate of its entry, and "tsu" means to pass through, with a secondary meaning of the Kanji, of magic, occult powers. "Ji" means temple with all its associative buildings layered and organized in some architectural assembly that relates to size or power of administration. Yet, Entsuji is contained in a craterlike side of the mountain, in an almost secret hideaway. It dips down from a pathway that encircles the rim of the mountain. You could miss it if you were not meant to go there. Numerous forks in the road may take you back on the same path, missing sight of the temple rooftops entirely. Again and again you could chose one or the other and yet run around and around and get nowhere.

A feeling of life pulsing beyond the ordinary realm radiated deep under the layers of my skin. It simply hovered for me on every crumbling adobe wall that surrounded the temple and its upper and lower pathways. It began when Miyoko Watanabe Sensei, my Japanese teacher, couldn't find the way from Entsuji Park. This newly built tribute to Ryokan surrounds the temple with scrub oak and brush pine and mossy floored bamboo forests and narrow trails that create the confusion of an open maze. One pathway led to the unmistaken roof design of Entsuji. Thatch! Deep thatch at a steep angle, hand set reed by reed. It speaks a grassy home, a roof of ancient times, some faraway place in the heart-mind. "Natsukashi," deep, warm familiarity, the Japanese say, nodding knowingly to one another. If we are listening and looking with an ancient heart, then everything resounds with this familiarity. It has an "I've been here before" intimacy that one cannot deny.

Watanabe Sensei with her son Seiji took us a few times around the same path and then said she was lost. Never having been there but without thinking, I took the lead and found the way because I could taste the character of Zazen, something pulling me into a vortex, circling inward and inward until we reached the steep walkway that dropped us into the bowl of practice—and we were there. The thatched rooftops suddenly sharpened above us and we felt the weight and mood of thatch and the presence of something remarkable. We were like drops of water releasing into the cup and we spread out almost immediately, each of us to wander alone in the temple yard.

Near the entrance to the Zendo and Ryokan-do, the monks' residence where Ryokan had lived, stands the statue of Ryokan in his early days as a young monk holding his empty bowl, his begging hat tipped over his shoulders and resting on his back. He looks strong and almost regal as he gazes at something showing confidence and vitality. He seems to be protecting a treasure, to be aware that there's more here than meets the eye. Now I felt aware of a circle of energy guarding the Zendo door and thought I could never go past it. It would not let any frivolous thought enter. I felt the presence of a strict and serious spirit. It seemed it would not let me enter and I never imagined I could dare go past it. The tactile quality of Zazen, the continuous meditation practice in a singular place as if it were an invisible sculpture hanging in the air was palpable.

The cement walkways had disintegrated such that they could not easily be swept without further exposing the earth, which would turn quickly to mud even in an easy rain. Two women tended small clusters of sedge in the yard in front of Ryokan-do. They knelt, wearing white sunbonnets and aprons that were meticulously clean in spite of the weeds, the abundance of hard-packed dirt, and clumps of moss. They chatted together quietly as they plucked at weeds. I walked around not thinking anything except bearing concern for the temple's well being. I remembered the labors of our Zen community back in California and how we had preserved lumber from old buildings with the idea of building our own temple. There we had torn up and redone floors so that our feet touched the old wood instead of carpeting during walking meditation. What intense labor it would take to keep Entsuji intact and how devoted the heart must be to maintain this old temple. Incense burned in a large stone cauldron directly in front of the Hondo, the Buddha Hall. Smoke circled through the leaves of a Japanese maple, so old that its limbs were propped up on crutches.

A sense of sympathetic care swept through me. I bent down and began to put together the stone walkway. I saw how the pieces fit together and thought that I could patch one area and it would help keep the walkway in place. Without thinking, I fell to my knees, working the pieces like a jigsaw puzzle, little by little, making a small walkway that would only hold together as long as no one walked on it or swept it with a bamboo broom. It didn't seem to matter. I could still taste Zazen in the air and wondered if perhaps monks were practicing behind the walls, listening to every moment and nuance of breath and scratch of stone as the pieces clicked in place.

Suddenly, I saw something white out of the corner of my eye. I looked up to see two feet in white Japanese socks, the big toes separated by the thongs of the sandals, and just above the sock-line, the hem of a black robe. At that moment I felt an array of sensations: embarrassment that I was so rude as to point out the condition of the walkway by trying to fix it, a cessation of any kind of thinking, a sense of wide, wide opening, the weight of the history of Buddhism, the entanglement of the history of Zen, no weight at all, supreme seriousness, an urge to be giddy. Looking up, up, up, I saw Niho Roshi's soft, kind face. All he did was invite with his head as if to say, "Come in. Come in." —No words, just a slight tilting motion with his head.

In a moment, Watanabe Sensei and Seiji were beside me. Seiji looked at me as we entered and he said, "You are a very lucky person." The Japanese say this when something unexpected and spontaneous happens. Such events can often occur to foreigners, as they may receive special recognition simply because they are rare. Around Entsuji, foreigners are occasional, but Americans are infrequent because Entsuji is off the beaten path. If you aim to find it, it helps to speak Japanese. To travel to Entsuji by train, you must take a bus to a certain road, and then walk a winding steep pathway through narrow streets. At a small stone neighborhood shrine, you turn left and continue up the mountain. At last you come to a pathway with a stone wall. Entsuji's gate that never closes is on the right, quietly, quietly there. There is little here that shouts Entsuji. You have to know your way. So, you enter and then climb a bit more to a pond, old and dark. On one side is a thick bamboo grove. On the other is a stone staircase that leads to the temple yard.

Entsuji is part of a pilgrimage tour, so each day, three-legged pilgrims, as we called them, these with two human legs and a tall walking stick that makes the sound, "thud, clump, clump...thud, clump, clump...thud, clump, clump." Sometimes by the hundreds, parade into the temple garden and ask for their books to be signed and stamped. The stamp proves they have personally visited the pilgrimage site and then they hold the healing of the temple and carry away its distinctive blessings. They will take the pilgrimage book home and place it on their home altars and share it with others in their families who could not make the long walk.

Now, we were inside. We were shown to a round, dark red carved table standing in an alcove next to the Dharma Hall where ornate gold filigree of chandeliers and lotus flowers decorated the altar. Above the shoji doors, woodcarvings of angels floating on clouds and paintings of celestial beings lifted us into another world. We sat in a circle on small futon cushions. In a few moments tea and sweets were brought in and served by a woman I would learn later was Obachan, Niho Roshi's mother. We began our talk. Watanabe Sensei translated and the discussion turned to Buddhism. What else would we talk about, strangers in a temple with the Temple Master? He hadn't invited us in to talk gardening. Niho Roshi inquired about my Zazen experience. I told him I had practiced with Kobun Chino Otogawa Roshi in Los Altos, California for about twelve years. Then I moved to San Francisco and practiced on my own. Had I sat Zazen at San Francisco Zen Center, he asked, and I answered no, I hadn't, I practiced by myself.

It was at this moment that I registered the unanswered questions that had hit me after my first experience in practice: Why must we endure such difficult practice if we are already Awakened? And should we practice alone or together? This burdensome question had plagued me throughout years of practice. Not only had we to endure the pain and discomfort of practice, we had to endure all the hard, questions and the seemingly strange people who were attracted to it. My questions felt raw and unruly, even foolish in the depth of Entsuji. They involved all the pain that I didn't want to endure in the effort to answer them. I clearly had unfinished business, but I didn't want to start again at the beginning. Still, I wanted to know. I wanted more than anything to know.

At some point the questions burst forth and Watanabe Sensei translated. Niho Roshi answered something—I'll never know what because I was incapable of hearing anything other than the fact that I was enveloped in the questions, the pain that I didn't know the answers, and the realization that at that moment I was completely prepared to give everything away to find out. No one could answer for me, not a word, not a murmur, not a hint.

Niho Roshi invited me to come back the following weekend. I said I would stay at the hotel over the hill near the entrance to Entsuji Park and walk over to sit Zazen on the Saturday afternoon. He agreed and before we left he invited us into the Founder's Hall, a room behind the altar. How dark and solemn it seemed in this preliminary room where many small vertical wooden markers and candles to indicate the names of dead temple members reached to the ceiling on tiered platforms. There were steps leading to yet another room higher than the altar. A massive carved black turtle sat at the left of the stair entry with a long scroll behind it.

We stepped into the upper room of the Founder, Tokuo Ryoko Zenji. A moon window was carved under the altar with a stupa of Tokuo Ryoko Zenji's ashes set directly outside. Tokuo Ryoko Zenji I would later learn was a great teacher who had been invited to Tamashima three hundred years earlier to establish practice there. He had founded other temples around Japan, but Entsuji became a powerful training temple and Kokusen Roshi and the training of Ryokan further enhanced its reputation.

As we came back down into the anteroom, we were shown the gold tablets glinting in the darkness at the very top of one tier almost at the ceiling.

"Those are the former abbots of Entsuji," Niho Roshi said. Then he was silent for a long time while we took in the atmosphere, our eyes moving along the row of tablets from one to the other tempting us to count the number of abbots who had served in the three hundred years. Then Niho Roshi spoke again, pointing to the space on the tier where the tablets hadn't completed the row.

"That's my space when I die," he said, without the least discomfort in his tone. "I'm number twenty-nine."

At least twenty years earlier, I had taken a course through University of California Berkeley Extension called "Zen and the Christian Mystics," taught by Jack Weller, who had been a friend of Kobun Chino Otogawa Roshi. During that course, we went for a weekend at Tassajara. This was my first experience sitting Zazen, although I had meditated all my life by right of having grown up in close Catholic training from kindergarten through high school. Prayer and meditation on sacred stories and mysteries was our practice because we had been taught to do such things from an early age. In those days every girl at some time had wanted to be a nun. Meditative mind had become natural.

At Tassajara, we took instruction in Zazen in the Zendo in preparation for joining in with morning Zazen and service the next day: sit quietly, focus on breath, listen to everything. The room I shared with two other women was adjacent to the *Han*, a huge wooden block that is hung on a thick rope and struck with a hammer so that the sound resonates for miles around. The reverberation of it terrified the air when it was struck, and in the early morning darkness it threw me upright out of a deep sleep. My body shook with terror as I climbed into my clothes and raced over to the Zendo for morning meditation. Someone pointed out a cushion for me to use toward the back of the Zendo. I folded into the posture and simply breathed and listened exactly as I had been told.

Forty minutes of Zazen flew by and we then practiced *kinhin*, very slow walking meditation. We settled in then for the second period of Zazen. Again I kept focus, easily breathing and listening to each moment, the subtle movements around me, occasional coughing or sneezing, and the whacks of *kyosaku* that raised the hairs on the back of my neck. The sound of *kyosaku* pierced the delicate spring air. Quiet footsteps roamed the zendo until suddenly there was a swish, a blood-piercing CRACK, and a swish. Some incredible encounter seemed to be happening in various pockets around the room. I could not imagine what would cause someone to place him or herself in such a vulnerable circumstance. And yet, here I was on the same kind of cushion except that it was announced that new people would not be hit. I trusted the leaders to keep their promise.

The *kyosaku*, or *keisaku*, is a long heavy stick that is used to strike people on the soft muscles of the shoulders to spur them toward Awakening. It represents the sword of wisdom, the means to cut through delusion. When people sit a very long time, the muscles become tired. A strike with the *kyosaku* can relax and revive the muscles that are fundamental to holding the mudra and posture of awareness. It is never a punishment; rather it is that which promotes the practice-experience of Awakening.

Of course, I was to learn this later. To be in the presence of the sound of *kyosaku* for the first time caused me to doubt the way of Zazen. And this practice was, for me, the final alternative. I had come to it because of suffering and I had few places to turn. I had thrown all my eggs into one basket. If I did not find answers here, it seemed there would be no other possibility. I had run out of avenues. I wanted to know what it meant to pass through the gate. If Zen had been going on for eons and others—thousands of nuns and monks and laypeople, matriarchs and patriarchs named and unnamed—had come through this gate, had been convinced of the possibility of ending suffering, what did they know? What did they experience?

For that second forty minutes of Zazen the tension seemed insurmountable. Yet the bell rang to finish Zazen and I came off the cushion refreshed. As I moved off the cushion to stand up, I turned and saw a man sitting opposite me pull the window curtain open to peek out at the morning light. At this, my mind opened and the light of the morning sky flashed throughout my whole body and burst into the darkened Zendo. An overwhelming river of compassion surged everywhere. What I thought was solid was now nothing but space and empty being. This simple gesture of a man looking out the window was an eternal gesture and yet it was as natural as every moment before it and every moment after.

The rest of that weekend I spent weeping at the beauty of each person's face. Fears of the future disappeared; anger and confusion fell away. Housekeepers came to our cabin and stripped all of the beds except mine. It was made up as though I were going to make the decision to stay. When a person's mind bursts open, everyone can see it, everyone knows, but in our practice such openings are natural and not to be celebrated or sought after. Awakening, however miraculous it may seem, is our natural condition, and so I went on with my life, returning to the city, transporting the people who had ridden with me in my car, seeing my children, and maintaining my everyday employment. Like the moon reflected in the water, Dogen Zenji says, "The moon does not get wet, nor is the water broken."

Everything is already naturally Awake and this is so in every particle. I had now tasted this.

Shortly after, I went to practice with my first teacher, Kobun Chino Otogawa Roshi, who was teaching at Haiku Zendo. I told him immediately about my experience, but I was concerned because the sound of the *kyosaku* had distressed me. I said that I thought the only way to overcome the fear was to experience the *kyosaku* directly. I trusted he would not cause me injury. Would he please show me how the *kyosaku* felt? He agreed and said he would show me during Zazen.

At the next session, each fiber of my body sat with a vital, taut alertness. Three bells rang to begin the period of zazen and there was no leaving then, just a waiting for the particular moment. Time passed and then a small swish of garments as Roshi got up from his cushion and moved agonizingly slowly around the zendo and then stood directly behind me. I felt him completely present at my back and I waited for the strike. And I waited. And waited. Waited.

Slowly in the silence of the empty no-striking *kyosaku*, his teaching washed through me, mind-to-mind transmission from teacher to student, the circle of lineage balanced on the shoulders in the immediate wisdom of Manjushri Bodhisattva. This was opening with the light of his teaching. Here without words the mind-to-mind transmission erased all fear and the gate fell away. Eye-to-eye knowing confirmed the emptiness and the abiding presence of the meaning of *kyosaku* in all phenomena. Transmission in this final place. No longer basket. No eggs.

That long ago I could not know how my life would lead toward Ryokan and his teachings. My own wandering nature was apparent in my choices. I'd been hurt and hurt myself in the consequences of the rootless life. It was no mistake that I landed on Kobun Roshi's doorstep. In some ways he was a spiritual Fool who led toward the Great Fool Ryokan. With enough Ryokan in him, Kobun Roshi was impossible to follow, just as it seems impossible to follow Ryokan. He defies a finite description, and his life cannot be explained or arrested in any ideological format. He's more like an exceptional person to encounter, an invisible of sorts who sits on the shoulder and listens.

To come then to find Niho Roshi later was more gold than anyone should have in one lifetime. Niho Roshi lives in the complications of a community temple with nearly 800 families to take care of. He is a wise dragon, physically fit and strong with his practice of T'ai Chi, and the same age as I am. His face is smooth and friendly, and his kindness makes him easily approachable. He has rarely a moment to himself and yet he moves with a keen evenness through his tasks and demonstrates a wealth of virtue. He is a brilliant human being who seems never to resist what is in front of him. Instead, he surveys any problem with a simple curiosity, crooks his head to either side while he thinks through a situation, and then he peacefully goes forward turning something complex into a simple move. Niho Roshi's proximity to the influence of Ryokan is also clear as he leads his community with graceful ease, somehow untouched by institutional posturing and demands. He allows people to be who they are and gives freedom to those who walk beside him. Perhaps the artifacts of Ryokan's life that surround Niho Roshi in his own daily life are a continuous reminder of an unusual life that once resided on those grounds. The endless flow of pilgrims who come to touch a moment of Ryokan's history is testament to a kind of hope that Niho Roshi recognizes in people's lives.

At the same time, I recall Niho Roshi saying that he thought Ryokan's spirit was in Niigata in the north, and not at Entsuji in the south. One could be fooled by the obvious display of statuary at the train station near Entsuji, by Entsuji Park, by the busloads of people who arrive yearning to soak in a taste of Ryokan's spirit, by Niho Roshi's paintings of Ryokan. Surely all this is more than mere promotion. Niho Roshi has examined the reservoir of Ryokan spirit at the temple and although he might feel Ryokan has gone north, Roshi is equally steeped in the mysterious play of activity that washes over the area and penetrates the lives of those who are gratified to be in the shadow of the hermit and at the origins of his priestly life. While he was resident at Entsuji, Ryokan travelled to nearby temples on pilgrimage, or to receive additional training from other Zen masters. Nearby Toshoji temple is many hundreds of years old. It was originally founded as a Tendai Buddhist temple and later assigned to the Soto Zen sect. Toshoji recently underwent restoration and is now thriving as a training temple for Japanese and international students under the direction of Seido Suzuki Roshi and with Niho Roshi's initial assistance. Because Ryokan had spent some time at Toshoji, pilgrims are apt to visit there and offer incense, which enlivens the Ryokan myths that simmer and propagate in the south. In the past, Toshoji had a strong institutional influence that Ryokan ultimately rejected. Ryokan's wish to separate from bureaucratic religion can easily be appreciated by most people who at some point in their lives want to abandon their ties to the establishment. This freedom is partly what we admire in the hermit. Niho Roshi values this quality in Ryokan, but Roshi walks a fine line that neither forces his life away from the institution nor makes him a hostage to regulations. He is his own priest within the system much for the sake of the many hundreds of people who treasure him as Abbot of Entsuji where he brings honor to Ryokan whose memory is cultivated.

In turn, Niho Roshi's balance in this mirroring of Ryokan's life touches me as I find myself aging and drawing further and further from the squeeze and hold of institutions. When the artist in us grabs hold, it's hard to stay attached, and I have far fewer cultural and societal demands to keep me in tow than those that weigh heavily on the Japanese. But this question is important: is it necessary to have a temple? So far, in spite of my personal efforts to finesse the requirements and Ryokan's rejection of leadership, my answer is still yes. The temple, as a visible sign of Awakening, as a response to our collective spiritual search and expression, is an inescapable need. Ryokan's juxtaposition to the religious establishment is the perfect reminder of balance. Ryokan begins his life at the temple Entsuji; it is his point of reference. As he proceeds, for all he distances himself from the institution, he makes a temple of Gogo-an. The more people we crowd into the temple, the more the regulations grow, the more complex it becomes, and the more food and organization we need. Ryokan was never without a temple, he just preferred one of a simple, uncomplicated nature. In this he is a pure poet, wanting to roam and lie hidden in the deep grass of the open fields. Now as I age, this too is my longing, yet there is no need to tear down the inevitable structures that priests and communities erect sometimes for need, sometimes for glory. In my heart and mind, the temple is still a touchstone that rescues me from the abyss of banality. I survive in the marketplace because I carry the temple within me. In wishing to stand apart hiding in the tall grass, I find myself in closer vicinity to the resonating bell sounding the temple's call, just as Ryokan did when he "reached for the holy book, written at the temple, Eihei." This is the temple Eiheiji which Dogen Zenji founded and where he wrote the sacred text *Shobogenzo* to which Ryokan refers. Ryokan is compelled to honor that sacred place which, through all of its activities, acts as a lighthouse of Awakening to the world. It was this call to taste that sacred presence of the temple that drew me in, that captured me, and that held the body of the Zendo and the light of morning Zazen. Gogo-an, because of Ryokan's life and practice, became imbued with presence. It is the timeless space of practice resonant at Entsuji for more than 300 years and the tide of its spirit that opened the floodgates to all who would follow.

Politics and Diplomacy

Words come sweeping out of your mouth, when your lips move,
Your arms are slow to act, be you anxious to use them well.
You often try to cover up with your ready-to-flow speeches
What your lazy arms have not quite succeeded in performing.
The harder you try to polish, the more you spoil your work.
The more words you pour out, the greater evils you provoke.
Let us not commit such folly as to flood the fire with oil,
To cool it down for a moment, knowing it will soon explode.

Do not drive after this or that thing in your mad pursuit.
Lock up your lips in deep reticence to do your daily work.
Never fill your mouth till hunger revolts in your stomach,
Nor rattle your teeth until you are fully awake and aware.
Ever since I learned what I know about the life of Hakuyu,
I have some means at least to sustain myself in the world.
Master your breath, so you may be tense with inner spirit.
No ills, then, can break into your heart from the outside.

Politics and Diplomacy

The old truth is that whenever more than one person is present, there struts the crafty head of politics. Only when we are completely alone are we free from the rub of differences that occur in relationships, however trusting and loving they may be. Something will eventually come out of hiding to show us our differences and challenge the harmony that we thought would carry us into the sunset. At some level, just to be alive means that politics cannot be avoided—at least not unless we are marooned on an island or committed to a life as a hermit. Ryokan seems to have been masterful at sidestepping the expected political, public roles that his father and his Zen master Kokusen Roshi had set out for him. Likely there were many tense moments in the Tachibana Family and in the decisions that fed into family life and influenced Ryokan. His father, the elder Tachibana, inherited his job as headman through marriage. His father-in-law had held the position before him. We can only imagine the tension inherent in this situation as the elder Tachibana continually had to please his father-in-law and at the same time keep his wife from the embarrassment of his own poor choices. As the eldest son, Ryokan may have been privy to some of his father's decisions and they may have been deeply painful or even have overwhelmed him. There had to have been toughness and even harshness in Ryokan's father in order for him to do the job he was faced with while balancing his familial relationships. After all, Izumozaki was an important port city, with shipments of minerals and gold coming back to Honshu from Sado Island and then transported across land. Izumozaki was also an important fishing center and depended upon its fishing fleet for its major income. Another important point is that Izumozaki was next to the town of Amaze, which competed with Izumozaki for government-supported transport industry between Honshu and Sado and other centers over land. There was great potential for corruption, intrigue, competition and in-fighting. The local boss would have had a slew of hierarchies to contend with and would need to make considerable maneuverings to maintain a superior position. Even if we were to consult the town records, we would have no way of knowing just how many challenges beset the elder official while Ryokan stood in the shadows watching, and growing in awareness. As Ryokan considered his father's actions, he was perhaps terrified that he would eventually be called upon to settle disputes, pay off officials, condemn prisoners, make criminal charges against families and the young, oversee public events, and handle a citywide range of administrative issues, all while his father and grandfather were watching and coaching from behind. Given the heavy Japanese sense of responsibility, the elder Tachibana was in the public eye, maintaining the peace and order of the town while at the same time insuring its economic success. Sado Island, about thirty miles across the Japan Sea and visible from Honshu, was also where criminals were sent into exile. Many of them came through Izumozaki for the journey to Sado under government watch. There must have been severe tensions particular to the town in this massive networking of relationships.

In his extensive book of translations of *The Zen Poems of Ryokan*, Noboyuki Yuasa gives a biographical sketch of Ryokan's family. The sketch mentions two incidents that led to the elder Tachibana's political decline. At one point Tachibana got into an argument with another town leader over his own leadership style that was seen to have been far too autocratic. At a later time, he discovered himself in a dispute with the headman from the neighboring town Amaze over the construction of a small notice board. He was miserably defeated in these incidents and could hardly maintain his position in view of the public embarrassment. In Japan, when one loses face, one cannot maintain leadership. Such inharmonious incidents create suspicion about one's character, and the loss of one's reputation simply cannot be reversed. Tachibana eventually resigned from the position as headman in 1786, after Ryokan had left to study with Kokusen Roshi at Entsuji.

The father's dilemma as leader may have been exacerbated by his own poetic temperament. The whole family was poetically inclined. The sons were clearly not administrators, given that Ryokan's brother would later take up the headman position and also fail. The elder Tachibana went by the pen name Inan and distinguished himself as a distant disciple of Basho, restoring the style of Basho's poetry among poets in his own surrounding area. Ryokan grew up in this charged atmosphere of politics and poetry, and the mixing of public and private life. Ryokan received excellent schooling in Confucian classics, literature, the arts, and other subjects that permitted him to be qualified as an administrator. He certainly had enough experience and background on which to base his choice of the monastic life and to later discover himself turning to poetry for artistic expression and at times writing it in exchange for seaweed and rice.

Oka Kamon, a biographer, suggests that Ryokan actually did have a time when he acted as an administrator after his father. It seems that an older advisor suggested to Ryokan that the only way to mediate in difficulties was to do it with cunning and guile. Ryokan rejected this strategy, saying there was no way he could mediate except by being truthful and acting with sincerity. Oka suggests that Ryokan made the choice to become a monk because he could not act in the world of politics with such openness and honesty. Therefore, his brother took up the job in his stead.

All of this complexity would have intensified in relation to Ryokan's marriage. There would be not only the shame for the family of Ryokan at his refusing his career, but further humiliation at his leaving a marriage. There is no information except evidence of the marriage in the town records, so we have no incidents with which to cobble together the pieces of the struggle Ryokan would have had. We can easily imagine it, however. He never alluded to his marriage in the poetry. If the girl had found a new life, Ryokan would probably not have mentioned it so as to protect her reputation. Shame is potent in Japanese culture and functions as a major means of controlling social behavior, so surely Ryokan would not have contributed further to the ignominy of her situation by writing or saying anything about that history. In the Japanese way of things, it would simply never be referred to, as if it had never happened.

There is further sensitivity to consider in Ryokan's in relationship with his father and in relation to his decision to take the robe. Tachibana's position in the community was deteriorating throughout Ryokan's life. Ryokan must have been watching this slow defeat. Ryokan knew enough about himself to know that he would not be successful as headman of a sizeable town, having to deal with all those political operators. In this, he would certainly not want to bring further embarrassment upon the family. And Ryokan was clearly not in competition with his father. He had nothing to prove. His study and his attraction to the depth of the Buddhist and Confucian texts has to have been a strong vocational pull. Politics was simply not his forte. He began the study of Zen as a layperson. We don't know exactly when he took his initial vows, the taking of the Precepts that establishes a person as a Buddhist, but it was several years before he was to meet his Dharma Transmission teacher and before he took the critical vows that established him as a novice priest, a wandering monk, a home leaver. Ryokan said, "Many a man becomes a monk and then practices Zen, but I had practiced Zen for a long time before I became a monk."

What makes us suppose that that was the end of politics for him? Earlier I said that whenever people interact, it is inevitable that there will be disagreements. Opposition is natural in human interaction in daily life and in the human condition. Monastery life is no exception. However much monks try to live peacefully together, there inevitably comes the moment when one is challenged by the testiness of another. Who has come through monks' training and not had a sleeve full of stories to tell? Hardly anyone who has been through Zen monastic training wants to remember this kind of story telling. A purposeful forgetting occurs that is something like a mother who forgets her pain in giving birth when the beautiful child is placed in her arms. This forgetting is a virtue. Would the soldier on the battlefield string out his petty grievances with his comrades after his life has been saved? Such forgetting is a sign of gratitude. How lucky we are that our parents put up with us. How lucky we are that our teachers stand firm and resolved and patient in their practice while we dance around in our immaturity. This forgetting is a sign of growth. This forgetting is a sign of forgiveness.

When Ryokan marched across Japan in the shadow of Kokusen Roshi on the journey to Entsuji, he was thrust into a new world of politics and daily life that must have strained him sorely, since for one thing he was not used to such hard daily labor. The hardship of training is visible in every piled up stone that forms the retaining wall around the steep embankments of the temple, but this toil is not visible in Ryokan's poetry. In that phase there was simply no time to write. This life was the making of the adult monk; he was learning to be comfortable in his discipline, soft in demeanor, rich in Dharma, he was leaving the world of attachment to hold his robe and bowl as his only possessions. Ryokan couldn't know that he was preparing his body, forming muscles that would sustain him in the years after Kokusen Roshi's death.

Kokusen Roshi was a famous teacher across Japan and entangled enough in the local tensions of the temples and his own teacher to feel the high-powered grip of politics. He was a severe teacher, a strong disciplinarian, a recognized scholar, and Ryokan loved him. Kokusen Roshi's style of teaching was to set his monks to work. Long hours of good hard work keeps young monks from thinking too much. Kokusen Roshi was believed to have said that he favored "rolling stones and carrying dirt more than any principles."

I shouldn't suggest that there was no harmony among the monks. Certainly there was, but the monks were pushed to know their mettle and something ultimately comes along to show you what your breaking point is. Zen training in Japan is slow and basic and takes many, many years. Through a certain amount of hardship you find out what you are made of. Some people are stronger than others; some are more virtuous. The strong help the weaker ones. Sometimes the strong do battle with one another; sometimes the weak torment the strong. The underlying core of this dynamic is enormous, unspeakable, enduring kindness in the nature of Awakening. It is the reason to be there. Each one in training knows when he or she has been stingy or has made life hard for another. The point is to drop pretense, ego, supposition, and false personality, the array of structures we have managed to acquire. To see one's limitations and the piling up of beliefs and projections heaped into an assembly that we think is ourselves and to see this mirrored against Zen practice convinces that compassion is at its core.

Ryokan became Kokusen Roshi's successor, his first Dharma heir. It was Ryokan who inherited leadership after Kokusen Roshi died and the responsibility for the future of the temple fell into his hands. Consider what it was like for the Sangha after Shakyamuni Buddha died. There was intense vying for position, maneuvering for leadership, politicking at its worst. The more influential the leader, the more severe are the politics. Ryokan was faced with this dissonance and flurry of such contention. He was not happy.

Perhaps we can say that he had had a stomach full and one quiet day he walked away and never went back. There's a secret tradition between monks called *hoko*. It's a sneaking out at night, a climbing over the wall to feel a taste of freedom. At Entsuji, up behind the temple and on the adjacent side of the mountain, there is a large, flat, prominent, and highly polished rock. Some call it the Zazen rock, where monks expand their practice by sitting out of doors in meditation under the hazy moon of Enlightenment in the long, long slow pulse of night. Others know it as the rock where monks who have slipped quietly out the back door with a beer or a bottle of sake hidden in their jackets, gather together in song and substance, telling jokes and laughing, letting down their hairless hair.

What monk hasn't wanted to walk away? I walked into the mountain once during my training at Shoboji. It was a mixture of pain and joy to feel the freedom of the air and the trees and sunshine, but most of all it was superb to have no eyes critiquing my walk or to have no monitor readjusting my clothing or chiding my style. It seemed at the moment like supreme liberation. The afternoon was warm and sultry in early August. Narrow pathways led through secluded rice fields. Birds flew high over stands of bamboo and pine. When I scrambled to the top of a bluff and found a place to lie down in the tall grass overlooking the valley where the monastery rooftops peeked through the distant trees, I heard the mournful sound of the distant bell calling for afternoon ceremony. My heart suddenly flipped over and I was filled with pain and remorse that I was not there to chant. I felt I had let my fellow monks down by abandoning them to all the effort they had to make for even one ceremony. More than that, I had made a statement of individuality by doing something apart from the group and this simply was not done in the Japanese temple culture. This is not particularly acceptable in American Zen culture either. One does not do things just on his or her own, does not make decisions, does not separate from the group, does not stand out, does not fulfill personal needs or wants. We are learning to become selfless and to honor all of oneself which is also the inclusion and recognition of other monks.

No matter how I felt, the hard part was to walk back and face the monks squarely with my absence. I had not just snuck away by the shadow of night, sharing in a particular secret tradition that other monks would have participated in. In a place where one is the only woman and the only foreigner, she is noticed when she isn't there. As I approached the kitchen, I could feel the silence and weight of their annoyance. They looked at me with crimped eyebrows, admonishing me with their hard, black eyes. No doubt they had been sent on a wild hunt to find me. No doubt they had had to run from one corner of the temple to the next, a good half mile from one point to the other, wearing the thin, little indoor temple shoes that give no support to sore, aching feet. No doubt they had been worried.

I had nothing at all to say. I made my body seem penitent and simply fell into the schedule of dinner preparation. Verbal apologies seemed useless. There I was and that was enough. After a while, Godo Roshi entered the kitchen and asked where I had been. I told him I had gone mountain climbing, *yama noburi.* He fell over laughing, his large belly shaking under his robes. This did not secure my relationship with the young monks. If they had done something similar they might have been severely admonished. If they had a history of disobedience, they might even be dismissed. Much would have depended upon Godo Roshi's mood.

What I had done was not so amusing. No one walked in the mountains during summer, not even the villagers. Once the wild spring vegetables were picked, monks were told that mountain walking was forbidden. On any given day in June, July or August, when the sun was high and hot, as many as two dozen snakes, red, blue, yellow, green, white, and black in various intricate designs and sizes could be seen lolling outside the kitchen door, sunning themselves on the rocks along the stone stairway that led out to the main gate. The first time I saw them I was startled and didn't want to do the chore that took me near them. I stood with the pail of compostable food scraps in my hand and wondered if this was meant as penance for my disappearance up the mountain. Had they saved this chore to teach me a lesson? I could feel the younger monks' eyes on me as I ventured along the path and I always felt I had to show my courage while training among young men, but I soon found that the snakes were not interested in me and if I walked calmly and quietly past the array of coils, they remained there undisturbed. I doubted that any of the snakes were poisonous, but I really had no idea. The young monks loved to scare one another with snake stories. What was true was that this northern, forested region was the habitat of the *mamoushi*, the viper snake that kills in an instant; there is no antidote for its venom. It can be small and silent and its erectile fangs can pierce an ankle and snatch the life of a human in a brief instant. Unlike the rattler of California where I had walked regularly through rattlesnake grass in summer, this snake gives no warning. When sitting around talking and relaxing, the young monks kept up a repartee, baiting one another with *mamoushi* stories or stories of bears coming into the grounds at night. These stories served to keep people out of the hills and to test their fears when they had to walk through the temple grounds in the darkness on fire watch.

Walking among the snakes reminded me of my utmost determination to finish training no matter what came in front of me. It wasn't that I was entirely fearless. It was more that I had entered training prepared even to die in the course of being wholeheartedly a student. Whatever challenges I met, I was determined to meet them. Many times my own determination got in the way of being graceful, but I wasn't about to quit because of snakes. The real snakes that troubled me were of the human variety. It is hard to say if the boys sent me out there to test me, but I had the sense that they had and that they themselves were afraid, so there was no way I was going to capitulate and back off. If I were to be swallowed by a boa constrictor, I knew the young monks were the ones who would be in trouble for having put me there. A certain level of protection went with being a foreigner. They couldn't bear the responsibility of having me die by snakebite. It would shame the temple and the Roshi. I got through a lot because my ego was big enough to equip me with some level of courage and to allow me to convince myself that I could and would do anything to prove myself and still survive.

Walking in the hills was a break with the whole structure of the culture. My going off on my own sent a message to the monks that I didn't value their stories and the intentions behind them. Their tales were there to remind one another not to go into the mountains after spring. My action suggested that I was more fearless than they, although I was really more naive. It suggested that I was above the boundaries that the stories and the regulations placed on them. It suggested that I didn't honor their feelings for me and the protections they provided through the warnings in their stories. The *mamoushi* were real and I could have been killed. Breaking from the group and disconnecting from its politics has its hazards.

Going back is very hard. Perhaps Ryokan felt that after a few days out, he couldn't face going back. We've all experienced that syndrome: it's easier to suffer the pain and anxiety of distance than to face the shame and agony of return. The gap begins to grow and before we know it, there is no going back. Then again, perhaps Ryokan's intention was to leave for good. He writes, "One fatal day, however, I left the temple at my own whim." It doesn't seem to have been a premeditated event, rather something that came over him in the course of time. We can't know exactly what was in his heart. We do know that he felt himself to be a runaway monk for the rest of his life. "Fully aware of what I owe to my teacher, I sit by myself, Shedding remorseful tears to the moaning river before me." The five years of wandering that followed his departure from Entsuji were full of darkness and dejection, as we learn in his later poetry.

> Tatters, nothing but tatters, are the garment on my back,
> And what else but tatters is left of my life, at this age?
> Seated on a wayside stone, I eat food given me in charity;
> I have long surrendered my house to the encroaching weeds.
> On a moonlit night, I sit up singing poems to my own ears.
> Led astray by the flowers, I roam away till I lose myself.
> Ever since I left the temple where I was once an inquirer,
> By my own sheer folly, I have sunk to this wretched state.

Current research is looking into the possibility that Ryokan went to China during his "lost" period. It was illegal to go from Japan to China during his lifetime, but certainly not impossible. People have always broken the law and there were no doubt small boats going back and forth illegally between Japan and China and Korea in those days. Ryokan may have followed in Dogen's footsteps, but he would never have spoken about it. Had he been caught, he would have been arrested and would have served considerable time in a Japanese prison. If he had gone, how wonderful an adventure it would have been for him to see a wider world. Having left Niigata and walked across Japan, his sense of the world had been expanded and his urge to leave the political intrigues would have increased. I would like to imagine that this happened for his expansion in the larger world, but as yet there is no concrete evidence for it. With Entsuji on the Inland Sea, it would be easy to find transport in a fishing boat even if it were a dangerous crossing. Whether a concrete picture of this period in his life will ever surface we can't say, but there is also no definitive evidence of his travels anywhere in Japan except for his appearance in Kyoto after his father's death. It is very difficult not to be noticed somewhere in Japan; in many ways, Japan is a very small country.

In our Western society we place a high value on independent spirit, on acknowledging our own feelings and wants, and on acting on what we feel is "right" for us. It's our heroic view; it's our heroic imperative. We hold most dear the self-reliant image of Walt Whitman striding along the solitary path and singing for his own pleasure, "Give me to warble spontaneous songs for my ears only..." or "Give me nights perfectly quiet as on high plateaus west of the Mississippi and I looking up at the stars." Oh how we love the solitary saint dismantling the mandala of politics.

Ryokan lived in a culture that celebrates interdependence and even co-dependence of persons, obedience to authority, duty, tradition and, above all, maintaining *Wa*, harmony. The Japanese insist on group cohesiveness, on maintaining social norms, and on restraining behaviors that would question the status quo or bring about change in the social structure. In Japan, there is an outside-in perspective in which the larger society is more important than oneself. A person first asks how he or she fits into the society. In America, we live in an opposite way, considering the social view from the inside out. Americans consider how the social order must change to suit the individual. Ryokan must have seemed very backward in his society: first he forsook his duty and obligation to his role as eldest son; then he left his wife behind; and finally he abandoned his obligation to the temple. Ryokan was at odds with his culture and he had to contend against the difficult pressures placed on anyone in his society. The conflicts set him apart and set him squarely on the hermit's road. He also felt that he was destined and suited to live alone.

Nevertheless, no one can survive without some connection to society and although Ryokan lived on the threshold, he did maintain touch. In the life of abject poverty, in the life of begging, he forsook the security that communal life in the temple would have provided. He gave up some of what was shared in his own society: belongingness, agreement, and tradition. What was shared became Ryokan's great legacy: his language in poetry and art, the geography and vow of the hermit's life, his belief and trust in the Dharma. In whatever way we attempt to explain Ryokan, we are always left with the inscrutability of his choices. In the face of his fragility, he seems almost superhuman, beyond what most of us could imagine daring. One wonders what deep powers flowed in the depth of his psyche to give him the courage to live such an extreme life, to make his choices and see them through. Most of us can't stick to a diet or even get a week out of our inconsequential New Year resolutions.

When we discover difficulty in our relationships and politics overwhelm us, it is then that we romanticize the solitary Ryokan, savoring his moments in idyllic bliss when he had no one to admonish him or nag. We long for the quiet without interruption where we don't have to answer to anyone else's whims or annoyances, and we don't have to wonder if our very presence and breath is the cause of someone else's irritation. On the other hand, when everything is peaceful in our relationships we invent the lonely Ryokan without the comfort of communal care. The one who shares cooking and cleaning and body warmth on a cold night is by all means our good friend. When all is well, we forget the isolation and monotony that come with being too much alone.

Our own situation may cause us to look to where we think the grass is greener rather than to understand that Ryokan had as much struggle with his life as any of us. He pushed against the surrounding politics and the spiritual institution of Buddhism by way of his confirmed lifestyle and his expression as a solitary monk. The teaching we receive certainly raises some questions: to what degree shall we engage in and support our social structures when they have become corrupted and no longer serve an honorable function? What are we supporting when we support a particular political orientation? Shall we become engaged Buddhists, activists who challenge the socio-political structure? How shall we vote? Shall we join organizations or shall we stand back and refuse aid? What do our taxes support? Are we all corrupted by the power of the group? Are we corrupted by the ego of the solitary way? Can we walk alone together, or together alone?

I don't think that Ryokan's life answers all these questions. After all, we have to answer for ourselves and with our own lives. Ryokan's juxtaposition against the prevailing authorities forces the questions our way and his life holds a mirror of examination for us to look into so we can make some hard inquiry. It isn't that he intended to make a statement with his life, but the social issues are highlighted as a direct result of what he did and didn't do. Had he intended to make a point with his life, we might be repelled by an ego that had tried to turn the world into his own image and likeness. Ryokan did none of this. He simply lived according to his own wits and conscience and left us to live our lives informed by his unusual and extreme choices. Plenty of people find him extreme enough to hold him at arm's length. After all, there is hardly one of us willing to abdicate our comforts, and it is a deeper challenge when such surrender is thrust upon us by way of homelessness.

When I returned from Japan, I wanted more than anything to live totally by begging. The mirror that Ryokan held up was a strong magnification, but he never intended that anyone should follow him exactly. Instead of simply seeing a straight reflection, he might counsel me to consider using his life as a convex mirror with which to see the wide angle of my life. Or he might suggest an acoustic mirror to reflect the musical sound of his poetry or the tap of his begging stick. Imagine me as a woman in her fifties walking the streets every day in monk's attire in an American town, tapping my begging stick with no idea where to stay, sleep, wash, use toilets, brush my teeth, get warm, get food, receive mail, as was the case with Ryokan. I'd be thought of as an unhinged woman and might actually go crazy. Grappling between cultural differences, religious differences, centuries of change, gender restrictions, age, language, training, all this becomes compounded in the perplexity of how to live and how to express the Dharma in my life. To live like Ryokan was a romantic notion, but for a few months within that longing, I felt a small taste of Ryokan's freedom in spite of the impending hardship. Establishing a Zen center was furthest from my mind. Like Ryokan, I felt ill-suited to the rigors of running a temple and taking on the politics of community life in the American milieu where people might not understand the texture of the Zen culture and training I had experienced in Japan and would ride over it, not intentionally, but out of the natural hubris of the American urge to express oneself without having a thorough background in the tenets of what Zen was transmitting. I never felt myself to be a spiritual leader and I wrestled with Ryokan's decision to leave the structure of the institution and make my way in some benign alternative expression. Yet I did sit Zazen and slowly a group formed and one thing led to another. It just gradually developed, but I cannot say that I chose it, although I do believe that the Buddha's robe is a central phenomenal appearance for any community and that a group naturally forms in response to its manifestation among us. I had completely agreed to wear the Buddha's robe. Ultimately, what I also chose was to teach at a community college so as not to be a financial burden to a beginning Sangha, and to live in the Zendo by *Dana*, that is, to receive gifts freely placed in my bowl which sits on the altar at the Olympia Zen Center. Whoever places *Dana* in that bowl shares in virtues and blessings that are the spiritual residue and teachings of Ryokan's life. This in itself is complete practice in our day and time and those gifts are the invisible spirit of Buddha, the secret gestures of the community's generosity that are made visible in the life of the robe. At the same time, as a community we contend with what it is to be human and to interact as human beings, imperfect, flawed, and vulnerable. It is natural to struggle with whether to stay together or to go alone in our imagined notions of Ryokan. Yet even if we go alone, we still need one another, for we crumble without the mainstay of community, for better or worse, richer or poorer, in sickness and in health. Politics cannot be avoided and the Buddha knew this best.

A Holy Poverty

In days old as gods,
When concord long forsaken now
Held the world over,
There lived an ape, and a hare,
And a fox besides,
All bound in honest friendship.
Awake at sunrise
They played on hills and moors,
And in the evening
Side by side they lay sleeping.
Thus for many years
They lived together as friends,
Till high in heaven
The sovereign heard their fame,
And wished to behold
What he had heard others say
In his own person.
Thus, disguised as an old man,
Feeble and sickly,
He came stumbling toward them
And demanded thus,
"If my old ears can still hear,
Differing in kinds,
You live united in your hearts
As one merry band.
Still, if you want to back up
The name you enjoy,
Then raise me out of my slough
And heal my hunger."
So saying, the old man dropped,
Releasing his cane.
Anon the three went their ways,
But after a while,
The ape returned from the hill
Rising high behind,
Healthy chestnuts in his hands.
He was soon followed

By the fox who came with haste
From the stream before,
Some live catches in his mouth,
All for the old man.
Now the hare alone leaped about
Flying everywhere,
But when he at last came home
Nothing in his hands,
The old man denounced him hard
For his ill nature,
His lack of truth in his heart.
In his deep remorse
The hare soon contrived a plan,
And said to the ape,
"Will you climb the hill again
To get some branches?"
And to the fox, "Can you build
A bonfire for me?"
The two obeyed as true friends
Should in such cases.
Then, into the flame, the hare
Threw himself alas,
Making for the strange old man
A great sacrifice.
As soon as the old man learned
The hare's loyalty,
His heart choked for deep pity,
He cast up his eyes
Straight towards sacred heaven,
And weeping aloud
He flung himself on the ground.
After some moments
The old man struck his breast,
And said to himself,
"I now perceive the loyal three
Are equally true,
All trusty friends in sad need,

And yet among them,
It was the good hare that made
The best sacrifice."
So saying, the old man brought
The corpse of the hare
To the bright hall of the moon
And buried it there.
This, as I have heard men tell
Through generations,
Is why on the cloudless front
Of the shiny moon,
We have a hare placed in glory,
And each time I hear
This tale so well know to me,
I cannot help soaking
In the warm tears from my eyes
The sleeves of my sacred gown.

Mortal as he was,
Once a hare offered himself
Before an old man.
How my soul pines after him,
Hearing his tale once again.

One mid-autumn night,
Watching the bright moon above,
Of its own accord
My heart turns to the old tale
I have learned time after time.

True as a mirror,
A humble heart taught itself
A great sacrifice.
That heart must be commended
Through countless generations.

A Holy Poverty

It is impossible to be with the life of Ryokan without considering poverty. I am interested in vowed poverty and imposed poverty and in how cultures, religions, and societies influence attitudes toward each of these forms of poverty. I want to ask whether our spiritual traditions lose integrity when clergy become unionized, professionalized, and salaried, and when living in ministry becomes a profession rather than a vocation. The life of Ryokan as we know it would not have occurred had Ryokan felt the need to be salaried, to be a professional priest, or to belong to the establishment. How do we create a Zen Buddhist ministry in the United States that can become organized enough to address the problems we face as a society, to hold the line against charlatans, to care for the health and welfare of the clergy and yet not become entangled in privilege and power?

Shakyamuni Buddha and his monks and nuns in the monastic order vowed to live in the virtue of poverty. Each day they conducted begging rounds holding their bowls to receive food from faithful lay supporters, and if there were leftovers, the food was placed in the garden for animals to forage. As the *Sangha* evolved, wealthy landowners set forestland aside for exclusive use of the monastics since monastics built small lean-to huts out of grasses and fallen tree limbs. Such highly impermanent structures, if they could be called structures, were the original Buddhist monasteries. One of the Buddha's teachings for the continuation of the *Sangha* was that so long as monks and nuns continued to dwell in forest lodgings, the *Sangha* would not fail to flourish. In this prescription for the living health of the community, Buddha points the way toward the virtue of poverty and simplicity.

Most of the Buddha's followers came from wealthy classes, but on entering the *Sangha*, they abandoned the connection to the caste system so one monk had no rights above another except by right of the day he or she joined the *Sangha*; they lived in equality while at the same time being guided by elders. For most, there was an abrupt lifestyle change as they went from a life of conventional convenience to a life of one meal a day and an undetermined diet, since they could not know what food they would receive on any given begging round. Dysentery and other intestinal ailments were common in the *Sangha*. The shift into spiritual poverty opened the eyes of many to the suffering of the poor classes, and this lifestyle put the monks choosing to live in poverty on equal footing with the suffering poor.

Some Theravada monks today continue to live in the forest and to live simply so that they remain awake to the problem of greed as an origin of suffering within each of us. Their vow helps all of us to remember to examine for ourselves the vital teaching of the Four Noble Truths and, as best we can, to live a life of awareness, respect, and generosity. There are very few able to take on this life and to live the pure austerity of renunciation, but because some do, we remember the meaning of the vow from an absolute standpoint. The matter of practicing poverty as a virtuous lifestyle has fallen out of favor in our Western culture and this has a profound effect upon the spiritual integrity of our wider culture. Gross materialism has made our culture comfortable and greedy and because so many of us have it so good, it is difficult to give up the comfortable life and it is difficult to relate to those who are really in need. Most of us cannot imagine what it is really like to live in abject, oppressed poverty.

Dogen Zenji, the teacher and founder of Japanese Soto Zen Buddhism, reflected the absolute poverty of the monastics who followed Shakyamuni Buddha. In his instructions to his monks, food from natural sources such as fruit trees and plants, food received through begging, and food which was donated by lay followers were the primary sources of pure foods which they must try to consume. Dogen Zenji also said that food should follow the conventions of the times, but it is a long distance from the practice of those three forms of receiving or obtaining food to shopping in Costco. Dogen's instructions for the food practices in their absolute sense are for monastics. The temptation for sanghas that are primarily lay in makeup where most people work at jobs outside the community or are married with family is to buy food that will be consumed during retreat in a supermarket. Cultivating a thriving garden is full-time work, which in water-challenged areas is poor water ecology or might not be feasible. Begging is thought to be totally inappropriate, particularly by lay people who are already well enough off to buy their own food. This raises the question whether the Dharma is injured because begging by non-monastics can cause negative feelings among non-Buddhists. Food donated by lay practitioners is very simple to arrange in this particular situation. And the question here is to live as best we can the spirit of the teaching and not become slaves to the letter of the law.

Spiritual practice concerning food was foremost in Ryokan's practice. It follows that whether one is a monk or a lay practitioner, the same mindful awareness of food is called forth in the chant as a preface to eating. This has not changed from the time of Ryokan; the same intentions around food are of primary importance. The need to know and value the effort in the production of food is basic to our connection to the world around us and the people of the world with whom we eat. We chant this verse from the Soto Zen liturgy before we eat, exactly as Ryokan did in his time:

> *First, innumerable labors brought us this food, we should know how it comes to us. Second, as we receive this offering we should consider whether our virtue and practice deserve it. Third, as we desire the natural order of mind, to be free from clinging, we must be free from greed. Fourth, to support our lives we take this food. Fifth, to attain our Way we take this food.*

> *First, this food is for the Three Treasures. Second, it is for our teachers, parents, nations, and all sentient beings. Third, it is for all beings in the six worlds. Thus, we eat this food with everyone. We eat to stop all evil, to practice good, to save all sentient beings and to accomplish our Buddha Way.*

Everyone is included in this partaking of nourishment—those who worked in the fields, those who drove the trucks to deliver the food to the market, the grocery clerks and checkers, all of the numerous labors. We are brought to examine our humility in this process and to understand the reason we eat and maintain the health of the body, who it is for, and what is to be accomplished. In Zen practice, the saying is, "A day without work is a day without food." People who live in poverty certainly know about this.

Dogen's teachings concerning clothing and the way of the robe, the robe of liberation, emphasized simplicity and poverty. The "tattered robe" was to be worn for the Buddha Dharma itself and in wearing it, one could become transformed from greed and delusion. Dogen quoted Lung-ya Chu-tun, a great seventh century Chinese master who said, "To study the Way, it is imperative that you learn poverty before everything. Only after you study poverty and become poor can you become intimate with the Way." Ryokan's tattered robes become more pure in poverty as they become more tattered. His spiritual beauty emerges in the letting go of any remnant of posturing represented by elaborate silk attire. He becomes completely transparent. With the robe personal comfort and show drop away.

> If my black robe is large enough
> How ready I would be
> To cover the whole world of sufferers
> With the robe I wear.

This is a sweeping, all encompassing fulfillment of his vow to save all sentient beings and yet it reminds us to be simple in our choice of clothing in our place of practice and to share what we don't use with the homeless.

Anyone entering the Dharma in search of fortune would have to be totally deluded because practice has a way of calling things into balance and making things turn in ways that provoke life lessons. Many Dharma centers across the United States are financially struggling, and many, many monks and nuns are barely receiving enough *Dana* to be able to eat. How fine and courageous was Ryokan's decision to live a life of poverty and obscurity. He could not avoid some level of notoriety in that he had done something so unconventional, so alien to the Japanese style of life, and yet so naturally true to the ultimate vow of the monk. Word began to get around about this anomaly. His virtue was pure and bits of myth began to build up around him. He did not hoard food or wealth. He did not enlarge his living quarters and acquire furniture and household goods. He did not even acquire students. The calligraphy he did was in exchange for food or provisions or done as a good gesture for friends, and he did not collect his art, publish it, or promote it. He sustained the vow of simplicity and in the face of remarkable physical discomfort, he continued. That's really all he did. He lived his vow.

Ryokan was critical of the ways in which the temples engaged in power and politics, and developed establishments and social structures that created position and wealth. He admonished those who took up false practices or built huge temples in the name of Buddhism. When our own temple flourishes we might think that our practice is superior to that of others and people start to revere us because of our association with a large and wealthy temple. Ryokan saw such ideas as a delusion and a shameful activity for Buddhists to engage in. He said it is a very difficult thing to truly practice the Dharma and not be misled by the cunning hand of power. "An unsurpassed, penetrating, and perfect Dharma is rarely met with even in a hundred thousand million kalpas," is what Ryokan chanted each morning along with all other Soto Zen priests in their vow to save all beings. The simplicity of the robe and wearing the Buddha's teachings is the primary practice and not the establishment of a fancy temple that leads toward fame and admiration.

Dogen Zenji too cautions us to be aware that the emphasis be on the spiritual practice and not on the building of the establishment where the practice occurs. The Zendo, the meditation hall, is composed of the practices of spiritual discipline and training and not of architectural magnificence. Dogen says to beware of building temples without knowing what we are doing. The primary purpose of the set apart place is for the practice of Zazen and not to be a monument to anyone's ability or reputation. Modesty in living, just as Ryokan lived in his thatched hut, should be consistent with living in the forest or in the open air under trees as the original monks had done. "The Buddhas and ancestors have never desired temples and pavilions," Dogen said. Yet in today's world most of us are loath to suffer the least discomfort in our living and sleeping. Central heating, air conditioning, insect spray, mouse traps, roach traps, the right bed—all these contrivances against discomfort distance us from the natural world and cause us to forget the true human condition and the right of all creatures to exist. Such privilege allows us to exert power in ways that diminish the recognition of Buddha Nature and our openness to the totality of existence.

The choice of spiritual poverty as a practiced virtue cannot be compared to poverty as a result of oppression but it does remind us that privilege exists and that the people who are oppressed are not invisible. In any system of dominance or oppression, a group because of race, gender, sexual orientation, age, ethnicity, or physical ability is prevented from obtaining the means to basic needs and rights and is prevented from equal access to those things that would improve their lives: education, health care, job training, opportunity, promotions, or fair housing. Allan Johnson in his book, *Privilege, Power, and Difference* teaches that privilege is obtained by a group not because of anything its members have done or earned, but only because they are part of a select and dominant group that has characteristics they themselves have defined to be essential for belonging. The oppressed suffer not because of anything they did, but because they do not have the characteristics of the dominant group. This is genuine suffering; by contrast, the vow of poverty in the monastic commitment may be difficult, but it cannot be seen as suffering. All that the monastic does is offered in spiritual sacrifice for something that has a higher spiritual aim. It is beyond the realm of suffering: it is joyful. There is nothing joyful about a mother who cannot properly feed or clothe her children because she can only obtain a minimum wage job in a fast food restaurant or work as a maid in a motel and is prevented because of poverty from providing adequate health care for her own children. There is nothing joyful about a mother or father who must leave their children in an unsafe situation with the fear that they will be raped or kidnapped while they seek work carrying goods across a mountain which will earn just enough to bring home a few bowls of grain. And no one thinks there is anything happy about children in rags splashing in sewage against a backdrop of high-rise corporate headquarters or expensive government buildings. What is difficult is that our systems of privilege and power help to perpetuate the suffering of the poor.

Until recently, preachers in the Christian countries celebrated poverty as a form of blessedness. The history of the saints is full of stories of those who found redemption through a vow of poverty, moving from a life of privilege to a life sustained by the spirit. Women and men today who follow the teachings of Mother Teresa as Missionaries of Charity, vow to live in ways that do not celebrate the development of modernity. They give away their worldly goods, commit to kneeling on the floor for prayer, walk up stairs as opposed to riding on elevators, and eat only a maintenance diet in regard for those who live on the streets of Calcutta and who know what it means to go without meals. Although the Missionaries of Charity saw a tremendous growth in their religious order in the time of Mother Teresa, many other religious orders have gone without vocations and a great number of them have died out. It would be quite unusual to find a family in the United States where the sons and daughters were encouraged to join a religious order as their vocational choice. No longer is this choice revered as a virtuous sacrifice and a sought after lifestyle. Any one who would chose such a life is considered an oddity. This is true in Buddhism as well as in Christianity as well as in any of the world's religious traditions.

The issue of the spiritual leader as an employed professional is common today and becomes problematic when an opportunity to teach is sidestepped because the lesson might not be what the community wants to hear. I recall an incident at an interfaith meeting during a long conversation about violence and guns and the fact that there had been several gun-related deaths in the area. The organization had created a program in which children would be motivated to turn in their violent toys, and guns in particular. People generally agreed that we had to go further to work with violence and youth. I suggested that all the clergy speak about gun violence to their communities and persuade the adults to turn in their guns too. This was met with an immediate, horrified silence and then a sudden shift of topic. The issue was abruptly closed down and never brought up again.

Later I learned from someone willing to tell me how naïve I was: not a clergy person at the meeting would be willing to do such a thing because they had too many in their congregations who were gun owners or members of the National Rifle Association. Were the clergy to speak out against gun ownership, they might lose their appointments, lose an increase in salary, and undergo severe criticism from their leading donors. They wouldn't take the risk. And for all I knew, they themselves had guns hiding under their pillows.

When spiritual leaders who are also teachers are under this kind of constraint, how can we expect people to undergo true inner personal development or for congregations to experience social development within the mystical body. If teachers cannot speak the truth as best they can, then there is no truth that can be heard. A salaried, professional clergy suggests that the community will not develop beyond its common desired level. If a teacher needs to be liked in order to keep her or his position, then the teacher cannot be effective or truly develop as a teacher. The issue is compounded when the spiritual leader has dependents, a wife or a husband and children, and would be in severe difficulties by being uninvited, excused, or dismissed.

The Catholic Church and the Episcopal Church sidestep these conventions by appointing clergy to work in various churches through their respective bishops. The Protestant churches and the synagogues mostly have the dilemma of salary and hiring and the expectations and tensions that go with the system of each local church or synagogue doing its own interviewing and hiring and firing.

In Zen Buddhism, there are numerous styles of clergy and community relationship. Some are teachers at a community for life, while others are hired or appointed for a certain length of time. They can be let go for committing an unethical act and then undergo examination and review via the findings of an ethics committee. They can also be let go by becoming unpopular and then pushed out by a clique of powerful members. The important issue remains whether the teacher can speak freely given the contingency of receiving support from the community. When the teacher is salaried, it becomes more difficult to act honestly and to teach openly.

For this reason, in the history of Buddhism the support of clergy takes place through *Dana*, the generous gift of support from the community to the cleric. This is not an ideal but an actual practice: these gifts are directly exchanged between the students and the teacher and not in any way considered salary. There is nothing implied by the gift; there is no expectation beyond the generosity, which creates an equality of Buddhahood between the two. The giver and receiver are one. The gift is freely given. In this way, the teacher lives in the vow of poverty because there is no promise that there will be a paycheck tomorrow. It does not have to do with the expectation of a certain amount of work; rather it has to do with the recognition of the vow of the Bodhisattva that the monk has made and in which the giver participates at the moment of giving. This is the practice as I understand it in my lineage, but it is not always the way it is done in other places. Poverty and the vow of poverty are not necessarily stressed. Today there are many Buddhist priests who are very well supported by salaries.

When did the practice of poverty as a virtue fall into disfavor? How did it happen? Where was the shift in values? Was it easier in times past to take up a life of poverty and service to humanity? Was it easier to do this when our culture accepted it as a worthy lifestyle? Have we now denigrated poverty so that we cannot see it as a virtue? Have we become so accustomed to having an abundance of food and goods that the smallest decline appears to be a deprivation? Can we no longer do without? Have we as a society lost our understanding of the nature of sacrifice? Mother Teresa would declare to those living in such materialism, "It is not we who are poor, but you." To have much, as we do in the US, to be able to share it so that no one should go wanting for food or health care, and yet to refuse to share it is to be truly poor.

My first Zen teacher Kobun Roshi often reflected on the absence of the homeless from the Zendo. He looked around at the middle class practitioners, well dressed, well fed, and almost all white. He pointed out how we live comfortably and have the luxury to ask the questions "Who am I?" or "What should I do with my life?" Homeless people cannot ask those questions. They want to know where their next meal is coming from. If you are sick, hungry, and homeless on the street, you don't care about examining who you are. You *know* who you are.

Once, while teaching reading to an adult man recently out of prison, I asked him what he wanted to be, what he wanted to do with his life. From the look on his face, I realized how utterly privileged and naïve I was to suppose that that question made sense to everyone. As an African-

American male who had spent ten years in prison and was then age 28, illiterate, uneducated, and battling with the temptation to return to drugs, dreaming up a life was not in his range of experience. Getting a job, any job, and getting one that wouldn't require him to have to be able to read immediately, was a challenge I could not imagine. I had always had the privilege of education. I could teach him to read, but I couldn't give him the privilege that would open the doors of opportunity to learn, to be educated, to rise out of poverty, and to live in dignity.

Tetsugen Bernard Glassman Roshi teaches the awareness of poverty and privilege in an immediate way by putting himself completely on the street as a homeless man and encouraging his students to do the same. In this way they might directly see the system of privilege and how it has disconnected them from the problems of suffering right in their midst. Sitting around talking about how people are suffering is a rather luxurious activity. We could only do this from a position of privilege. Go out on the street and be suffering and see how the world responds to you, he urges. See how you feel yourself. See how you become invisible and unable to share in the division of the world's goods. Maybe then there is an opening to understanding and some who venture onto the street will come back and make progressive and equitable changes.

Going homeless in this way is a very distinct experience from giving up worldly goods and living in an ashram, in a rectory, or a temple, or a convent where three or two or even one clean, regular, hot nutritious meal is very likely guaranteed, where the linens will be washed and clean, the library will be open, well stocked, and available, the washing machine and dryer will always take care of your clothes, where there will probably be no rodents or bugs, and someone will always call you by name.

Ryokan had none of the luxuries of temple life when he returned to Niigata and lived at Gogo-an. He celebrated his happiness in his choice of the monk's poverty, a life most complete and free. He endlessly expressed his happiness at living without the accumulation of possessions and without the anchor of an institution. Ryokan deplored the great suffering in the world of those living in hunger and yet never saw his own vow as one of suffering even when his begging bowl went empty. Contented to live the life he'd chosen, he celebrated the life beyond desire.

> Void of fleshly desire, I find satisfaction in all things.
> Nothing is big enough to cure man's desire, once awakened.
> Wild vegetables are quite sufficient to gratify my hunger.

The gown I have on my flesh keeps me wrapped against cold.
I range all by myself, stags and harts keeping me company.
I sing loudly to myself, children answering me in harmony.

These are not the words of a man wanting or being denied anything. With each great religious saint there has always been choice, and choice is not available to the world's oppressed poor. Children do not choose to go hungry.

I remind myself that to be able to provide certain services in the world, one must maintain one's health. Without it we cannot help others. People who teach or perform social or public service jobs are out in the trenches every day so they becoming discouraged and tired. They must have enough to support and sustain them so they do not suffer to the extent that they cannot help others. But the question becomes: what is enough? What is too much? When does having become greed?

American Buddhist clergy, particularly Zen clergy, are aging and we are suddenly confronted with how to take care of retiring monks as if their aging were some kind of mystery we have never heard of. We have enjoyed and benefitted from their teachings, their sacrifices, their pioneering efforts, all given during their prime wage-earning years, and now they are getting too old to keep up the same level of work. They deserve to retire and still have a place to live and enough to eat, but we have not prepared a way for them to be supported in any sensible fashion. What are we thinking? During the time of their teaching, they were practicing the virtue of poverty, but now they are faced with imposed poverty because there are no support systems to give them a simple, dignified life in old age, which even Ryokan received. We are putting them out to pasture without any grain in the field. The answer is quite simple, of course. We have to contribute to their retirement. All of us must come out of hiding and put money in the monthly kitty so they can have a place to live, eat modestly, and be warm. We live a shared existence. If we fail to do this as a Buddhist society, as Buddhist practitioners, as people of Zen, then we are not prepared to receive and live the Buddha's teachings. Support for our aging, retired clergy should be as freely given as the teachings were given to us without thought of recompense.

The Buddha, who lived on as little as possible, would come to say that the origin of violence is poverty. When people are prevented from obtaining their basic needs and they see others around them able to obtain their basic needs, they become angry and violent because they are prevented from also having these things. Mahatma Gandhi in his passionate drive for social justice would come to say this same thing. The clinging to privilege that drove the caste system prevented true political and social reform. Any system that is so entrenched that it cannot allow itself to take care of other human beings is a system that generates violence.

Some critics of the capitalist system, a system that is based upon privilege and power, point out that if we want to save this planet from ecological destruction we must learn to use fewer material resources, we must create less waste, and we must create maximum allowable levels of wealth. In order to establish any of these practices, we will each have to remember to do them. In an article by Andy Rowell, he remembers the heroic life and death of Ken Saro-Wiwa, who stood up to Shell Oil's greed when he asked that his country Nigeria receive a more equitable share of the oil that was drilled in his homeland and shipped away to the rest of the world. Saro-Wiwa was ultimately murdered because of his campaign against the oil giant. Rowell reminds us that we have to learn to remember. He writes, "Czech novelist Milan Kundera once wrote that 'the struggle of humanity against power is the struggle of memory against forgetting.' The powerful stay in power whilst those who seek to confront it rise and fall. Someone who makes the news today quickly becomes yesterday's forgotten hero..." (Spin Watch, March 27, 2005)

The teachings of the Buddha and the wisdom carried forward in all the streams of Buddhism which have produced profound teachers and teachings must not be forgotten in the face of the terrible forces of comfortable living, materialism, capitalism, and privilege. Are Buddhists in America, on the whole, on a dangerous spiritual path because we have become conditioned to maintaining the systems we have inherited? After all, the very system we are living in supports our lives, builds our temples, and instills in us the privileges we enjoy today. This same system supports oppression. Our true inheritance is the teaching of the Buddha who demonstrated against the class system of privilege. Ethical living demands that we live modestly, that we practice generosity in giving, that we promote and foster sound ecology, and that we question and challenge the systems of privilege that deny equality by right of race, religion, ethnicity, gender, sexual orientation, or physical ability. These issues must be reexamined and must be challenged again and again by each generation and by each one of us in all our encounters. If the origin of violence is poverty, then the origin of poverty is privilege.

Ryokan was well aware of the poverty around him and the fact that he was supported at all is a tribute to the people in the community around him. He wrote several poems about an incident that occurred while he was away from Gogo-an and a thief came and stole his belongings. He had walked up the steep hill from the town through the tall cedars to Gogo-an when he caught sight of the robber who was just making his getaway. The man jumped out of the hut carrying a sack full of goods and ran into the cover of brush and trees, leaving Ryokan startled and nonplussed. Ryokan entered Gogo-an and saw that almost all of his very meager belongings were gone. When he noticed that his sitting cushion remained, one story that seems to lionize his virtue says that he picked it up and ran into the woods calling after the man to try to give him the last thing he owned. "You forgot the cushion," Ryokan shouted, "Come back. You forgot to take the cushion." With that, he writes a memorable poem about the moon in the window:

> The thief left it behind --
> The moon
> At the window.

This is one version of the story. Yet there are poems that reveal a more complex Ryokan, one with as much virtue as the story, but one that shows his powerful range of feelings without having to name them. We know them by the language and images in the poem. He had so little, and to lose a small amount has to have disheartened him. Sure he was sad to lose some possessions, but he was also sad that someone would be so destitute as to have to steal from his meager supply. He was sad about the condition of the world and that men are reduced to such petty actions as thievery. He writes:

> O, the woeful state of this world and man's frozen heart!
> I know not where under heaven I can find my life's peace.
> Yesterday night, beating drums were heard in the village.
> Alarm, they say, at a thief's approach, to scare him off!

But there is response in this next poem that is far less popular than the "moon at the window" poem. Ryokan had been robbed of a few articles that helped to make his life tolerable. A leaning block was one item, which is a small rectangular bar stand that allows someone to sit on the floor at a table while resting on one arm on the block. It is something like the arm of a chair with a base on it so that it stands alone. Having a leaning block allows a person to sit on the floor, lean with one arm, and write for long periods of time because it relieves some of the stress on the legs and the back. The cushion in question is likely a small futon for sitting at or kneeling on at the table. Here is the second poem:

> A burglar made away with my leaning block and my cushion,
> But who could have hindered him from entering my cottage?
> On the night I was robbed, I sat down at my black window.
> Passing showers made empty sounds in the bamboo thickets.

Here is a far more bereft Ryokan left in the shadow of darkness with nothing, not even the romantic moon, just the black window on a moonless night with the sad, sad rain. He can't say much about it. In one sense he seems thrown off balance by the incident. There was no way to lock the sliding door to Gogo-an, and he wouldn't have locked it even if he could, so a burglar comes and robs him. What can possibly be said?

The poem that is popularly championed from this event, the "moon in the window poem," the brief haiku that gives a contrastive flavor and suggests Ryokan was a fully transcendent creature, beyond feeling and need, able simply to let go of whatever had been given to him. I don't doubt his deep-seated goodness, simplicity, transcendent nature and freedom from attachment, but I do hold that he was not detached from the occurrences around him, and he experienced a full range of emotions that saw the complex nature of theft in a world marked by the desperation of the penniless alongside others who enjoy affluence and the privilege of position. "Oh the woeful state of this world and man's frozen heart!" How can he come to peace within himself when humans are so wretched—the privileged frozen in clinging to possessions; the destitute frozen in the need to rob?

But "the moon in the window" poem that is far more celebrated seems, at least to me, to sidestep the condition of those suffering poverty in the world by idealizing the outcome. I don't wish to undercut the beauty of the poem and its effect upon many people, and I feel certain that at some point Ryokan came to that directness of the moon and its light resting with gorgeous grace upon his splintered floor as a symbol of Awakening, but not without many tears and an awareness of the full latitude of suffering that pressed in upon the people of his time.

What does this holy poverty of Ryokan teach us in this time and place? Surely his non-acquisition, non-hoarding, and non-attachment to goods are ample reminder to root ourselves in the spiritual. His concern for the welfare of those around him is a prompt for us to show mercy to the suffering masses and to share what we have. Ryokan makes the best of things by seeing spiritually into the situation and resisting any thoughts to condemn or assign blame. He knows the man has committed a theft, but he also sees the man's desperation. He sees the larger picture of society and its karmic intricacies and he remains human and nonjudgmental. He does not set himself apart nor does he stand in an arrogant haughtiness looking down at the man from his holy perch in order to shame him for his lack of virtue. In the face of something difficult, he continues to dwell in equanimity. Ryokan knows that the Buddha's Precept not to steal, not to take what is not given, means that the mind and the object are one. When we own nothing, nothing can be stolen. Ryokan strives to be good. Dogen Zenji says,

> "Those who feel no compunction to be the best that they can be are human beings who are truly poverty stricken and lacking in good fortune and astuteness. Those who do their exploring and training are among 'those persons' whom we should by all means undertake to know, for, by doing so, we will consequently come to see Shakyamuni Buddha." (*Shobogenzo, Kembutsu*).

The Solitary Hermitage

My hermitage is named after the Five Bowls of Rice.
My room is naked, except for the gong, as they say.
A thousand cedars stand together outside my window.
An iron pot, my rice-cooker, has some kitchen dust.
My hollow furnace is seldom heated by cooking-fire.
Yet in an east village I have a friend, an old man,
He often knocks at my gate beneath the bright moon.

The Solitary Hermitage

In art and in the history of Zen, the image of the hut has served as a symbol of solitude, a place where a monk may go to celebrate the moon, to commune with nature, to reflect on life, to have respite from busy temple life, or to be at peace away from the madding world. Bodhidharma went to his cave, Hakuyu to a mountain lean-to, Basho to a retreat, Han Shan to his hut. Ryokan went to Gogo-an. Many temples in China and Japan have mountain huts hidden from view where monks and nuns may enjoy a time of solitary life. Such practice brings balance to the daily routine, and in the American Zen climate, the laity also have opportunities to share in a time of solitude. As a matter of fact, it may be that given the noise, bluster, and insistence of today's technological world, times of solitude are essential to inner balance and spiritual health.

The small hut named Gogo-an is a distinctive example of old Japanese mountain architecture consisting of tongue and groove fittings and two essential uprights attaching to joists that reach out from the top of the frame to hold an extraordinarily heavy thatched roof. Situated deep on Mount Kugami in Niigata Prefecture, the hut has become a pilgrimage site to modern seekers of the solitary experience, because Ryokan lived there during the central part of his priestly life in the late Edo Period. Ryokan's life and Gogo-an together have emerged as teachings that reveal the development of spiritual maturity as a necessary factor in fully addressing the demands of the solitary way.

For many of us, the moment we recognize our teacher, such as Ryokan's recognizing Kokusen Roshi, we feel a sense of urgency to forsake our material lives and enter practice. For some, we do not take this step because we cling to our possessions and become frightened and unable to let go. We think of all the possibilities that can cause failure and dissatisfaction rather than the power of our own embrace of the Dharma. Others feel this call but recognize that it is a greater work in the present moment to meet responsibilities until such time as we can choose another life. However and whenever we meet our teacher, we carry within us a seed of the solitary mind and the development of what it means to keep one's own counsel. The Buddha told us to find out the truth for ourselves and surely this journey develops as we face ourselves in the mirror of the teacher.

The immediacy of Ryokan's decision to enter a deeper level of practice and to follow Kokusen Roshi shows his spiritual maturity at a very young age. At that point, Ryokan had already stood up to his father and ordered his life toward the freedom to take action and choose the Dharma. Nothing stood in his way the moment he sensed the call to act. His character is revealed early on in this determination, courage, and simplicity of going forward with complete commitment. In this, he did not look back.

Ryokan trained at Entsuji temple for thirteen years until Kokusen Roshi died. Ryokan was Kokusen Roshi's favored student, but when it came time for Ryokan to assume leadership at Entsuji, he left the temple for short periods of time and wandered off alone, until one day, he simply didn't return. Ryokan had been devoted to Kokusen Roshi, but this didn't stem his suffering from deep loneliness during his time at Entsuji: he missed his family and friends. His mother died while he was there and he was unable to return home to grieve with his brothers and sisters. Kokusen Roshi's death in 1791 must have exacerbated the pain of loneliness and grief, and it pushed Ryokan into deep life-questioning and exploration. He knew he did not have the inclination to be a temple leader and deal with the institutional requirements and restrictions of the Soto hierarchy; nevertheless, he had all the capacity and determination to accept responsibility for his priestly vows, to live a life of begging, and to wear the robe through an expression that more closely resembled his own understanding of the Buddha Dharma. For him, this would naturally tend to take the form of the solitary way.

After five years of anonymity, somehow Ryokan received word of his father's death by suicide in the Katsuura River in Kyoto in 1795. Ryokan arrived in time for a memorial service seventy-seven days later, and then in 1796 at age 42, determined to return to his hometown of Izumozaki. He walked back the 400 or so miles and arrived without notice or fanfare. His family was perhaps embarrassed by his disheveled state and some townsfolk didn't recognize him. After all, he had been gone for twenty years and had been living in the out of doors for a long time. His robe was torn and tattered, his begging bowl seasoned and weathered. He found an old shack to live in close to the Sea of Japan and about eight or so miles from his hometown. When his family learned of his presence, they wanted to take him in, but he refused and said that he had enough food and clothing. Of course they were worried about him, and he was an odd ball no doubt, but gradually he became accepted and people began to watch out for him.

The years on the road had influenced Ryokan to settle down. Living through begging had been hard on his health. He was 43 years old, and it was another eight years before one of his friends in the town obtained permission from Kokujoji Shingon temple for Ryokan to live permanently at Gogo-an, although before that he had been living there intermittently. The hut had been built by Kokujoji temple for the guest priest Mangen. The name Gogo-an refers to the five servings of rice that Mangen was served each day. "Go" means five, and "Gohan" means rice. "An" means hermitage. It would be too awkward to say Gogohan-an so it was shortened to Gogo-an. Gogo-an can sound as if you are saying "Five Bowls of Rice" but the kanji actually mean "Five Bowls of Rice Hermitage." Gogo-an was already one hundred years old by the time Ryokan came to live in it. Field mice had eaten small holes through the thatch, and insects from the woods had bored into the floor planks. Wooden doors that lifted out of their tracks had become warped so that they could no longer completely block the extreme wind, rain, and snow that swept along the Bunsui Plain and onto the shelf of the mountain where Gogo-an stood.

Despite the condition of the hut, Ryokan was ecstatic to think that he would have a place all his own, where he could live simply and peacefully in familiar terrain and close enough to people he knew. His vow to live as a Soto Zen priest was unbroken. He firmly believed in the simplicity of begging. We can only imagine how lonely he had been along the road, and how hungry he was to be in company again with friends. He was soft spoken but quite gregarious and fond of good company. He was well read and literate and appreciated good conversation that explored philosophical ideas and language. His happiness at arriving at his own home was boundless and the poetry he wrote in those first years is filled with the joy and ecstasy of settling into a stable situation. It is at this point that Ryokan and the sense of place become integral. Wherever it was that Ryokan had wandered, it could not have been easy. He speaks of his life on the road in several poems and we sense his difficulties. He had to deal with extreme heat and cold, occasional severe storms, monsoons, hunger, and the uncertainty of a next meal. Years of homelessness take their toll on the body. The idea of having a reliable space and a roof to be under must have seemed sublime. Others could find him at Gogo-an and he could receive letters and enjoy visits from friends.

Gogo-an was under the ownership of Kokujoji temple not so far along the path, and so the space was already recognized as a priest's place of retirement. It was appropriate for Ryokan and it must have given him some stature with the people in the town. It was a respectful arrangement, for unquestionably it was difficult for the townsfolk to watch Ryokan struggle without a place to live. All the town's people knew him and were aware of the situation; there is talk and gossip in a small town. Something had to be done. When he finally had a place to live, everyone could feel taken care of and could be relieved of their angst about his homelessness.

It is important to understand that in order for a hermit to be a hermit, it is necessary for the society to accept this lifestyle. The surrounding community completely supports the hermit by respecting his or her privacy, by honoring the intention of his or her life, by keeping a look out for his health and welfare, and, in Ryokan's case, by making sacrifices to maintain his life. Aside from food, Ryokan received clothing, bedding, paper, and ink, and any other articles he might have requested from friends. In a world where the hermit life is accepted and honored, the community makes a tacit agreement to observe and care for the life of the hermit without the hermit feeling watched or beholden to the community. In return, the hermit lives the life that others cannot and balances the community by creating the full spectrum of the self in existence. This arrangement requires trust between the two. The community has to trust that the hermit is balanced and sincere in intention and not misusing the community for selfish ends. The hermit has to trust that the community is aware of him and that they remain truthful in their acceptance of his position and function in society.

In Western terms, Gogo-an is 12 feet by 12 feet and opens with sliding wood doors on two sides. The back wall houses an altar at the center and on the right is a tokunoma, a small alcove for the display of artwork, which usually consists of a hanging scroll with a flower arrangement placed on the floor in front of it. Another alcove is to the left. In the back of the wall is a small door that opens to the outside. This door could be used during the winter for passing things through without having to open the large heavy doors, or as extra ventilation for cooking.

There is a small walkway porch around two sides. Outside, attached to the right part of the hut is an outhouse, just large enough for someone to fit inside without turning around. The floor of the hut is wood and in its present form there is a ceiling so that the rafters that hold up the massive weight of the thatch are not visible. This was likely not the case in Ryokan's day. The under-thatch would have been visible. Several large trees tower over the hut, and bamboo grows among the large pines, as almost everywhere in Japan. Bamboo prevents erosion, purifies the soil, provides food by way of bamboo root, and is used to make simple tools and household items. Every part of the bamboo plant is beneficial. After living in the hut a while, Ryokan would encounter the problem of bamboo growing through the floorboards and ultimately through the thatch.

I have climbed numerous times to Gogo-an in summer and winter. For true alpine people, Mount Kugami seems more like a hill, a volcanic, unconnected mound that forms an obvious hump on the landscape. Mount Kugami itself is about a thousand feet high and Gogo-an is about halfway to the top. The distance involved may not seem like much but the extremes of the weather in the area make this a difficult place to get one's feet down and engage in daily life. Summer foliage closes off the view of the Bunsui Plain, which is a large open stretch of fertile land that tucks in behind the coastal hills which protect agriculture from the sandy winds of the Japan Sea. Small rivers wind through the plain and provide irrigation. The land stretches to the south and west from the City of Niigata and is dotted by villages, towns, and hamlets with occasional small temples here and there.

In winter, winds sweep up the mountain as if aiming straight for the hut. The view is extraordinary and peaceful, but the bitter cold is unrelenting. Given these conditions, Gogo-an takes on an archetype of place that speaks of fortitude and courage against the extremes of life's challenges. I imagined myself living there and climbing the mountain day after day, begging in town, and visiting with friends. In summer, the mosquitoes make a high-pitched whine in the ears while the blistering heat and humidity leave your clothes perpetually wet and sweat trickling along your back. In winter the winds hum low dirges into the bones. This is Snow Country and snow piles upon snow; climbing through the drifts is exhausting and dangerous on hilly terrain, and there are no plows or other travelers to establish tracks. I wondered how long I would last in such a life without heat and adequate clothing, even in the nineteenth century when I wouldn't have known of our modern comforts. How easy it might have been to opt for a room in town, to forsake the robe, and to live with the family, to be in a place where food was available and one could huddle together with other humans for understanding and warmth.

In spite of these considerations, Gogo-an became Ryokan's temple of freedom, his sacred place of solace and practice to truly live his priestly vows, not in terms of the institutional religion, but in the radical way he felt was most complete and free. Life became simpler for Ryokan. He climbed the mountain as he wished, did his begging rounds, played with children, visited with friends, partied and drank sake, played *Go* with the men from town, expressed a luxuriant freedom to live naturally, and at times in his quiet, secluded Gogo-an he wrote poetry. He stored his extra food in a jar and took care to move the insects out of the way before eating or offering food to visitors. On the walls on the closed side of Gogo-an he hung his calligraphic work to dry.

Many of his poems tell of life at the hermitage and what Gogo-an meant to him. The hut symbolized his true temple, his spiritual home in the mountains where Buddha Nature was completely expressed through him. Ryokan identified with the Chinese poet Han Shan and his hermitic life on Cold Mountain. For Han Shan, Cold Mountain became the archetype of the spiritual place where he could express Buddhist and Taoist philosophy and understanding through poetry. Like Han Shan, who may have suffered from a deformity that made him unable to serve in the army, Ryokan identified with the inability to serve in public life.

Gogo-an became a place of protection from the outside world, the world of bureaucracy that Ryokan eschewed. It was a place outside of time and untouched by the demands of organization and temple policy, a hermitage above the clouds, too high on the mountain for anyone in the outside world to be bothered with. After a day of begging, Ryokan could climb to his refuge, write and read poetry, write essays (an art that is promoted in Japanese culture), study various Buddhist texts, receive occasional visitors, and be faithful to his solitude. Still, it would be naïve to suppose that this was all idyllic. The best of the hermit priests and artists have acknowledged the challenges that confront solitary life. Such a life calls for the spiritual and emotional maturity that understands how the hut functions as one's true interior. Dogen Zenji reminds us that the visible world is the manifestation of the spiritual, Buddha Nature. The hut then is that which appears as Ryokan's interior home made visible in the world. The spiritual interior is the beginning of that which we see before us. Sometimes we have to build a temple to express what we envision; sometimes an existing building completes us. Either way, because we have a developed a spiritual interior, we have the eye to see what is possible and our intention becomes manifest. With all this it remains a challenge to stand wholly on spiritual ground when one is hungry, lonely, and cold. A period of tremendous training and self-development would be necessary.

Perhaps we could say that one of the functions of the Sangha is to help us polish ourselves. Those who live the solitary way are those who have matured and have advanced far in their polishing. They no longer need the daily activity of the Sangha to help them understand their tendencies. Perhaps they have released themselves from arrogance and pettiness in their interactions with others. There is a danger that we won't see our own weaknesses if we practice meditation alone, especially in the beginning. Without others around, we fail to interact and see ourselves in performance. There is the tendency to develop ego and this becomes intractable if we have not accepted the "other" in the Sangha as our teacher.

Living in solitary practice suggests that we have come to know ourselves and that we understand the difference between solitude and loneliness. For this, we will have come to a stable intimacy with ourselves and our spiritual practice will be well developed so that we can maintain spiritual life day after day when no one else is looking. We will have learned to practice listening at a deep level, and we will have learned to understand fear. The community trusts that we can do that. We have to become ruthlessly honest about our own condition before we can maintain balance in solitary life and before solitary life can truly generate beneficial spiritual development.

For many practitioners today, our lives are bound by the workplace and by our dependence on technology. We have less and less time for meditation, introspection, and simple pleasures. Solitary practice can seem like a faraway dream and yet for some of us, it may be the most spiritually restorative form of retreat we can take.

The hut symbolizes that spiritual place where we can release ourselves into silence and survey our lives from a different vantage point. It represents a space outside of our usual demands, a place where we will not face continual intrusion and interruption, a place of hope in which we can actually hear the sounds of natural life as well as our own small inner voice calling out for help. It is the protection we manifest in order to release the wounds and snares that cling to us. Isn't this what we hope for in ourselves through practice: that we mature spiritually and truly enjoy life that we live and love well in the activities of daily life? Moreover, it is true that we don't have to wait to be fully mature before we step into an experience of solitude. As a matter of fact, a solitary retreat may be the very thing to throw us into deep listening, an experience that teaches us about our own loneliness, that helps us see the ways in which we are holding on to our old histories, or that enables us to discern our vocation.

This very recognition of wishing to provide a spiritual place for solitary practice and a place to honor Ryokan led us at Olympia Zen Center to build a close replica of Gogo-an. Niho Roshi acknowledged the value of the project and assented to the idea of the building. I requested his permission since I did not wish for the project to be an appropriation of the Japanese celebration of the unique Gogo-an which is such a powerful symbol of Ryokan. Winona Ward, now deceased, the mother of Fletcher Ward, came forward with the wish to dedicate the building to her late husband, Hugh Ward. Numerous other fine people came forward to bring additional financial support. Pat Labine put us in touch with a talented builder named Judy Fleming who created the structure from photographs taken by Fletcher and me on a trip to Japan. Bob Fischer took two weeks of his vacation to work with Judy and her assistant on the foundational footings. The first day on the job Bob said to Judy, "Where are the blueprints?" Judy pointed at her head and said, "Don't worry Bob, they're right here." Bob was a bit unsettled by this, but he soon learned to trust Judy's extraordinary building skills, bringing his own abilities to the tasks as she gave directions. Judy is as thin as a rail and stands about five feet five so one would not imagine by just looking at her that she was up to the task. She worked with a cigarette hanging out of her mouth and an open can of Coke resting on the nearest crossbeam. Ryokan would have loved her.

Jikyo C.J. Wolfer and I prepared daily lunches and persuaded the workers to take a break in the middle of the day when we sat around and talked. We had excellent summer weather and every day the work went forward. In deference to the actual Gogo-an and because of how it is situated on our land and the position of the moon, the doors of Gogo-an at Olympia Zen Center open to the front and right side rather than the front and left as in the Japanese original. The original Gogo-an is one of a kind even in Japan, and I wanted to honor that uniqueness by facing our doors in the opposite direction. Since there never were any blueprints, we have nothing to offer people when they ask to have copies so they can copy our copy. Gogo-an should remain unique.

The wood of our Gogo-an is mostly cedar and the interior is rendered in tongue and groove design with no nails. The building stands along our Path of the Ancestors, a trail through the temple grounds that honors the patriarchs and matriarchs from Shakyamuni Buddha to Niho Tetsumei Roshi. It is located at the point where Ryokan is placed historically in the lineage. Outside the hut is a stone circle that honors the truths of the Buddhas and the Moons, and acknowledges our Native peoples who inhabited the land before us. The thirteen Buddhas and the thirteen moons that appear in every year coincide in their truth aspects. In the very center of the circle is a large stone to represent the Buddha and the Moon of Infinite Space. Our hut is available to anyone who feels the call to be in quiet residence and retreat in the experience of the rustic nature of the hut. The standing statue of Ryokan as a young monk in training faces the center door. Here, Ryokan's eyes are wide open, waiting, ready to host and listen to any practitioner in any condition who comes in earnest to restore inward harmony, to pull back from the hard demands of life, to meditate, write, relax, or be refreshed. There are no criteria for retreats. The field is wide open.

Bob Fischer was the first to test his resolve in living at Gogo-an through the entire month of January. In addition to the two weeks of his vacation which he gave to help Judy put in the foundation, he took a whole month of back holiday for this solitary retreat. He believed strongly in the purpose of Gogo-an and chose the coldest month to be in practice to test himself and to find out what he was made of. We started out the month with a ceremony in the Zendo to wish Bob well and to let him know that we were in the background, aware of his retreat and supporting him spiritually and physically with anything he needed. Bob planned out his approach to dealing with the cold by wearing numerous layers of clothing and sitting Zazen under a blanket which he hunched up tent-like around himself. Whereas Ryokan had been surrounded by mounds of snow and ice, we in Olympia enjoy a more moderate climate of incessant, bone chilling rain with temperatures that can hover close to freezing. Bob used the kitchen to heat hot water and lived on freeze-dried foods for the entire month. For two hours in the afternoon, he walked our long hiking trail to warm up and move and stretch his body. He did not talk to anyone the entire time unless he needed something specific. Slowly, as the month wore on, the light in Bob's eyes became brighter and brighter and his face softened with a beautiful transparency. Bob was simply immersed in quiet solitary practice every day allowing the tensions of life to drop off and his own practice to fill his heart. Most important was the experience of focusing wholeheartedly on Zazen and his own sense that he could survive in the world without all of our technological paraphernalia. There is a certain triumph in knowing that one can actually set out and do this and not fail. Most of us no longer know whether we can survive in the world without all of the devices that eat at our time and energies. At the close of the month, we once again received Bob in the Zendo for a ceremony to complete his retreat. For our part, those who bore witness to Bob's practice felt we had also completed something important that was a gift to the Sangha. For the entire month, our awareness was with Gogo-an and with Bob, feeling the interiority of each day, carrying him in the heart's core, and receiving the gift of the awareness of solitude which is what the practice of solitude is. We were given the gift of Gogo-an within as if the hut had taken up residence in the mind and we could step inside the indwelling Gogo-an and receive the mercies of practice. The reverberation of this practice went everywhere. Ryokan's practice became the image we lived by and this happens whenever anyone stays in our Gogo-an.

Others have come to spend time in residence at Gogo-an to take time to work out personal issues, to fulfill solitary requirements for their training in other traditions, or to have an experience with their children in a sacred space that is a little more luxurious than camping in a tent. The presence of the hut on our temple grounds is a powerful reminder of the meaning of the vow and our interior spiritual practice. Wherever we go, the hut abides quietly at humble attention and continually invites us to enter the interiority of the soul, the daimon, the kernel, the essence we want to touch. This is the central import of its meaning: to call us to remember what is most important in our lives, that we are Buddha Nature. We are completely affirmed in this space and made whole through the presence and atmosphere of Ryokan's profound spiritual practice of acceptance. I have no doubt that the people of Izumozaki, or any people in proximity to Ryokan's Gogo-an, experienced the spiritual residue of his life, as a part of them was continually aware of Gogo-an and Ryokan as a solitary force acting along with their spiritual functioning. We are reminded that we are always in company and are never separate from all of the activities we often think we do independent of others. There is solitary practice, but we are never alone even in that, and we actually have nowhere to hide.

Ryokan, even from an early age, showed signs of spiritual maturity. He exemplified kindness toward everyone, compassion toward those who were suffering, joy for the recovery of others, and equanimity in every relationship without discrimination. Life at Gogo-an allowed him the slow blossoming of Awakening and he could express the Dharma of a great teacher living a natural life. He wandered through the high grassy meadows on the lower plains and sat in the thickets of yellow mustard on the weedy slopes in spring sunshine. Sometimes poems would come to him and he would pull out his small traveling brush and stone and write some lines on the spot, rolling the paper afterward and tucking it into the loose fold of his robe, although most of his poems were written in the residence. He stood under a tall pine or a cedar tree and let the tree life shower him with energy and wisdom. He bathed in the stream, fetched water to the hut, inhaled the mist of autumn mornings, endured the cold drizzle of early winter. In all seasons, mountain life spoke to him through the voices of wind, fox, deer, rabbits, snow in its quiet falling, rain pelting the roof, insects buzzing at night. All of this life fueled moments of pure joy. Yet sometimes the sounds cast him into loneliness.

Ryokan planted a spring flower garden with "autumn bush-clover, pampas, pansies, golden dandelions, a small silk-tree, plantains, morning glories, hemp agrimonies, asters, dayflowers and forget-me-nots." I don't know how he acquired the seeds or the seedlings—perhaps they were gifts from friends or the townsfolk. He hoed a section of earth just on the flat space where the hut sits, and he lovingly planted the garden. Every day he walked down to the stream and filled a bucket with water to bring back to the garden, tending the plants with devoted care. In truth they grew to be the most beautiful flowers he'd ever seen and he was overjoyed to have them near Gogo-an where he could sit on the edge of the porch and lean against the post letting the day go by as he enjoyed the sweet beauty of colorful blossoms so high on the green mountain. But once, to his utter dismay, a terrible rainstorm swept over the area suddenly in late May, a drenching heavy squall with winds that raged and forced the rain to pelt his tender flowers, tearing them to pieces, reducing his garden to a useless mud hole. For days he was grim with a terrible depression but soon pulled out of it when he realized he could not stop the wind and the elements no matter how much he loved his flowers.

Ryokan could not have survived without the supreme toughness that mountain life requires with the unexpected storms and bleak and demanding winters, without a resolve and determination to completely live his vow. At the same time, the solitary life taught him about the nature of loneliness, about not owning goods, about generosity, love, kindness, and impermanence. Without a firm practice and grounding in the basic virtues of Buddhist practice, called the Paramitas, and the grounding of Buddhist texts, Ryokan could not have survived in such a spiritually elegant way. The six most important virtues or Paramitas are Generosity: giving of oneself with open-hearted attentiveness; Morality: understanding and actualizing the deep meaning of the Buddha's Precepts; Patience: steadfast perseverance and cheerful willingness no matter the circumstances; Enthusiasm: practicing with vigor, diligence, and assiduity; Zazen: with one-pointed attentiveness, opening to the vastness of Being; and Wisdom: lucid insight into the fundamental nature of the Great Matter of life.

The solitary hut in balance with the active life of the Sangha, along with living the Paramitas and the Precepts, helps to mature us in meditative practice. Deciding to practice when no one is looking is an essential interior working that has to come if we are to truly understand the Buddha's final words to us to "find out for ourselves." Persistence is a major lesson for us to see in Ryokan's life—that we persist in our spiritual search, persist in our practice of Zazen, persist in our vow so that Buddha Nature manifests a healthy life of spiritual stamina and grace. It is no wonder that teachers and temples create opportunities for nuns and monks who are monastic, or for long-term lay practitioners to retreat to meditative silence. We all need the self-care that comes with respite within this difficult world. The image of the hut is carried in the deepest recesses of the spiritual heart and serves us as we learn to walk and listen in solitude, to live in simplicity, and to follow the Buddha Way.

Ryokan left Gogo-an after twelve years at age 62 to move to the Otogo shrine, closer to the base of the mountain. Even the Otogo shrine, a Shinto site, was no simple walk. The path to it went up a steep hill and then down a long, sharp dip, ladder-like, into the hollow of the shrine; yet the secluded nature of it was equal to Gogo-an. The decision to move came only after a long period of reconciling himself to the practicality of old age. He could no longer climb up and down Kugami's steep slope in all the weather that the North Country brings. He still had much solitude at the Otogo shrine, but it was not his beloved Gogo-an that was also himself. I want to quote a passage from Dainin Katagiri Roshi's *Returning to Silence* and boldly substitute the word "hermitage" for "room," for it expresses the power of place.

> "The hermitage is not something different from us. We are the hermitage, the hermitage is us. Then we and the hermitage communicate with each other in the rhythm of identity-action. We have to take the best care of the hermitage we can, because the hermitage is not a material being apart from us. The hermitage is a great being called Buddha-dharma. Buddha-dharma means the unity of Buddha and us, Buddha and the hermitage." (172)

In his chosen life of poverty Ryokan had expressed love to his fullest capacities. He had lived a life of emptiness and simplicity in a monk's hermitage. He had not disappointed himself in his own capacities to remain faithful to his vows, to his teacher Kokusen Roshi, to Dogen Zenji, to the First Teacher, Shakyamuni Buddha. As a solitary, he was elegant in the tenor and mature texture of his spiritual activities. There was a triumph in succeeding on the mountain. But, as he walked down to the shrine with his meager belongings, surely his thin face exhibited an unmistakable sentiment. It was a moment of sadness to leave his hermitage and yet Gogo-an, as the manifestation of his spiritual nature, was still his deepest ally, his cosmic refuge, his wistful home.

> My house is buried in the deepest recess of the forest.
> Every year, ivy vines grow longer than the year before.
> Undisturbed by the affairs of the world I live at ease,
> Woodmen's singing rarely reaching me through the trees.
> While the sun stays in the sky, I mend my torn clothes
> And, facing the moon, I read holy texts aloud to myself.
> Let me drop a word of advice for believers of my faith.
> To enjoy life's immensity, you do not need many things.

The Art of Begging

Early, on August the first,
I set out to beg in a city.
Silver clouds sail with me.
Golden winds ring my bells.
At dawn I see the thousand gates and doors thrown open.
At noon I feed my eyes with cool bamboo and basho tree.
East or west, I will not pass a single house unvisited,
Not even the slimy haunts of drunkards and fishmongers.
Straight glances of honest eyes break a pile of swords.
Strides of steady feet scorn the heat of boiling water.
Long ago the Prince of Pure Eating preached how to beg,
And the Beggar of Beggars truly acted out his teaching.
Since then it is two thousand, seven hundred years and more.
Yet am I no less a faithful pupil of the First Teacher.
Therefore I beg, a bowl in my hands, a gown on my back.
Have you not read or heard
Of that noble one of high repute, who solemnly decreed,
Equal in eating, equal under the divine law we must be.
Look out, everyone lest you should run loose unawares.
Who stands secure against the lapse of countless years?

The Art of Begging

Takuhatsu is the spiritual activity of Zen Buddhist monks to receive charitable offerings for support of the temple. It is the tradition in Zen practice for monks to go on rounds, holding their eating bowls to receive offerings. The person who gives, places the offering in the bowl and the monk acknowledges this by chanting a verse that acknowledges gratitude, as the giver and the receiver are one. They then bow to one another in mutual gratitude and respect. Both parties are recipients. Together they are the teaching.

In takuhatsu, the monks offer the teachings by means of their own example. In exchange for this, they are supported by those who trust in the truth of the teachings. In addition, almsgiving is considered a virtue, which increases good. The monks through takuhatsu provide an opportunity to practice this virtue.

On the narrow stone paths that curl up the hill in Tamashima near Entsuji, or Izumozaki, Ryokan's hometown, there are echoes of the hermit begging. His woven sandals leave soft imprints on the dirt walkways. His robe rustles, just barely, if you draw near. The ching-ching of his begging stick resonates against the old walls of the cities. His clear, deep voice intones *Hannya Shingyo*, The Heart Sutra. When he is given an offering, we hear him chant in acknowledgement of the exchange. We find solace in his presence, are comforted by the opportunity to remember this moment of practice as refuge—Buddha, Dharma, Sangha—the oneness in giving and receiving.

Ryokan as teacher of *takuhatsu*, a true student of Shakyamuni Buddha who first led monks on begging rounds, speaks of the lineage he follows:

> Long ago the Prince of Pure Eating preached how to beg,
> And the Beggar of Beggars truly acted out his teaching.

105

Since then it is two thousand, seven hundred years and more.
Yet am I no less a faithful pupil of the First Teacher.
Therefore I beg, a bowl in my hands, a gown on my back.

Ryokan began his begging life at Entsuji temple. It is customary for monks to walk among the villagers and hold their bowls open to receive support. Food or money might be placed in the bowl and in this way the monastery and the townspeople are united in the life of the Dharma. At Entsuji, you'll begin at the *Sodo*, the living quarters, hat in hand, leggings laced up, straw sandals tied around bare feet, robes hoisted and tied high on the waist so as not to gather too much mud and road dirt, half gloves modestly covering the hands. At the main gate you will stand in a circle and chant a blessing to begin the begging. Then, straw begging hats put on, single file, each one lines up and descends the mountain on that same trail that Ryokan walked, along the steep hillside with homes on either side, passing by the homemade shrines and altars with their offerings to the Buddha. Eventually the path feeds into the road that crosses the river. Herons sulk on the ropes that are strung between the boats and their pylons.

The town of Tamashima has modernized since the time of Ryokan. Almost every town has its form of shopping mall, a long road of shops side-by-side, walls touching, sometimes half a mile long. Tamashima is not so extensive. Most of the shopkeepers live in apartments above the stores. The front side of their rooms looks out onto the street and they have entrances on the street side, and cross ventilation, as well as staircases that feed into the shops.

Japan works on the honor system. There is very little theft and only a few items are subject to thievery such as umbrellas and bicycles. Train stations are known haunts for pickpockets, but foreigners rarely are victimized. This is because foreigners make a huge outcry when they discover they are victims of a pickpocket, whereas Japanese people are embarrassed and will keep silent. Pickpockets don't want to call attention to themselves so they will select people who tend to remain quiet. For the most part, shopkeepers trust that no one will sneak into their stores and steal their goods. So they tend care of the home upstairs while at the same time listening for the arrival of a shopper. This is a peaceful and practical system.

To perform *takuhatsu* through the shopping area, monks spread out and take either side of the street, stopping at shop doors while chanting, and waiting for the shopkeeper to make an offering. Most shopkeepers are ready and make an immediate offering, but those who don't want to give will escape up the stairway to avoid being seen by the monks. Americans have their own methods for escaping from beggars by turning their eyes away, ignoring them completely, or crossing the street to avoid eye contact. Anyone who doesn't want to give has a route of escape.

If we near the heart of Ryokan, we cannot miss this echo—the living breath of his teaching. The music of his footsteps that brush the cobblestone path is present in our own steps. If we catch this rhythm, we are not bound to Tamashima, Izumozaki or Bunsui. We hear the presence of Ryokan in America. Yet, when we enter Zen practice in America, we do not see the practice of *takuhatsu*. How deeply can we follow Ryokan? Can the practice of *takuhatsu* actually take root in America?

We tried for a period of time to continue the tradition of *takuhatsu*, but in America the practice of *takuhatsu* is not so direct and simple. As a matter of fact, we no longer practice *takuhatsu* in the form expressed here. As we continued to practice, we met further and deeper derision from the very conservative wing of our city. We began to be laughed at, pushed aside, and then ignored. I began to feel we were doing a disservice to Buddhism, putting this misunderstood practice and Buddhism and Zen in a bad light. It would be wrong to persist just out of stubbornness if Buddhism were being disparaged. We had, at last, to content ourselves with the forms of begging we do which are indirect and never face-to-face in the directness and honesty of *takuhatsu*. That is, we beg through the mail in our fundraising and we have a begging bowl on our altar. These are the methods that many faith groups take on. There is nothing wrong with them, but they do not express the Dharma in the same way as face-to-face giving does.

Ryokan's choice to practice humility and poverty through the actual practice of *takuhatsu* is against the law in some places, as it has become in our town. We do not see monks begging on the street, yet we see the homeless, the disabled, and the forlorn.

Begging is no longer a religious activity. The word "begging" has taken on distasteful overtones, for it is thought to be the practice of those who are too lazy to work, of those who are homeless, sick, infirm, or drug addicts and are "ripping off" others. It is seen as something vile and repugnant, and yet in these difficult times, there is more and more of it out of hunger and desperation.

Takuhatsu and begging appear to have different meanings and different intentions. *Takuhatsu* is a religious gesture, an activity of prayer for the benefit of society. Both the monk and the public are recipients or beneficiaries of Dharma. To give to the support of a monk's life, is to express full trust in the life and truth of Dharma. To give alms in this way is itself virtuous and expresses recognition of the living Dharma. The one who taps the begging stick and the one who puts an offering in the bowl are both participating in the one practice of *Takuhatsu*. Both are as one supporting the Dharma.

I recount a time when we practiced *takuhatsu* in Olympia. After zazen and morning ceremony, we ate a modest breakfast of oatmeal and tea and still felt hungry, as one should not go begging on a full stomach. The rain held off but it was misty, windless, and raw. Streets and alleys were full of puddles. Only students who had especially requested that they have this opportunity were participating, and two were doing *takuhatsu* for the first time. We were not trying to create a spectacle, we were simply practicing. Students wore their street shoes and standard Japanese temple work clothing that they had borrowed from me. They each wore *rakusu*, little robe, and a *takuhatsu* bag to collect offerings and identify our affiliation, Olympia Zen Center. I wore the traditional *takuhatsu* clothing of the monk: my robe was hiked up and tied at the waist so that the white cloth leggings showed from below the knee, half gloves covering the visible portion of the forearm, towel around the head to keep the wide straw woven hat from slipping, and grass sandals over Japanese socks with the big toe separated from the other toes like mittens. We all carried begging bowls. I also carried a tall stick with three rings on top that would make a clear *ching-ching* as it tapped along the pathway leading the procession.

Takuhatsu is one of the deepest traditions of our lineage in Soto Zen, which manifests alongside the poet/priest Ryokan who spent his entire life relying only on the fruits of *takuhatsu* for his food and sustenance. My teacher, Niho Tetsumei Roshi, is abbot of Entsuji, where Ryokan trained as a monk. It was along the narrow streets near Entsuji that the sound of Ryokan's begging stick first rang against the mud walls of the old farm buildings. Later he returned to his hometown where he wandered throughout the Bunsui Plain, living his life completely as a mendicant, practicing *takuhatsu* from town to town. The tradition of *takuhatsu* is unbroken.

I, too, was raised in a begging tradition. The 1940's and 1950's were still close enough to the Great Depression to appreciate that begging at one time was commonplace. Catholic monastics practiced begging in Brooklyn, New York. It was not unusual to see clerics sitting outside shops holding coffee cups to collect coins, and as I realize at this moment of writing, in those years it was only women I ever saw. Nuns maintained this religious practice supporting their communities through this work. In our neighborhood in Brooklyn on Thanksgiving, children had the practice of dressing in old, torn clothing and going from door to door to beg for Thanksgiving. This served to remind the householders that kindness to beggars, especially on such a holiday as Thanksgiving, was virtuous and to remind the children that all people were worthy of notice and that sharing the goods we have is what we are to learn to do. Thus, we children collected a few coins for the missions and took home some slices of apples and a handful of nuts.

In Olympia, before leaving the Zendo we faced one another in a line and chanted *Hannya Shingyo*, The Heart Sutra. We emerged into the cold winter air, and felt a sudden vulnerability. There was no hiding, no way to disguise what we were doing. We were suddenly visible to everyone. The mixed nervous feelings about practicing *takuhatsu* in America rose with the wisps of fog that caught around our ears as we walked in single file.

A little more chanting and moving down the hill into town we intoned "Ho," only it sounded more like a deep "Hooooooooooooooooooooo" coming from the belly in a long vibrating stream. We breathed at differing times so the echo was continuous. Cold hit the hand and the fingers numbed around the bowl like frozen lotus petals forming a winter cushion for a Buddha.

Only a few Zen communities in America are practicing *takuhatsu* in this particular ancient form. In Olympia we have no models, only my experience of practice in Japan to go by. We have had long discussions about why, although it was practiced and taught by Shakyamuni Buddha and all Zen monks since, *takuhatsu* has not been transmitted to America. We have asked why Americans embrace zazen meditation and yet do not incorporate *takuhatsu* in their practice.

Begging is no longer legal in our city nor is aggressive panhandling. The word "panhandling" is an American colloquialism developed from a practice of the homeless, meaning literally to use a pan with a handle for begging. In America, religious begging has all but disappeared. The Salvation Army, the last of the religious street beggars, comes out at Christmas with the unmistakable Army bell at the door to the supermarket. As late as the 1950's, religious organizations practiced begging on city streets in New York. The religious went from door to door, or they stood at train stations or outside factories accepting donations. This behavior was then acceptable and recognized as virtuous practice. As begging became popular, but not completely acceptable, during the hippie movement, young people took to the streets demonstrating the need for changing values in society. They did not hesitate to ask for money and people were curious and generally responsive. But as the hippie movement faded, it gave way to the homeless who became more and more visible on city streets. As the numbers of the homeless increased, the practice of begging persisted and the public became impatient with the continuing visibility of the poor. Other areas were beset by Hari Krishna followers who had aggressive and confrontational methods. Some cities passed ordinances to prevent beggars from annoying others. Begging is now illegal in some places and restricted elsewhere.

The disappearance of begging as an activity of the religious may have to do with the increased wealth of the American religious communities. Few religious groups practice poverty today in the style in which Ryokan lived or, for that matter, St. Francis of Assisi, in the Western Christian tradition, who taught his monks to store no more food than they could use for one day. Each day Francis and his brothers practiced begging, and any left over food was given to the poor. Today, most of the religious live in comfortable housing with guaranteed meals and an income. Begging has been institutionalized in the form of fundraising and is conducted by every church and nonprofit corporation in America. Giving is no longer the direct matter of going from the donor to the begging bowl. We make appeals through the mail, requesting donations for every imaginable cause. If some are moved, they send a check. There is no contact, no communal prayer, no immediate direct eye-to-eye gesture.

As we walked, we reached the main road alongside reasonably heavy traffic for a Saturday morning, which also proceeded in single file. People saw us and stared. They were not sure exactly what we were doing, but our demeanor was unmistakable. Our begging bowls were held out. We were deep in meditation. We crossed the streets with the traffic lights and passed in front of motorists who now saw us head-on, not just with a sideways glance. We were right there together. Memories of Sangha discussions felt woven into the fabric of these black sleeves. The insistent *ching-ching* of the stick kept us concentrated and we were a living Sangha, moving in a single body through the city.

Our first direct encounter other than with people in cars occurred at Bread and Roses, the Catholic Worker soup kitchen. About ten men had gathered on the sidewalk talking as we turned the corner and walked toward them. Likely, we appeared as a small attack force arriving out of nowhere. There was no precedence for this; no picture that they could turn to for reference. We moved at a moderate pace, chanting *Enmei Jikku Kannon Gyo*, an appeal to the Bodhisattva of Compassion. They faced us and stared since this was their block, their territory, and many who stood here then would be begging later in front of other shops, or huddling in doorways of businesses that had closed for the weekend. Shopkeepers would ask them to move, saying they were bad for business and that they kept shoppers away.

I looked out from under the hat and my eyes met one man's eyes. They were deep, tired, and watery from being in the cold. His look was full of question but in an instant we both knew something: the *takuhatsu* I was doing was engaged in prayer; his *takuhatsu* was engaged in a raw kind of desperation that fights back incessant hunger and cold. I could go home and shower; he could not. I had a place to sleep; he might not. Yet a dimension to begging seemed to wash through him and was revealed in his eyes, was made spiritual, was lifted out of the stereotypical attitudes he had to face every day. It seemed a reminder to him that the great saints begged, that Christ loved the poor, and he seemed to intuit the ennobling nature of his life at that very instant. We had seen inside the other in a stark moment of truth.

There are other dimensions to this encounter too. I had dared into this territory of begging without the crisis of hunger. I had dared to ask for participation on the street where Christ's children and Buddha's children walk together. What we felt was more complex, was layered with nuance and the pain of not meeting fully in the intuitive happening, which quickly passes. We were pulled along by the simple action of walking, by the silence of going forward step by step in our meditation. We tried to give the man a paper that explained what we were doing, but he didn't want to take it. He shook his hand and his head together. He was not afraid of us. He seemed more afraid of what we represented. Finally, another man accepted. We went on our way.

As we got closer to town, the resistances and encouragements that Sangha members expressed in the course of several discussions appeared and dissipated one by one. The support to do *takuhatsu* had been powerful. Niho Roshi urged me to practice it in America. Others, who themselves could not go, had expressed it as deep, pure activity that they knew takes courage. They were somehow in awe, unable to express exactly what *takuhatsu* meant, but they sensed the rightness to begin.

Other Sangha members feared we would be perceived to be like the Hare Krishna. Because we live in an area of fundamentalist Christianity, they feared that through *takuhatsu* we would be misunderstood. To be misunderstood means to be discriminated against, I suppose. Perhaps some feared that they would have to defend their practice in some way. They might be seen as guilty by association.

Others spoke of what it means to face the homeless, what it means to be associated with such a massive problem and to stand face to face on the street with all the vulnerability of feeling and be unable to come to terms with it. Some resisted asking for alms in such a fundamental and direct way, knowing that there is no expectation on either side. Usually we make some kind of bargain when we ask for money, but in *takuhatsu* there are no promises, no expectations. It is the most direct way of almsgiving and the gift is pure.

Some felt that by begging we might take what would otherwise be given to a homeless beggar. We tend to give where wealth has already accumulated. We want to identify with success, with accomplishment, and therefore we will be generous where we can see some sign of economic protection or the legitimate use of our money. We want our gifts to be insured. We want accountability for our judgments of worth. Thus, we will give to the successful organization but not to the homeless.

Perhaps the deepest, most debilitating notion, and one that hits the entire nation and not just those who worry about *takuhatsu*, is the fear of being perceived as or associated with the poor. The fear that we will find ourselves on the street begging someday is real for some people. The thinking is that so long as we ignore the poor around us, we can pretend that it won't touch us, won't show up on the doorstep, won't shake the stuffing out of our plans and our children's welfare, and won't find us knocking helplessly on the door of the shelter in the middle of the night. A more crippling fear is to have the hobby of shopping and accumulation of goods ripped away in a sudden mortgage failure, no longer to be a consumer, no longer to participate in the culture of the mall.

Some mentioned the problem of the visibility of *takuhatsu*, of appearing publicly as poor. They were new to practice and were not ready to say that this was their route, their way, their life and home. Some wanted only to come and sit and go home. They were not yet prepared to be Buddhists, at least publicly practicing Buddhists.

Takuhatsu is a deeply visible part of practice. It means going into the public arena, the market place, dressed as a monk and yet if you are dressed in this way your face is not seen. It means having society see you in relationship to what you own and profess. But, the Zen clergy as well as the Christian clergy have become invisible today. This may have several graces such as allowing the laity to feel its own spiritual strength and equality, or giving the clergy some anonymity in their personal life; the other side is the loss to society of what a visible clergy means. To be visible means that there are those in society who are willing to live as examples for people to emulate. It means that the clergy willingly and openly live the precepts from moment to moment in all conditions. It means that the young have some notice of the potential of spiritual commitment, someone they see who lives inside yet outside of society, someone visible to whom they can turn, someone who will advocate for them. It means that when someone sees clergy, they have hope. This is the meaning of the visible robe of Buddha: *hope*.

Takuhatsu is not the same as what a homeless person experiences of being invisible to society, of swallowing the meaning of hunger, confusion, cold, hopelessness and bare survival. It finds itself in the same root experience, yet *takuhatsu* confronts the self from a different angle. In *takuhatsu* there is the assumption that we recognize Zazen as the primary way, that the practice of Zazen brings healthy change, balance and harmony, and therefore that we enter society with bowls open to receive support to continue this work.

It sounds as if I advocate for a separation of clergy and laity or that I suggest that clergy have some power or spiritual inclination that laity doesn't have. Quite the contrary. True, the basis of *takuhatsu* is the belief that monks carry the Dharma. Monks do not carry any more Dharma than laity, but monks are those who make lifetime vows and whose vocations compel them to foster the Dharma such that they arrange their lives to practice in intense and consistent ways. In a very democratic society such as America, we have not created any separation of clergy from the laity. Suzuki Roshi speaks of Americans as being not quite monks and not quite laity. But we clearly have not wanted to make a distinction, nor should we. Dogen Zenji teaches there is no difference between monks and lay people. And yet we delineate teachers, make hierarchies, establish levels, have additional vows. Among other things, to be a monk means to be visible in the community, just as one is visible as the bank teller, the UPS driver, police officer, bus driver, postal clerk, or gas station attendant.

Were all these complexities too much for the first Zen masters who came from Japan? Was it impossible to understand the dynamics of this culture in relationship to *takuhatsu*? Is this why they did not transmit *takuhatsu*? Is this why some Japanese teachers today laugh a little to themselves, make a face and say, "No, no, no. *Takuhatsu* is impossible for Americans"? Perhaps *takuhatsu* is too deep a confrontation with the culture. Is it too direct? Is there something in our culture, some distaste for begging that recommends against it?

Perhaps some Japanese Zen masters were reticent to carry out this aspect of practice in America for several reasons. For one, we are a violent nation. In *takuhatsu* we have no protection. It is deeply vulnerable work. Americans are verbal, outspoken, and will not hesitate to belittle or ridicule what they don't understand. In *takuhatsu* we have no cover from the rude or the obscene. Japanese teachers may have seen this as too controversial, too problematic outside their own culture. They may have felt that to establish practice at all, it had to be acceptable to society. It had to find its way into daily life, into the mainstream. *Takuhatsu* may have seemed too radical for the American mind. This, they may have felt, was a purely monastic practice that has yet to take root.

Will *takuhatsu* take root in America? First, a deep visible monastic stream must flourish. While householder Zen and lay practice continue to be established, such practice must rest on a foundation where training and a clear understanding of practice have firm ground and are solidly planted in the monastic stream. Perhaps monasticism itself will take on some redefinition, but it still must be the core ideal. In lay practice we are always at risk of becoming a "Sunday only" congregation, using the cushions occasionally, but not when it interferes with the primary schedule of daily living. Something larger than us has to happen. Americans must discard any notions of casual practice, must give our lives, fully committed to the Dharma. We cannot see Zen practice as faddish or exotic. It is work at its core. Many men and women must give their lives to become these very roots. Deep practice must become natural in the culture, a respected and familiar expression.

It is the very matter of establishing a monastic stream that tells us why the Buddha begged. He went in search of poverty, to live among the least, to learn non-attachment and acceptance. The alms-round permitted the monks to practice poverty and humility, to learn how to overcome vanity; and it allowed the laity to benefit, to merit, through acts of generosity. Monks further learned acceptance since they were completely dependent upon what was offered. They had to eat what was put in the bowl and they ate just once a day. There is a story of Makakasho who was said to have eaten a leper's finger that had dropped into his bowl in an extreme practice of acceptance. We are told stories of St. Francis and Ryokan, who ate food which had been shared by insects and grubs, having gone beyond any discrimination regarding the condition of the food. To them, this simply was Buddha's and therein lies the nourishment.

As we walked further downtown, people stepped aside as we came by. Our voices reverberated off the back walls of shops where doors stood open. Customers looked out as we passed. The low vibrating chant penetrated each portion of brick and mortar, of plaster and wallpaper, display shelves, cabinets with antiques, dress racks, glass cases filled with jewelry, taverns where there were leftovers from early morning happy hour, card stands, books, incense, stacks of futons, coffee urns, bubbling pots of soup in restaurants. The words were healing. Yet, we saw ourselves reflected in shop windows, our images like double exposures against the sheer massive piles of goods stacked in shop windows. We ourselves were startled by the contrast. We sensed the impact on others.

The practice of *takuhatsu* does not teach us to be dependent upon society, asking for something that is not earned or pressuring a community for an entitlement to food or goods. Rather, it teaches us to be dependent on nothing, to live our original homelessness, to include the homeless in thought and deed, to share everything, to accept what comes to us, to be generous, to be humble in society, to recognize the timid, to resist fame, to be modest, to resist the acquisition of goods, to throw off ego, to have the courage to be fully visible in practice. And as we practice *Takuhatsu*, that is what we teach and that becomes our culture. But it is also easy to imagine that these are the very lessons we resist the most.

We walked beside the marina and were photographed by a tourist against the backdrop of the state capitol building, a dome that is the copy of our capitol in Washington, D.C. I saw the photograph in my mind's eye, the name "Entsuji" written in Japanese across my hat and the capitol dome above. In this incongruous image it still seems to make sense, the collision of cultures, time, no more nor less than this direct activity, the same incongruity that is at the heart of practice. We followed the boats to the farmer's market where we stood in one area for half an hour. One of us gave the handout to the curious who walked slowly away reading. In a moment they came back and made an offering. Some, when they understood, returned. One man gave us a bagel that we later gave away to a man on the street.

Making money or filling the bowl in *takuhatsu* is not the point. The point is the practice of acceptance, humility, poverty—a way to address the arrogance of our material times. When we see that we are all dependent upon the same Emptiness, that we are all homeless, we can fully exchange the deepest meaning of this practice. Our giving away, our receiving is the same act. The spiritual act of *takuhatsu* reminds us where our true treasures are and that the begging bowl and the hand filling it are always Empty.

We had a long walk back up the hill to the Zendo. We did not chant on the return, but walked silently, observing the smallest seedlings that were tucked here and there in crannies of stone and fence that lined the avenue. Unexpected details in the landscape seemed surreal. They filled the heart. Two young missionaries from the Church of Jesus Christ of Latter Day Saints crossed the street to find out what we were doing. We stopped for a moment and traded stories. We agreed on this: rain rains on us together; and our feet share the same wetness. The faithful gray sky and rain of the Pacific Northwest persist. Then we walked home.

After we chanted, we washed our feet and placed the offerings on the altar. We drank tea, ate lunch, felt stiffness and soreness set into the muscles and joints. *Takuhatsu* is hard work, and is cleansing and purifying. Without doubt those who go out to do *takuhatsu* want to go again. They want it to be their regular practice. The deep matter of monkhood has been touched. Each of us is calmed and thoughtful. We sense Ryokan in our midst. We begin to appreciate the life of a mendicant, the life of simplicity in poverty. Poverty: not an end in itself, but a means to a life in the Buddha, the One most complete and free.

Ryokan's familiarity with the townsfolk never guaranteed a full stomach. Once he wrote: "This rank absurdity of mine, when can I throw it away? This abject poverty I shall take to the grave with me. After dark, along the dirt road of a decaying village, I carry homeward my begging bowl, weathered and empty." We see that *Takuhatsu* is Emptiness itself, not the practice of acquiring goods or food. Ryokan expresses this even when something does arrive in his bowl: "After a long day of begging in the city, I go homeward, fully contented with what I have got in my begging bag. Holy man, which way lies your home, your resting place? Somewhere beneath those clouds, is all I know about it." The echoes of Ryokan's begging stick are the teacher, resonating wherever practice is, across the ocean to America, to the forested land of the north. The weathered bowl waits, the sandals rest at the gate. How deeply I regret they are not put into action.

Children and Friendships

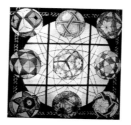

Bright as a gilt bow,
Spring had come, bringing flowers.
Begging was my aim;
I walked down the village street.
I found on the way
Children absorbed in their sport,
A handball bouncing.
I joined them then straight away.
And all the long day,
One two three four five six seven,
As they kept bouncing,
I sang by their side,
And as long as I sang,
They went on bouncing.
Thus we sang, and thus we bounced,
One misty spring day,
Sweetest of the sweet spring days,
Till darkness wrapped us complete.

Children and Friendships

Ryokan found nourishment for his soul in the life of children and friends in the village. He also found the prevalence of the death of children a source of great pain. It was a dark time in Japanese history, filled with plague, fires, floods earthquakes, and dire poverty. Hundreds of children died in these events and Ryokan would say that for all his life and practice he had never found a way to put an end to so much pain and suffering. Poverty was widespread in the area and people began either to sell their children or adopt them out because they did not have enough food to feed them. It was preferable to let a daughter go to another household where, even though she may work her fingers to the bone, she would at least have meals, and the family would have one less mouth to feed. The great pain of letting a child go to another family in a faraway village ate into the hearts of these struggling people. Parents who were distraught and desperate saw their children walk away from the family, and young friends were torn apart. It was enough to have your house burn down, and then to be forced to give away your children. All of this is impossible to conceive of, and yet the world still witnesses such sadness.

In the midst of this suffering, Ryokan did what he could to alleviate some of the pain and grief in the local families; in this way he assumed an important role in supporting the spirit of the area. He played with the children and helped them forget the strained look on the faces of their parents. He lifted the hearts of the parents and friends who knew that with him their children were in good company. He functioned as a teacher, steering the children toward good manners and morals. He practiced kanji with them and supported their studies by talking with them and teaching them about the world around them. He showed them how to respect nature and one another. He served as a folk healer, bringing herbs to the sick, and he took several students in the study of poetry. In these exchanges with friends and children, Ryokan could have an uncomplicated and supporting relation to the family unit and a way to express his enormous love and care for his fellow humans. Now, without having to shoulder the problems of a town administrator, he could genuinely take part in the internal life and health of the village in the way that he saw was his role as priest, friend, kind-helper.

> In the holy shade,
> Beside this secluded shrine,
> Children about me,
> I play one quiet spring day,
> Praying the day have no end.

Play and prayer were nearly synonymous in his generous vocabulary. Many of his poems are about playfulness with the children, but not always, as so many died during his lifetime. He writes with deep tenderness for the parents who are holding a memorial for the death of their baby:

> Just one year ago
> We snapped off to amuse you
> A tiny plum spray.
> This year, we break another
> To decorate your gravestone.

But then he could turn to a lightness of heart as much to comfort himself as to say that life is not all darkness and sorrow. He had a healthy laugh, and he loved fun.

> One misty spring day,
> Longest of the long spring days,
> With village children,
> A handball I bounced, singing,
> Till gloom buried us at length.

> Come along, toddlers,
> Let's march together, shall we?
> To the mountainside.
> Wait one more day, and too late
> We'd reach for cherry blossoms.

In recognition of Ryokan's relationship to children, a meditation week for youngsters is held every year at Entsuji temple in the month of July just at the finish of the school year. As many as 500 children from third grade to middle school are invited to early morning Zazen before they continue the day in school. They arrive on the mountain carrying a sitting cushion at 5:45 a.m. and take a seat in one of the buildings. All of the buildings must be used to accommodate so many children: Ryokan's house, the Buddha Hall, and the Zendo. There's a feeling of great anticipation: all of the children are in uniform; only the girls with designer hairclips and decorated socks with little bears and dolls embroidered on the cuffs show any variation in their dress. Some boys are shoving one another and trying not to laugh. A few parents escort them and quietly tolerate their impatience and fidgeting. In each of the buildings they are given instruction by one of the members of the Zazenkai, and Niho Roshi, perhaps Inoue Roshi, and Niho Seiju Sensei, are seated on the teacher's platforms in each of the buildings overseeing the young meditators. The children will be invited into the space where Ryokan has lived and they will be taught to sit. Because of Ryokan's love of children, this annual Zazenkai is to promote the development of practice for young people, to remove the mystery and awe of the temple, to put children at ease in the sacred practice of Zazen, and to develop the character of patient listening and acceptance of others.

Once when I was a monitor for the children's Zen practice, a huge insect flew into the section where I was helping the children with their posture and their legs. The black darting flyer must have looked to the children like the size of a soaring golf ball, as it certainly did to me. It would hover and then suddenly dash in an unexpected direction zooming at their heads. They couldn't scream, but a quiet and obvious hubbub was affecting the area and they clutched one another and hid their heads inside the sweaters of their neighbors on the cushions. I unfurled the long sleeves of my robe and began waving them like a flag on a pole hoping to chase the monster outside. No luck, and my waving only made the students all the more unsettled and terrified. I looked up at Niho Roshi on the teacher's platform and he looked at me in disbelief as if I were a misplaced character from a trivial Oscar Wilde comedy. But I pressed on and at last captured the innocent intruder in my sleeve and took it outside. The young meditators were relieved but giggled uncontrollably nearly till the end of the meditation period. What was remarkable was that no one scolded them, made them feel bad for their natural response, or even tried to quiet them, as they were in Ryokan's playful arms where there was no judgment on anyone's behavior, particularly children's.

Ryokan easily takes up the theme of children in many of his poems and this is a special subject, with the playful monk tossing a ball back and forth with the young ones who live in town. We may take these plain children's poems on a simple, lighthearted level, but as Professor Yuasa says, Ryokan takes this to a mystical level as he "found a supreme religious experience in the simple act of playing with children." It's as if he becomes a spiritual parent to the children, nurturing them in complete acceptance. In one very famous poem, Ryokan shows himself at play while revealing the depth of his mystical state:

> The silk ball in my sleeve pocket is worth my soul.
> Its best bouncer, proudly, is no other than myself.
> Should anyone question me on the secret of the art,
> By way of reply: one two three four five six seven.

He says there is nothing more important than the care of children in playful exchange, seeing to their happiness and influencing their world. His soul depends on this exchange. That he is the "best bouncer" implies that he is free to inhabit the world of children in ways that others cannot enter. Ryokan has not the daily encumbrances of home and business to keep him away from children's games. He can focus fully on the emotional health of the children when he is with them. He is best because he has given up the world and may offer the children someone in whom they can find hope in the Buddha, even as he is bedraggled and foolish. And then, if we don't understand how important this is, he says he will tell us what true balance and harmony really are: the simple order of the universe articulated one moment after the next, the art of life, taking each moment as it is, "One two three…"

Ryokan had a nephew named Umanosuke who could not get his life in order. He wasn't a child; he was a young man ready to find his way in life but his mother, Ryokan's sister-in-law Mitsuko, couldn't control him. He drank heavily and caroused with people who would do him no good. Mitsuko climbed up the long road to Ryokan who was surprised to see his sister-in-law standing outside Gogo-an.

"I need help with him, Ryokan," she said, "Umanosuke drinks and becomes unmanageable. He's wasting his life. Won't you please speak to him and tell him to stop this behavior."

Ryokan was taken aback. "I don't know what it is I can do," he answered.

Mitsuko begged and Ryokan at last agreed to go to the house. He packed his few things and walked down the long road with Mitsuko planning to stay over at her home so he could find a chance to speak with his nephew. Later in the evening when Ryokan was sitting quietly in Zazen posture in his room, he heard Umanosuke stumbling in the hallway. The shoji doors slid open and Umanosuke entered with a bottle of sake in hand. Ryokan didn't move. "Come on, uncle," he said. "Let's drink together and have some fun." He fell onto the floor beside Ryokan, trying to get Ryokan to take a swig of the rice wine. Still, Ryokan remained still and silent. "Come on uncle, it's fun. Let loose. You don't need to sit Zazen. Let's drink." As Ryokan refused to respond, Umanosuke gave up and left the room, stumbling against the wall and slurring some words of anger.

After a few days, Ryokan prepared to leave, having been silent all the time. Umanosuke had slept late and Mitsuko felt disappointed that Ryokan had not been successful in speaking to him, but she had to let Ryokan return to Gogo-an. It seemed there was nothing to do. Mitsuko prepared a lunch box for Ryokan along with other food that would last him a few days. They went to the front door where Ryokan sat to lace up his straw sandals. Umanosuke suddenly appeared and Mitsuko asked him to help his uncle with his laces. In his good nature, he immediately agreed and knelt down at his uncle's feet. As he did so, great tears fell out of Ryokan's eyes onto Umanosuke's hands. Umanosuke was completely startled and looked into his uncle's eyes, which were filled with love and compassion for him. Not a word was spoken between them, not a word of rebuke from Ryokan, not a word of contrition from Umanosuke. It was a look so deep and compelling that it penetrated Umanosuke's very soul. From that moment everything changed. Mitsuko and Umanosuke stood together and waved as Ryokan ambled along the road toward his mountain home. Umanosuke's life turned around, he stopped drinking and chose a better way.

Ryokan did not impose his lifestyle or his practice on children or friends; rather, he left people to be as they were, knowing that sermonizing or proselytizing doesn't change much. He had many friends in the village and enjoyed companionship with a number of men. A set of translated letters are to be found in Ryuichi Abe and Peter Haskel's, *Great Fool Zen Master Ryokan* demonstrating not only Ryokan's closeness to his friends, but also his reliance upon their goodness for his needs. This wonderful, full-bodied text gives the range of Ryokan's reach into the community of his contemporaries and presents a multi- dimensional human being and profound Buddhist teacher who knew and understood the world around him. Numerous poems express the warm sentiment he held in his heart for the good people in his neighborhood. They lent him books and got together with him for rich conversation. This tender poem was written to a poet friend who came to visit him at Gogo-an and stayed overnight:

> In the shady grove
> Outside my pine-built cottage,
> Rain began to fall, drizzling.
> My beloved friend,
> You must stay here in my house
> A while longer till it clears.

When friends came to visit, Ryokan always offered to share some of his food. They'd find any excuse to get away and not eat from Ryokan's cache because no one knew how long the food had been in the big iron pot he used to store any extras.

"Oh please stay and have a little meal with me," Ryokan would say.

The friend would answer, imagining the maggots wriggling in the pot, "Oh no, Ryokan, you need your food. I couldn't impose."

"Nonsense," came the reply, "there's plenty to go around and you'll need some energy for the walk down the mountain."

"Ah Ryokan, you don't understand. My wife is already cooking dinner. She's been at it since daybreak and if I'm not hungry enough to eat with great gusto, she'll be deeply hurt. She'll think I've been out partying. I wouldn't want to hurt her."

"Well, if that's the case, of course, we'll just have tea."

"Oh that's kind of you Ryokan. I knew you'd understand. I'll come another time and we'll enjoy a meal together."

If another meal came up, the man would be sure to bring some rice balls from home that were freshly made. Ryokan would be delighted to receive this gift from one of the households, and the next time he went down the mountain he would be sure to knock on the door and offer his thanks to the woman who had made them.

Ryokan well knew that friendships, loyalty, honesty, and right speech were the hallmarks of life in relation to kindred spirits, who were the most important gift anyone could receive. Even though he was openly frank about things he needed such as undershirts, socks, rice, pipe tobacco which he loved smoking, oil for his lamp, miso, and vegetables, he didn't so much depend upon these or the care he received as that he lived in a state of gratitude for what friends did do to support his life. He didn't make himself a dependent but rather he became a bodhisattva to whom others could choose to express generosity and thereby participate in a good and harmonious community. He wrote many letters to friends and was invited to their homes for short periods for social gatherings. It seems he would take advantage of these times to commiserate with the people of the village on subjects such as poetry, medicine, or current events, or to check on the welfare of the families. Among his friends were numerous scholars who engaged in excellent discussions of classical poetry and Confucian and Taoist philosophy. Following these visits he would write letters of thanks for the care and the gifts he'd receive. Many of these friendships were cultivated with more frequency while he lived at the Otogo shrine where he was closer to town and could more easily keep in touch with people. Often he found himself an overnight guest enjoying the hospitality of his friends and benefactors. It was a happy time for him. He was well regarded by the community and looked to as a spiritual teacher. Oh to have been a fly on the wall at any of the gatherings to hear the dialogue, repartee, laughter, and deep exploration of ideas.

Ryokan writes a long poem about receiving a surprise gift of a fur piece from his good friend and brother. Never has Ryokan touched anything so remarkable and soft and he spends the days wearing it around his neck and spread out beneath him at night. He feels sure it is a dream, so he keeps it with him for fear it will disappear. At last he realizes he can put it underneath his kimono and undershirt and put it right up against the skin of his back and for the first time in years he feels warm even though it is the middle of winter and icicles are hanging from the eaves.

> I took the risk of
> Wearing it beneath my shirt,
> Yes, my body shirt,
> The one I slept in,
> Right next to my fleshly skin,
> And as I lay still
> I was amazed by the warmth
> Of the sleep I had.
> So warm was the fur, in fact,
> That at midwinter
> Spring seemed to have come to me
> While I stayed dreaming in bed.

Then he realizes he has nothing to send as a thank you gift that is greater than the treasure of his own life and his own precious breath. But he instructs his brother and friend, not to brag about the importance of the gift and he ends the poem in the midst of the words of caution.

> About me I have
> Nothing proper to send you,
> But my living breath.
> Yet, I warn you in good time.
> Brag not about it, my friend.

He seems to say that the gestures between friends register so deeply in the heart that boasting would destroy the purity of the action. The giver and receiver are one; so showing off about what one has done could undermine the bond of friendship. Friends don't actually give a gift to someone else; they give the gift to the friendship and both share and benefit equally in the exchange. Ryokan's cautionary words also imply the magnitude of the gift, its meaning to Ryokan, and the depth of his gratitude.

Some parents take up practice even if their children do not, and in this they still are modeling commitment and virtue, thereby teaching in a quiet and important way. Many old friends also return from great distances to say hello, to check in after years of absence. To keep the spirit of the hut alive while they are away is the work of the continual river of spiritual friendships that swim in the river of Dharma and form a long chain of connections through time. Ryokan is one of the foundational points in this river, a barometer to test where we have been and to ask what we have done with our lives. After we've gone away, we sometimes need to return in order to see where we have been. A friend asks us such difficult questions and a friend opens her or himself to receive such inquiry. What have I done with my life? This is what Ryokan, by his presence and friendship, was asking his nephew, Umanosuke. What are you doing with your life? Living in the vicinity of Ryokan's hut and in the spirit of his life prompts the question, thus the reverberation of Ryokan's friendship and vow is unleashed through time and spreads over the many continents of interconnections. Those lucky enough to touch and be touched by the life of Ryokan can carry that spiritual friendship into and throughout their lives.

Eyes of the Constabulary

In its innocence, the heart is like water pure and bright.
Boundless it presents itself to the sight of its beholder.
Should a proud desire rise, however, to disturb its peace,
Millions of wicked thoughts and pictures will bog it down.
If you take these fancies to be real enough to engage you,
You will be led farther and farther away from tranquility.
How sore it is to see a person crazed about earthly thoughts,
A heart bound closely by the cords of the ten temptations.

To hear the words of truth, you must wash your ears clean.
You will not, otherwise, stand true to what you will hear.
You will ask what it is I mean by washing your ears clean.
It means to rid yourself of all you have heard beforehand.
If only one word of your previous learning remains within,
You will fail to embrace the words, when they come to you.
Resembling what you know, a plain lie may seem acceptable,
And a simple truth, strange to your ears, may sound false.
How often, alas, we have our judgments made in our hearts,
When truth lies outside, in a place beyond our conception.
Let us not commit such folly as to steep a stone in water,
To hide it for a moment knowing it will show in due time.

Eyes of the Constabulary

Poor Zen Master Ryokan had no one to vouch for him during the times he was taken into custody and suspected of being a criminal. His robes were dilapidated, torn, and dirty from sleeping in the fields. He didn't look like he belonged to any temple at all. Who would believe him? He would be put in a room where he would wait and wait, then be given some water, tea and rice. And still he would wait and wait. If the criminal that the police were seeking was eventually apprehended, then Ryokan would be let go. At times, Ryokan's behavior over a period of such detention was instrumental in proving his innocence. If need be he could show his papers from Kokusen Roshi, but Ryokan was disinclined to speak on his own behalf. He accepted his situation and waited it out. He was in no real danger; he wasn't about to be hanged. Perhaps it was also the case that the jail provided him a respite from the rain for several days where he could recuperate from the difficult effort of homelessness and wondering where he would find his next lean-to and bowl of rice.

Various arrests occurred throughout Ryokan's life as he wandered around the Bunsui valleys and ambled here and there at some distance on his begging rounds. He was well known in his own town, but when he roamed outside to further reaches, he became suspect. Criminals were know to hide behind the monk's begging hat, collect money from unsuspecting people and then make a clean getaway with enough to keep them in food for a substantial time. Ryokan was unperturbed by the accusations of criminal behavior. He quietly stood on the grounds of his innocence and allowed the police to sort things out. He made no attempts to remove himself from the situation and this very likely disturbed the police who were forced to care for him as long as he was in their custody.

My own brush with the constabulary in Japan could hardly compare to Ryokan's many experiences, yet it taught me a general lesson in composure when coming up against the power of the police force. Before entering monk's training, I lived on the top floor of a high-rise apartment in *nishi-guchi* Okayama, the west side of the city, while I taught at the women's college. On weekends I packed up my things and rode the train to Entsuji where I sat Zazen and engaged in temple activities with the Zazenkai, the group of lay practitioners connected to the temple. Most of the members were middle-aged or older men with only a few younger ones and two or three women. A man named Masan Miyake, who was integral to the Sister City organization between Kurashiki and Christchurch, New Zealand, and Kansas City, Missouri, spoke excellent English and served as a translator for Niho Roshi and me. He was also a long-time Zen practitioner and was always there with his generous assistance with language. He transported me around in his car from time to time and helped me with many things while I was in Japan. Along with Zazen, the Zazenkai members worked in the garden, and ate breakfast together. Sometimes we raked the entire side of the mountain, burned massive piles of leaves, built ornamental bamboo fences, reorganized storage rooms in the temple, helped set up tents for events, or prepared materials for handouts. The Zazenkai essentially did whatever was needed to support events or projects that the temple master undertook. When our work was finished on Sundays, Miyake san would always drop me at the train station at Shin-Kurashiki for my return to Okayama.

These activities would not have been unfamiliar in Ryokan's time, except that his teacher Kokusen Roshi, whose name means Stone Wizard, was famous for having his monks move large stones around the temple grounds to build supporting walls to prevent erosion. The stones also secured the walls that serve as a back fence and create a walkway for the lay temple members to reach the cemetery. All of this is hard work, manual labor, is a means to create cooperation among practitioners, to help us become less self-centered, and to still the hurried, talkative mind. Practical Zen they call it. Practical Zen!

Back home after the weekend, I would shop, cook, do laundry, prepare lessons, read student homework, score exams, and get together occasionally with friends. Other teachers lived in the same building on lower floors. Seventh heaven I called my floor. From the window I overlooked the bustling city of Okayama, which from this observation point looked like Liverpool—a vast concrete sea of buildings, train lines, neon lights that glared through the night, construction sites for new high-rise apartments, and a steady stream of cars along a main thoroughfare. Just below the balcony where I hung my laundry to dry, an all night convenience store kept the thrum of activity pulsating with its automatic sliding door that opened with the touch of a finger. Groups of young people would park their bicycles, buy junk food, and then stand around outside in their school uniforms joking and laughing.

On the opposite side, a long balcony ran along the building on every floor and provided an entrance to each apartment with staircases and an elevator at one end. Now and then I would walk up the seven flights for extra exercise and stand at each landing for a moment enjoying the view from this side of the building. The buildings disappeared into the tops of trees and the greenery fed into a large park with a sports arena and beyond into the hillsides with mixtures of bamboo and maple. Several large private homes with classically stylized gardens stood to one side below the apartment building. From the upper floors I could see the sloped tiled roofs and the delicately manicured patterns of grasses and stone, sand and gravel in the pricey estates.

Several times I stood on this side of the balcony, sketchbook in hand to represent a sense of the hills. These few rough drawings captured the experience of being where I was at that moment, giving a sense of place rather than depicting the accuracy of the scene. Drawing allowed me to stand aside from words and helped me to stay in touch with my body. In a land where I was illiterate and mute, sketching now and then gave me an additional means of expression. The sketches were never meant to be anything at all, just a way to remain in contact with myself.

One day, one of the Japanese teachers told me he had read in the newspaper that morning that there had been a big robbery in my neighborhood, in one of the houses next to my apartment building. Someone had entered the home, held the owner at knifepoint, and stolen about two and a half million yen, about $25,000 in cash. The owner reported that the thief had a foreign accent and had spoken halting Japanese. Everyone was abuzz. Such things rarely happened in Japan. It was not a crime-ridden country and although you certainly locked up your apartment when you went out, there wasn't an expectation that you were in danger of any kind. To a large extent you could rely on the good will of the Japanese people. The idea that someone had gotten away with such a crime was a serious matter and a grave embarrassment to the police.

Days went by and police went from door to door asking if anyone had seen anything suspicious. Had there been anyone new in the neighborhood? If we could just give them the slightest information, it would help. On a Friday night, I had a classroom full of students over for a party. The police knocked on the door again and took a look around to see who was there. Still, we had nothing to say to help them out. Others had had the police at their doors, but it was my door that they persisted in knocking on. They would stop by at various unexpected hours to ask again if I knew anything. Repeatedly I answered, "No, I haven't seen anything," and "No, I don't know anyone who would do such a thing."

The persistence of the police gave me the distinct feeling that I was being followed. When I would go to the train station, the same man would appear standing watching me and then follow when I got on the train. I saw a pair of binoculars from the window of a facing building directed at my living room window. All of this sounded neurotic when I told friends, but they agreed that the authorities would stop at nothing to uncover who had committed such a crime. This was particularly true because a foreigner was thought to be involved. The authorities went to the school where I taught and questioned my department chairwoman. A nun friend was forbidden to visit me. My apartment was suddenly off limits to anyone connected with the school and I found my evenings rather quiet. One nun who visited me for tea and a little taste of sane, non-convent, relaxed life was forbidden even to approach the building. It convinced me that the building and I were under surveillance.

I began to recall the actions I had engaged in that would lead the police to my doorstep. There had been the organizing of the Peace March during the first Iraq War. I wanted to lead the rally for the sake of the American and other foreign people living in Okayama. Most of us were against the war and we wanted to feel we were doing our part in the anti-war movement. Most of the Japanese people I knew were also against the war, but because the American government had declared war, the Japanese government was compelled to follow; the Japanese people could not speak out against their government even though they disagreed. This was particularly true for teachers.

In trying to make arrangements to march, I'd gotten a lead on someone who could help me with the organizing. He in turn took me to meet some of his friends in an office building in downtown Okayama. These gentlemen turned out to be members of the Buraku Liberation League, a human rights organization that spoke out against oppression and on behalf of those considered to be unclean, invisible, or untouchable. A single member was called a "burakumin" with the word "*buraku*" meaning "villager" and "*min*" meaning "person." *Buraku* people were those who had engaged in the "dirty" occupations such as butchery, garbage collection, or caring for dead bodies. They were poor, uneducated, and had lived in particular areas in cities. They were discriminated against so that they could not advance in occupations or education, nor was it likely that they could marry outside of their class. The existence of outcastes can be traced back to the Middle Ages, but the feudal period in Japan saw a rise in the system that fostered this subclass of people. There were approximately three million Japanese in this situation. Try as they might, they could not bring themselves out of the fate of the downtrodden. Because everyone in Japan is registered with the government, it is easy to find out the history of an individual and determine what neighborhoods they lived in. An underground real estate book that identified people who came from these addresses remained in existence and secretly circulated among upscale corporations, banks, the wealthy, and the not so wealthy. If it were known that you came from one of these addresses, you could lose your job, be denied marriage, be excluded from social organizations, and find yourself not accepted in a school. There would be no explanation except that you would discover yourself being shunned. Many *buraku* people simply kept silent and lived their lives without expecting to progress or to enjoy the same opportunities of other Japanese. The Buraku Liberation Movement came about in response to the plight and mistreatment of this group.

There were those Japanese who were openly hostile to the *buraku* and who posted vile graffiti suggesting that *buraku* should be gassed and burned. There were no civil rights protections against the outward display of such discrimination. The organized *buraku* in turn were accused of using unconventional tactics to confront those who discriminated against them and because of this they were deeply feared. For instance, they would wait outside a place of employment where they knew a *burakumin* had been fired. When the CEO of the company came out, the league members would suddenly come out of hiding and, wearing masks and costumes, they would surround him with cat calling, play drums, and attract a crowd. Holding placards, they would dance around him and call him names. Even in America where you could slough off accusations, no one wanted to be accused of discriminating against minorities. In Japan this it is supreme embarrassment that one could not easily recover from. Saving face is everything. People did anything to avoid being confronted by *burakumin*, but, of course, that didn't stop prejudice and ill treatment of particular people, it just drove the prejudice further underground.

It was this intractable situation that Shakyamuni Buddha met in his own society by way of the caste system. One by one the mistreated came to his door asking for refuge against the unremitting corruption of discrimination. The monastic order represented liberation because it saw all its members equally deserving enlightenment, care, and nourishment. The caste system did not exist in the monastic order as created by Shakyamuni Buddha. He opened the door to everyone—beggars, lepers, thieves, whores, princes, paupers—men and women, old and young, infirm, and vital. Ryokan lived out this model. When he went begging, he begged from everyone alike. He said, "I will not pass a single house unvisited, not even the slimy haunts of drunkards and fishmongers." Everyone must be and is included in the Dharma.

I sat quietly in the office while the *buraku* gentlemen photographed me and decided that I could help with work they were doing with similar anti-oppression groups in the Philippines. They explained how they had expanded in Asia and were using other groups to strengthen their combined cooperative impact. They said they could gather help for the Peace March and that the foreigners could march in front and that they would march in the rear supporting the Japanese voice. I was to apply for the permit with the police under the guise of being a foreigner and they would remain in the background as secondary support, but they would march with us in the rear of the group and hold up their signs at the rear.

When I left the office I knew I was in trouble, caught in an impossible situation. I felt sure that if I used their support and tactics I would be sent out of Japan very quickly and forbidden to return. I sought the help of a Japanese friend who advised that I immediately cease any connection with these people because it would only result in trouble for me as a foreigner. Japan's battles were its own and although they were kindly toward people working wholeheartedly in their country, they did not take well to interference in their problems. And it wasn't that they weren't working those problems out. There had been legislative movement in the direction of anti-discrimination, and groups that were complicit in maintaining lists of *burakumin* were making efforts to destroy their discriminatory records.

The Soto Zen temples themselves had been forced to erase records that identified any of their members in the class of *burakumin*. Under Tokugawa rule from 1603 to 1868, the temples had been ordered to keep clear records of untouchables so that they could trace the family history through birth and death registrations. When a lawsuit came about in the early 1990's that implicated the history of discrimination in the temples, the Soto Zen administration was ordered to remove *burakumin* labels and erase any trace of that history. Thus, the Soto Zen administration educated the temple abbots and priests and ordered them to remove all discriminatory tags. A side issue in this was that the hierarchy was also forced to open the way for women to receive fair treatment and to begin to remove the obstacles to allowing women to receive training for the priesthood.

How torn I felt for I had always been a supporter of the oppressed. I had been particularly feminist in my declarations, and I had many times in my life spoken out clearly on behalf of minorities. In this instance, I had to learn that without adequate language to sort my way through this, I could not engage in this work in a country in which I was a guest. Some friends said that the First Iraq War was dying out anyway and that therefore the peace march would have no meaning anyway. Yet I was determined to march for peace. I ceased the relationship with the man who had brought me to the burakumin. The police did grant a permit allowing us to march from a central point in the city, through the shopping center, and back to a point where we held a rally and gave speeches on behalf of peace. We played a marching *taiko* rhythm through a boom box as we walked. At the speech rally site, a *taiko* drummer played and gathered the occasional Japanese who were courageous enough to pause and find out what we were about.

As fate would have it, the day we marched was the day of the large military land offensive against the Iraqis and the war was suddenly again front-page news. The national television station filmed and interviewed us and we got lead coverage on the evening news. We all mused on the amazing timing since the application and processing of the permit to march had taken at least two months. I wondered whether the nuns were watching that night to see us, their foreign teachers fired up in front of the cameras, rabble-rousing and making trouble. The police would not have forgotten this activity in their robbery investigation.

One Sunday morning at Entsuji, a former police chief came to Zazen. This man was aware that I practiced at Entsuji because I'd met him at another temple where he practiced. He knew me by name and knew his way around Entsuji. During our teatime, the subject of the robbery came up and we fell into discussion about it. I felt sure he had come to Entsuji to find out whether I was harboring another foreigner. Criminals had been known throughout history to hide out as religious mendicants where they would be less apt to be suspected. It is easy to keep one's face hidden beneath the wide brim of a begging hat. It is easy too to stay at a temple and remain hidden from the world. If some foreigners were looking for a hideout, the temple would have been perfect. But this was surely not the case. I simply had no one I was assisting. He could go back to the city and report to the police that there was no one hiding at Entsuji.

The police continued investigating and weeks later one night at three in the morning, my phone rang. I got up and turned on the lights and talked briefly with the caller long enough to point out that it was 3 a.m. in Japan. The next morning at 7:30 sharp, the doorbell rang. There stood three policemen, two in uniform and one in plain clothes. One seemed rather burly for a Japanese man. I wondered if they were planning to have to tackle an oversized foreigner. At any rate, I invited them in. They took off their shoes and we all sat on the floor while I was questioned. One of the men looked around in my bedroom and kitchen. The plainclothes man said he was from Interpol and that they were looking for the foreign man who had robbed a house in my neighborhood and held a knife at the owner's throat, threatening his life. They wanted to know about the sketches I had been doing on the balcony. I stifled a laugh and picked up my sketchbook to show them. Pathetic little drawings they were—enough to make someone feel sorry for me that I would take the time to do them. The were hardly the mapmaking that could be used by a thug as the layout for a break in! I asked them why they were bothering me and they led me to believe that because I was a single woman, I must have a man hidden somewhere in my life. There was no such thing as a single woman who would go to another country alone, live alone, and conduct her life independently of a man. Most likely I was hiding someone somewhere. Women just did not do this kind of solitary living.

The next day, I strode into my department chairwoman's office and demanded that she intercede and request that the authorities stop pestering me. Employers have this kind of power in Japan. They can protect their employees. The nun looked at me with a kind of suspicious contempt. The equation went this way: the authorities knew best and they were following me, therefore they had reason to follow me. I must be harboring a criminal and lying about it because the police were investigating me. I was bringing a bad name to the school, no one should come near me, the police knew best, and they wouldn't do this without a reason.

She sat at her desk tight-lipped and cold.

"This is outrageous," I said. "I'm a middle aged woman, I am an employee of this school, I have no boyfriends, and I certainly don't go around planning robberies."

"The police have to do their work," she responded, "and that building you are living in is no longer an acceptable address."

"This school chose that housing for me," I said. "You have the relationship with the landlord, not I."

"Perhaps you don't choose suitable friends," she said.

"My friends and the people who visit me are perfectly fine. As my employer, you have an obligation to protect me. If you cannot be effective in stopping this investigation," I said, "I will get on the train and go straight to the consulate in Kobe."

She sucked in her breath and conceded. "I doubt that will be necessary." She did not actually say she would do anything, but I knew that she had no choice but to get the police off my back.

Indeed, that was the last I saw of the police. Whether they continued to follow me or track my banking, I have no idea. I simply was aware that the intensity of their probing was over, but I also knew my time at the school was limited. Being a Buddhist became uncomfortable while teaching in a Catholic school and it was something of an embarrassment to the sisters that I would choose Buddhism over Christianity. As much as I attended the school assemblies and put forth a good face, they knew that underneath I was a rebel, a deserter, a heretic of sorts, and they preferred that I not stay. They had to find a way for me to go. They did not know that I had been planning my getaway for a long time and that my escape was already written in the stars.

Being suspected in a country like Japan is considerably different from being suspected in other countries where I might have been arrested while the police did their investigations. In some countries you could sit and rot in the jail cell without outsiders knowing you were there. You would be powerless to get free. Japan has more grace, and a foreigner working for a prestigious women's college would certainly not be ill treated because it would reflect upon the school. The individual is identified with the employer and it would be very rude for the police to treat someone as a criminal, particularly if it turned out to be a false claim. The authorities would have to make enormous apologies.

In my case, I had no fear that I would actually be arrested in Japan. I had not done anything illegal and I couldn't be taken into custody without evidence, but there had been subtle pointers via the peace rally, my occasional bouts at sketching which Japanese would rarely do in public, and the odd assortment of people I sometimes engaged with—loners, misfits, undesirables. I had plenty of upright friends too, and perhaps the mixture helped to create suspicion.

I always ask how I can bring attention to the privilege and oppression around me as well as around the world. Many such as I in the circumstances leading up to the peace march would fail to stand up and reveal the systems that keep oppression in place, but the Peace March did speak to what we were able to speak to. Had I chosen to work with the *burakumin*, I would not have been permitted to continue to live in Japan, and I don't know where that would have gotten me. The intractable nature of a system that permits privilege to continue has somehow to be acknowledged and revealed in order to bring progressive change. I meet situations one at a time, choose as best I can, and recognize that I cannot do everything at once. The system is global and has been in place for as long as recorded history and the battle against privilege and oppression must continually be fought. Ryokan's quiet pathway is but one way, and he would be the last to insist that it is the only way. The important point is to live authentically and to be unafraid to choose and to act.

Ryokan writes in the opening poem,

> Let us not commit such folly as to steep a stone in water,
> To hide it for a moment knowing it will show in due time.

Isn't he teaching us to be honest, not to entertain the folly of discrimination which must ultimately be faced and overcome through social justice? He tells us to listen to the words of truth. Racism and various forms of discrimination continue in the United States just as offenses against the *Burakumin* and the *Ainu*, the original peoples, continue in Japan. Our practice should be never to hide from the poisons of discrimination that may fester within us, but rather to dwell in clear listening and open dialogue with the words of truth.

While Ryokan must have experienced some sense of alienation during his arrests, I suspect that it deepened his compassion for those who experienced harassment, or who found themselves in criminal activity out of the desperation of poverty. Ryokan's character was so innocent that he could only imagine that a person who would take up criminal activity would be someone who had lost all hope. My own fairly minor experience of being suspect drew me into a sense of the true protection of the Dharma. Ultimately, I demanded my rights, but in a deeper sense, I had no fears that I would be swept into an untruth that would land me in prison. This attitude may have been naïve and foolish on my part, but it was grounded in a faith strong enough to face up to power. This may not help the thousands of minority residents in the U.S. who discover themselves unfairly accused and locked away because they do not have the means for a fair defense. It is up to us who live in freedom and have some relative privilege to challenge the laws and attitudes that permit racial unfairness, or any kind of unfairness, in our penal system and to address the problems with the mind of a Buddhist and as Ryokan says, with a "heart like water pure and bright...hearing the words of truth." Zen practice does not mean that we just sit still and do not respond to the world around us. It teaches us to keep a magnanimous openness to all of experience and to address the world with a pure heart, speaking truth to corruption. This is the true meaning of Ryokan's name: "Ryo" means "magnanimous" and "Kan" means "good."

Way of Ink and Brush

To Issairo

Early in the morning, one of those burning days in summer,
I sought shelter from the heat, high at a mountain temple.
In hushed solitude, by the parapet of an elevated terrace,
A gentle breeze from the pine woods fanned my sacred gown.
It was not long, as it seemed, before I saw birds go home
Amid the whole range of mountain peaks aglow with the sun.
I also dragged my feet down the slope upon my bamboo cane,
And slipped into my grassy house at a most leisurely pace.
A spray of yellow leaves arrested me in front of a window,
And by a short poem tied to it, I discovered to my regret
That you had paid an unrewarded visit in my short absence.
For hours after that, sweet thoughts of you so whelmed me
That at last I took my brush and wrote this poem on a fan.
Kindly accept it, my friend, a poor meed for your journey.

Way of Ink and Brush

Were we to locate Ryokan at all, it might be in his calligraphy where one cannot hide behind the ink. And it isn't that he was trying to hide, it's that his nature was polished by purity of character and thus he became transparent and no longer subject to being read in the usual way of identification. Yet, in his calligraphy, even his transparency is visible. Ryokan was recognized in his lifetime, at least in the area where he lived, for unmatched and spirited calligraphy.

Ryokan is known for using a particularly long-haired brush, which helped to create his unusual style. It is extremely difficult to handle such a brush because the mixtures of heavy and light strokes that help to create the beauty of Japanese calligraphy require a light and flexible hand. The brush must literally dance on the paper. If the weight of the hand is too great, the hairs of the brush become entangled and begin to split. The stroke is easily ruined. Ryokan seemed to have painted with a very light touch, letting the brush dance up and down with great skill. One could not lose concentration for even a second and would have to profoundly enjoy the activity to succeed as skillfully and honestly as Ryokan.

His friends in town were keen to take advantage of his skill. People who ran shops asked Ryokan to paint their signboards because his calligraphy was easily recognizable and Ryokan's handwriting attracted business. If Ryokan lost a game of *Go*, he paid his betting debt with calligraphy. Since he was a poor *Go* player, it was easy to get a piece of calligraphy out of him. It became quite desirable to own a piece of Ryokan's art, but truly this recognition went right over Ryokan's head. He was aware of it but it did not influence him to paint more, nor to get better at *Go*.

For a time, I kept a correspondence with Keibun Otogawa Roshi, the brother of my first teacher Kobun Chino Otogawa Roshi. Keibun Roshi lived in Japan and taught me to use the brush and ink as the only tools for writing. He wrote letters to me in English on long streams of narrow rice paper, and he raised philosophical issues of practice and life for discussion. The ink was always uneven, dark at the point where the brush had been dipped in ink and then softened into grey as the words seemed to pour in a stream off the wet stone. He said that if I wanted to learn the nature of the brush, I should use the brush for everything including notes to my own self and my family, and for lists to go shopping. The brush should become so familiar that it would become as natural as holding a pencil or pen.

Keeping a desk alive with ink and brush is no easy matter in a modern home and in a culture that doesn't celebrate the brush, unless a person is very well organized. I am not. I tend to live with an open-ended creativity, letting things drift and gather as they will until at last I am forced to tidy up and start the process over again. My letters to Keibun Roshi were written with ink and brush, but I have never succeeded in the purity of brush for all the other writings in my life. Cheap ballpoint pens and half sharpened pencils are found about my house. Yet, at this moment, sitting to write this essay on the cold hard keyboard of a computer and thinking of Keibun Roshi, now dead, I almost have an inclination to write this essay using a brush. To do so would entail much. Immediately, time is suspended in the physical action of making ink and dipping the brush hairs into the black liquid pool on the stone. For a while, I would not care whether I ever finished the essay, and I would feel each word in the rhythm of its making. Everyone who read it would see each change of thought and every nuance of gesture. The breath would be visible in the ink and the muscles and hands palpable in the lines. One's whole character would come forward to accompany the words, with grammar and vocabulary somewhat irrelevant.

One of our long dialogues by letter concerned the question of whether a person should leave footprints behind after death. We were thinking primarily of artists or writers and whether they should create with an idea of leaving a legacy of their work. Keibun Roshi wrote that we should live in an invisible way and not seek to hand a body of work into the future. We should not seek fame, but live totally in the present so that our thoughts and actions are loaded, like the brush is with ink, in the expression of Buddha Nature. We should not be concerned whether anything we have done will live beyond us. In other words, the mind should not attach to anything. If something we have done lives beyond us, it is none of our business. Fame does not actually belong to the person who becomes famous but only to those who make others famous.

Through Keibun Roshi's teaching we can clearly see Ryokan living out his creative life without any intention of fame. Ryokan's renown in our present age comes about through the work of others and not by his own hand. His fame is our doing and while he was alive, he was saved from the burden of having to live up to the greatness we impose upon him. He resisted notoriety although toward the end of his life, he felt flattered by the esteem placed upon his calligraphy. Yet he had no notion of what might come after, whether his poetry would live on beyond his own years. Jan Chozen Bays writes in her book *Jizo Bodhisattva* about her own teacher Maezumi Roshi who was asked if something continues after death. Maezumi Roshi replied: "No. It is the vow that continues." This vow stands beyond any notion of fame or continuity because the vow of the Bodhisattva is fully lived and cannot be saved up from the past or apportioned for the future. It is, as Chozen Bays says, "...a propelling energy. It propels us into the search for an end to suffering and into finding ways to help others." There can be no suggestion of concern for the small self in it.

When I first went to Japan, I knew that I would take up a particular art. After all, why be in Japan and not take advantage of study? First I searched out a Kabuki teacher, wanting to learn theatrical performance. Then I learned that women are never permitted to perform in public. Kabuki was actually founded by women but ultimately taken away from them in the Tokugawa Period in the 1600s, when they were thought to be performing lewd dances. Men then took on all the roles of women and to this day only men perform on the Kabuki stages in Japan. No, I couldn't engage in that kind of exclusionary practice.

Taiko was my next search. The passion of drums seemed to suit me; at least I wanted the taste of *taiko* spirit. Why not do something so unusual, so different from what I might take up in the United States? Then I learned that teachers accepted students who were young, most often male, and not someone middle aged like me who happened to be a woman. Playing *taiko* would be a difficult commitment because I would have to contract for at least a year just to begin. I was past my time for the required muscle power. *Taiko* centers were far from my apartment and lessons were expensive and beyond my reach. Even small drums were breathtakingly priced and then, where would I practice? No, perhaps in my next life I would take up drums.

I had studied painting prior to going to Japan and when I got beyond the urge to explore the exotic expressions of drama and drumming I realized that I would never be in a better situation to be able to study Japanese *shodo*, calligraphy, and *sumi-e* painting. The best materials were available and teachers were plentiful. When I was told of Shoen Tokunaga Sensei, an energetic and creative teacher whose teaching studio was in Okayama, I went for a lesson. From the first meeting, I found myself engrossed in the training and homework which Tokunaga Sensei offered. She herself brushed an interpretive style of calligraphy and allowed for much inventive exploration with the brush. Not an absolutist, she allowed for and nurtured experimentation, yet she wanted to see excellent fundamental posture and technique with the brush.

Tokunaga Sensei stood about 4 feet 10 inches and smiled broadly at every chance and her eyes flashed with energy. Her English was halting in the beginning, but her sister- in-law, an English teacher, and her brother, a medical doctor, spoke excellent English, and Tokunaga Sensei had the finest support for her English study. Now that she had an American student, she wanted to improve her language skills. The combination of my intense study and her excellent memory cinched the relationship. I fell in love with calligraphy and practiced every day. Tokunaga Sensei expanded her vocabulary and slowly we learned to communicate half in my Japanese, and half in her English, and fully in the language of art. She became my teacher, working together for three years until I went into training, and she still is my teacher to this day.

I learned the sacred elements of *Shodo*: brush, ink, paper, stone. I envied Tokunaga's brushes, all Japanese and of the finest hair of deer, sheep, horse and the horse's tail, as well as hair from the bear, goat, ox, badger, camel, and squirrel. She taught that human hair, if it has never been cut, makes the most excellent of all hair for a brush. The first cutting of a child's hair can be captured and made into family brush treasures.

Tokunaga Sensei took me along with Edwina, a friend who was also an American English teacher, on a trip to Kyoto to visit an ink factory where *sumi* was manufactured. Tokunaga Sensei went on ahead to visit her family, and Edwina and I debated whether to go given the sudden snowstorm that hit the previous evening. Bullet trains ran sporadically and we had no snow gear. Eventually we decided we would brave it and so we trundled off to a shoe store and each bought a cheap pair of snow boots that I have to this day and wear in the garden. By the time we got to Kyoto the snow was melting, but not on the side streets, in the park, and on the rooftops, which provided a most brilliant fairytale vision of the city.

We arrived at the ink factory, run by the same family for centuries, and saw the small room where little glass pots with wicks soaked in rapeseed oil were lined up on racks and burned like devotional candles at an altar. Atop each pot was a small cap that collected the soot as the wick burned. Every half hour or so, a man would come into the room and brush the soot into a collection pot which he would then take into another room where the soot would be combined with resin, set aside to cure, and made into clay. The clay would be put into molds and hung to dry, sometimes for as long as six months to a year depending upon the fineness of the ingredients. Like certain delicate wines, the longer the clay bricks are allowed to cure, the better they will be. The air in this candle room was as toxic as any I've smelled. The soot and rapeseed oil brought an immediate cough from anyone who stepped inside.

The men who worked on the ink were visible to visitors through a window where we looked down on them and saw them work the clay into thin coils and press it into molds that they tied together in bundles so they could be set aside for curing. Above the window was the straw marking this place where they did their work as a shrine, a holy place. Each man had a shaved head and wore only a pair of boxer shorts. The room had to be hot in order to keep the resin and the clay supple to avoid any premature drying or cracking. The men wore no masks.

From head to toe the workers were as black as the pitch that they worked with. It seemed that their skin had become this color permanently, like that of coal miners, from working so long on the ink, and that they had given their bodies over to the making of *sumi*, a sacred element of writing. Their lungs too must have become black because they wore no protective clothing. The realization of their sacrifice brought out the most heartfelt response in me and I began to sob, thinking that this was what it took so that I could rub a stick of *sumi* on a stone and make some feeble brush marking on a piece of paper. I don't believe Tokunaga Sensei quite understood my tears, but Edwina said, "You never quite know what's going to hit home, do you?"

To this day I am inconsolable when I think of how little I appreciate the implements of art, the centuries of work that have gone into their perfection, and the care that allows them to get to my hands so that I can paint. Ink, paper, stone, and brush—all are noteworthy and vital in the expression of *shodo* and *sumi-e*. Later in the factory showroom, we regarded beautiful sticks of ink, artworks in themselves, and watched Tokunaga Sensei pick out the finest of inks in preparation for painting for a new exhibition. We smelled the fragrances of the *sumi* and learned to distinguish them just as one who knows can tell much from the fragrance of a wine.

The following year when I entered Zen monastic training, I learned that Godo Roshi, the training master, was also a master calligrapher. His work in rendering the lineages was sought from all over Japan. Zen priests are expected to be proficient in calligraphy and this was part of my training. Godo Roshi's style was deeply traditional and I was forced to conform and learn the way of perfection or receive slaps on the hand for holding the brush improperly. I embraced learning the very basic strokes in this most formal way. During my year of training with Godo Roshi, we did extra study in brush since Roshi knew how much I enjoyed it.

When Godo Roshi would be called out of the painting room for a phone message, an old, occasionally drunken and disheveled monk living at the monastery would come over and give me secret painting instructions completely counter to the neatness and care of the Zen master. "Don't listen to him," he'd say, "never try to be neat. Paint from your heart and don't worry about being careful." Then he would wildly brush the same characters in his own style, amazing me with the beauty of his naturalness. We hid the work under the table when we heard the Zen master returning to the room.

Godo Roshi knew quite well what was going on. The old monk and he had been good friends from their own days of training and before I left, the three of us got together one day and we each rendered the same calligraphy in our own styles: Godo Roshi's pure, clean lines with excellent quality of ink, black and solid and strong; the old man's style, wobbly and uneven, yet vital in its sincerity and naturalness, the ink muddy, a little weak and grey; mine still tentative, painted with a foreign accent, but the ink somewhere in between Godo Roshi's and the old monk's.

However difficult it was, after countless slaps on the hand, stacks and stacks of discarded practice paper, discouragement because the brush would not behave, and the ultimate acceptance that I could never quite write like a Japanese calligrapher, I learned from Godo Roshi how to slow down the path of the brush and allow the ink to have its full say. He and Tokunaga Sensei both taught me the two most difficult points of painting—not that I've mastered them—which is how to put the brush down on the paper and how to take it back up. The rest seems easy in comparison. The metaphor of beginning and ending is in what the brush has to teach and endlessly plays out in the life journey.

Coming back to America after years of formal study and having learned a few "under the table" techniques, I wanted to find my own way in the element and tools of *sumi* and paper, a way that would bridge with a Western style. As I had painted in abstract expressionism in years past, my emerging style seemed to fit the pieces I had become: a little East, a little West, a hybrid, a mix of teachers, cultures, and even, perhaps, a wealth of sobrieties.

All of this seems far more contrived than the simple clarity of Ryokan's calligraphy, rendered without a suggestion of pretension or sophistication. He is sure of himself in his utter spontaneity. His ink glows with inner spirit and integrity and his heart is as pure as a child who brings a scribble reverently to the parent without any idea of what he has done. In this work, there is no place to hide and there is no hiddenness. Because Ryokan ascribes the fate of his talent to that One in Heaven, we get a glimpse of the infinite in the words that are written through him:

> What destiny has put together myself and this writing-brush?
> Having laid it down, I take it again at my friend's request.
> Failing to unriddle this mystery, I have none to comfort me
> But the infinite He who has tamed the sins and walks heaven.

Ryokan was given paper and ink by various people around town. He might have traded his brushwork for more supplies. We don't know all the kinds of tasks he did around town, but they were said to be many and were helpful. When people had some extra paper or ink, they would give it to him. But he also practiced kanji with the children by using a stick in the dirt. This way it could be practiced endlessly and erased after each gesture. The children memorized the order in which strokes were written in a kanji, so no paper or ink went to waste and Ryokan could save any paper for his poetry.

Once when Ryokan was asked to brush calligraphy to create a banner for a festival, he wrote it in the native style, simple and basic, rather than the literary style, so that it could be read by everyone and not just by the educated class. As a selfless man, he looked out for everyone and certainly did not care about a legacy of fame, although he was well aware that the locals knew about him and valued his calligraphy.

> Since I shed my black hair and took vows as a holy priest,
> My feet have carried me for years through grass and winds.
> Till today they thrust at me everywhere a brush and paper,
> Telling me but to make, but to write poems for their sake.

One of Ryokan's most famous paintings occurred when he was asked to pay a debt with a painting. Ryokan brushed something and the fellow complained that he couldn't read it and he passed the brush back into

Ryokan's hands. "Please paint me something that I can read," said the fellow.

Without much hesitation, Ryokan unrolled a clean sheet of paper that was in front of him and brushed *"Ichi, Ni, San,"* One, Two, Three. Three simple characters with six brush marks. This was extremely simple and the first kanji that a child learns. Although the shopkeeper may have seemed miffed at first at something so profoundly simple, it became a true art treasure. I had the opportunity to see this calligraphy in person at a special showing of Ryokan's art in Okayama during my first years there. When I stood in front of this brilliant creation, tears ran down my face at the utter simplicity and beauty of Ryokan's character, which beamed off the page. It seemed to radiate a silence around it, as if Ryokan were completely present behind the form of his characters having just brushed the work a few moments before.

Ryokan didn't take students and he didn't preach, yet we have his teachings through the brush and ink in direct, visible form and we are partners with him in the act of creativity as we soak in his character in proximity to his work. Such art in Zen practice is referred to as "ink traces" because it gives us a record of the past and allows us to communicate at this moment in time with the teachings of great artist monks. The elements of brush painting are rooted in ink and brush picked up from stone and exploded on paper, releasing the power of spirit in formless form, and expressing the ungraspable and inexpressible. Imagine through his whole life, Ryokan writing only with a brush!

The plainness and clarity of the characters in Ryokan's brushwork tell us how Zen training is reflected in all that we do. The aim is to drop off the fragments of personality that express ego and to allow the radiance of Buddha Nature to shine forth as a presence. The ease of the characters in Ryokan's painting becomes a teaching for us as we realize that his True Nature is what came forth on the paper. We are drawn into his brushwork and we see our own True Nature reflected back at us. The point of his work is to bring us to see our own undeniable Buddha radiance. Because this work lacks any guile, any trace of dishonesty, its purity of execution and power to transform us continues throughout time and space. This is what Zen paintings are about. Can the artist paint Awakening so that we are Awakened when our eyes meet that Awakened expression? This is the aim when we stand with the loaded brush poised in silence over the paper in Emptiness-presence. Then we move and throw our entire being into each stroke. The black ink on paper is charged with light and we cannot look away.

Way of Poetry

Whoever reads my poetry, and calls it poetry by its name,
I know he is in grave error, for my poetry is not poetry.
After you have learned my poetry is unworthy of its name
I will sit down to discuss with you the secret of my art.

Way of Poetry

The literary history of any culture and language is layered in complexity: the evolution of poetic form and convention is an aggregate of centuries of artistic exploration. What comes across to us in English as simple, magnificent lines extolling nature, is built upon the scaffolding of centuries of Japanese artistic mastery. These Japanese conventions originated in the 4th century C.E. even before Japan had its own written language. Japanese poets borrowed a syllabary from the Chinese language and used it in phonetic form to be able to record their oral poetry. The poems of more than four hundred poets were anthologized from these early times around the year 749 C.E. in a collection called the *Man'yoshu*. About one hundred years later, Japan adopted its own written language and the *Man'yoshu* soon became unreadable. In yet another one hundred years, Emperor Murakami ordered that the *Man'yoshu* be translated from its original phonetic and semantic mix of Chinese, thereby reclaiming its own important literary history into the new Japanese written language.

The *Man'yoshu's* poems date back to 350 C.E. and express the dominant themes of love, loss, and separation. The name "*Man'yoshu*" means "A Collection To Be Handed Down Throughout Ten Thousand Eras" or "A Collection of Ten Thousand Leaves." It is a monumental anthology of over 4,000 poems consisting of twenty volumes with more than four hundred known authors and many more of them unidentified. The collection encompasses all of Japanese life, including nature, folktales, love relationships, and not just imperial court poems, which speak of the deaths or funeral laments of important royal personages. Poems in the *Man'yoshu* consist of long poems, *chokka*; short poems, *tanka*; head-repeated poems, *sedoka*; and serial stanzas, *renga*. Other inclusions are verses in the form of hymns to the Buddha's footprints. This is a verse form based on twenty-one poems that are carved on a stone engraving of the Buddha's footprints (at Yakushiji temple in Nara), which praise the Buddha and offer some of his teachings.

Another important collection from the classical period is the *Kokinshu*, a collection from the 8th to 10th centuries that includes all short form poems or *tanka*. The *Kokinshu* includes twenty-one collections, and it centers on the seasons and love, with the form determining styles of poetry that would last until the late nineteenth century. The next in classical importance is called the *Shinkokinshu* or "New Collection of Poems Ancient and Modern." In this collection, as in the *Kokinshu*, poems are linked as if to tell a story. For instance, the love poems are arranged in such a way as to suggest the moments in the course of a love affair. This anthology of court poetry was commissioned by the imperial household and came out in 1439 C.E. There are no overtly Buddhist poems in either of the last two compendiums. These early collections form some of the groundwork of Ryokan's poetic output, but he is also influenced by the poetry of Eihei Dogen Zenji, the founder of Soto Zen in the 13th Century, whom Ryokan follows as a priest in the Soto Zen lineage, and to Tang dynasty poets Wang Wei, Li Po, Tu Fu, and particularly Han Shan of Cold Mountain.

Ryokan's birth name was Eizo, and from the time the boy was able to read, he had his nose engrossed in literature and poetry. Sometimes his parents scolded him for not responding quickly enough to the calls to dinner or to participate in some activity. He immersed himself in his books, missed his sleep, and struggled to get up in the morning for school. If his own name were called, he wouldn't hear until it was spoken with enough emphasis to it that he'd finally look up and respond. This is typical young teen deportment, as we all know, when young people are lost in their own worlds and sometimes only half present. Given to dreaminess, he would lie about looking at clouds floating over the trees, probably wondering about life and language. As he grew, his reading and study at school included Confucian ethics and he was said to be an excellent student who truly applied himself to his subjects. Along with his close young friends, he read poetry early and developed a fondness for literature: "We often played together on the banks of the Narrow Stream. Already, literature was our concern, and we often sat down in an earnest conversation, not caring how time crept away." As mentioned earlier, Ryokan's family members were all interested in literature and poetry, so books had been available to him and likely there was conversation around literature in his home, particularly with his mother who spent more time with him as a child.

We don't have a sense of Ryokan's writing as a young man, but a few poems appear at Entsuji from his early twenties, when he would have had little time to sit down and write. He did study various Buddhist texts and the writings of Dogen, which Kokusen Roshi required for his certification as a priest in order to run his own temple. Whatever he read and studied in poetry, language, philosophy, and wisdom, contributed to his inner development already considerably advanced for his age and his time. I have to wonder if this deep background added to his sense of isolation and loneliness while at Entsuji. Young novice priests may not have been as well educated as he was. There would be kibitzing and small games and jokes when there was free time, but the novices were unlikely to be mulling over philosophical questions or discussing differences in the metric rhythms between Li Po and Han Shan. Their exchanges would likely have been more trivial.

Once Ryokan left Entsuji and established his own direction as an itinerant monk, living from village to village and begging from door to door, he was free to pick up his brush and say poetically what he pleased. It is likely that writing poetry saved him from complete dejection during this dark period of wandering and insecurity when he could not seem to gain stability in his life. Wandering monks were people who went from temple to temple to receive teachings of various masters in order to deepen their understanding of the Dharma. We have no record of Ryokan living for a periiod in this way as a regular temple visitor. He does not refer to this period in his poetry, nor do the temples have a record of his having visited them. If he did stay in Japan and didn't go to China during those lost years, as contemporary research is trying to discover, he may have hunkered down to sleep in country barns, in fields, or in lean-tos behind people's homes. He had time to think and write and let loose some important expression that was aching to come out. One thing we must remember when reading Ryokan's poetry is that he wrote from experience and not under the constraints of traditional poetic meter and form. He did follow some of the rules, but he also pushed the envelope of tradition, experimenting with language to search out his own interior feelings and condition. Perhaps this is why we love him so much.

Ryokan studied the Chinese poets closely and may have identified with their hermetic lives, the thatched huts that they found themselves in as they aged, and the unusual circumstances of their lives. Han Shan on Cold Mountain lived in a thatched hut before he moved to the cave to save himself from housekeeping and the tiresome repairs that were always required of grass houses. Li Po took up wandering for years and years in exile, writing poetry, living as an outcast, and refusing to settle even when pardoned by the government for his challenge to imperial authority. The lifestyle of the wanderer was too pleasurable in the relaxation of a simple life of freedom to travel, to see friends, and to write poetry. Tu Fu, one of China's greatest poets, declined the civil servant career. He did come back to it later, but spent the happiest time of his life in a thatched hut at Flower Rinsing Creek, during which he reached the high point of his creative output writing 240 poems in four years. There was nothing humdrum in the lives of the Chinese poets. They were sometimes penniless, threatened, homeless, exiled, unhealthy: all circumstances in which Ryokan too found himself. He would have felt a sense of camaraderie in the hagiographies of these eccentric poetic masters.

As for the debt he owed to other poets in the poems themselves, there are shades of familiar images and echoes of language from the whole range of the tradition. What Ryokan did was to read the Chinese and Japanese poets closely, to learn from them, and to use them as springboards for a fresh expression out of his own experience. The Chinese and Japanese poets all disobeyed the stringent rules of prosody and made the language new in their own style as they pushed against prosody to bring it into the light of their own time. Ryokan did the same. This is what we do in American poetry as a tradition filled with ethnic diversity. We search out the flavors of other cultures, widen our vision, and season our language with the music and richness of multiple heritages. Poetry is, in essence, a continuing conversation with one voice bouncing off the other in the procession of time, and each person has a unique voice. Yet we all owe our insights and images to those who have gone before us. We pay tribute to the language traditions when our utterance reverberates with the art of our ancestors but finds a new stirring in the thrill of invention. This is not to say that we copy from them; it is to say that we have absorbed the richness of their music and given them continuing voice through us via their influences. They are made new by our effort to express ourselves with some level of originality. It is similar to finding one's own way in life and yet looking a little like your mother and father. Ryokan says, "Ancient sages left their works behind, not to let us know about themselves, but to help us understand our own stamp." If many ghosts dance in Ryokan's poems, how glad they must be to have their bones still rattle.

Ryokan most deeply valued Han Shan, called Kanzan in Japanese. He says:

The volume of Kanzan's poetry in my house, I esteem more
Than the sacred sutras or countless commentaries on them.
A brush in hand, I have made copies on my bedside screen.
And now and then, I brood on them, feasting on each poem.

Another important influence on Ryokan was the great Japanese poet
Saigyo, who also influenced the poet Basho. Saigyo lived a solitary life in
the 12th Century on Mount Koya but he also made many writing trips
into Northern Honshu that later inspired Basho in the 17th Century in his
Travels to the Deep North. Saigyo's poetry expresses sorrow, loneliness, sadness, and melancholy due perhaps to the suffering of the times in which he
lived. At the age of 22, he inexplicably withdrew from society and became
a Buddhist monk, something with which Ryokan would have identified.
But Ryokan's poetry is often bathed in a sense of loneliness to such a degree
that we get the impression that his sorrow is larger than his own ability to
cope with it. While there is no doubt that Ryokan's humanity permeates
his poems, the expression of loneliness as an artistic aesthetic is also to be
considered. It prompts me to ask about the resonance of suffering in his
poetry. We identify with his struggle; this is almost what draws us to him,
and yet Ryokan is transcendent in his vow to live in the fashion of the hermit in the thatched hut Gogo-an on Mount Kugami, huddled in a blanket
surrounded by heaps of snow in the black, dead night of icy winter. Is the
poem a work of art employing loneliness as a traditional Japanese artistic
theme, or is the poem the presentation of his life, the rugged nature of his
experience? Perhaps we could say that it is both, a typical Zen compromise.
It's important though to hold both sides. If we say that his loneliness was
of an overwhelming nature, the level of his suffering topples us, and he
many times points out that he is living out his own choice. If the suffering
had been too much, he was free to make a change. At the same time, if
the loneliness were merely a poetic device, then the poems would not reach
us; they would fall flat and have little impact. Humanity was imbedded in
Ryokan's voice, which was an aspect of himself that we can receive as his
teaching. He was a man suffused with compassion and brotherly love; his
very being is his teaching without his having done anything purposefully.

In the *kanshi* poems we get the deepest sense of his life laid out in
detail, a chronicle of his heart and mind in the struggles and triumphs
of his life. A *kanshi* is a Chinese style poem written in Japanese. There
are periods in Japanese literary history when the *kanshi* poem underwent
popularization and Ryokan's time was one of those periods. Ryokan could

not care less about slavishly following forms of poetry; he broke the rules, but he still needed structure, some basis on which to hang his ideas. The *kanshi* are long philosophical poems in which he had the leisure of the wide field in the poem to work out his true declaration. Of course he also wrote in the tight forms of *haiku* or *waka*, but he was not as much at home in these forms where the emotional temperature is rather cool and great restraint is required as he was in the *kanshi*. His poems are always clear and simple in their diction, straightforward, resisting any sense of cunning or artifice aiming to say what was deepest in him in the true reality of the moment. For examples of such moments, numerous *kanshi* begin the chapters of this book.

Ryokan's subjects were similar to those found in Chinese poetry. He wrote poems about the joys of solitude, the near defeat of loneliness, begging, being poor and lamenting his own life choices, and philosophical poems about the nature of life. Just a few lines demonstrate these subjects, which are profuse in his work:

"Beneath its cool shade, I make poems, long and short,
Not for a moment leaving this quiet seat by the tree."

"This rank absurdity of mine, when can I throw it away?
This abject poverty I shall take to the grave with me."

"Cold or hungry, go I must as many a saint before me."

"Laugh, whoever is tempted, at my sad bowl and flask.
Reconciled am I to finding myself in a ruined house."

"My begging bowl is loaded with a heap of white rice, and
I rise far beyond the glory of the rich emperor.
Hoping truly to follow upon the heels of holy sages
I march along from house to house, begging for alms."

"At a weedy cottage I found the restful life of a recluse.
I have since lived alone, turning to songbirds for music,
And for my friends I have white clouds rising in the sky.
With nothing to worry me, not a care to disturb my peace,
I live from day to day till the day dawns no more for me."

"Deep enough have I probed into the truth of our existence
To know the glory of spring flowers is but a form of dust."

These last few lines seem to help explain the enigmatic opening lines of this chapter, "My poetry is not poetry." Is Ryokan saying that everything is "but a form of dust" and that what is true poetry cannot be spoken? The real poem is not the lines that we are able to put to paper but the essence of the life that we lead, the essence of the Zen life, the mirror of Buddha Nature. Ryokan says that when we understand this, we'll know that his poems are just moments of the dusty world, and then we'll be ready to encounter him in understanding his real art. And this is his real art: the centrality of his vow.

The quality of the poems is equal to the brilliance of the calligraphy as a means to locating Ryokan, to being able to grasp and glimpse his character. It is true that he refused to publish his poems and kept most of them packed away. In this way, he hid himself from the terrible prospect of fame. He secluded himself from praise and the ramifications of public life. But if we look at his work now, we can find the one we want to meet and know, even though he will escape when we try to catch him. We may find him and find his hiding place, but he cannot be tagged.

I must admit that when I sit to write a poem, or when a poem flies into my mind, I do not think of Ryokan or try to imitate him. That would be as impossible as it is to forge his calligraphy. I am not Japanese. I am American and I can't be anything else. The poet Robert Hass once taught a class at San Jose State University and asked everyone to write a *haiku*, and then he pointed out the amount of imitation of Japanese images in the poems we produced. He was getting us to find our own American voices and not to parrot another culture to make ourselves sound cute. He was questioning whether we could succeed in haiku so long as we were caught by any Japanese affectation. It is difficult to be an American and discover a mythic base that can hold the body of poetry so that it has presence beneath and surrounding its words. One must become very wide and have something to say. Walt Whitman, for instance, infuses *Leaves of Grass* with his mythic vision of America. The way to do this then and now is to be completely oneself and to discover one's own voice and what one has to say while not ignoring all that has gone before. If one is to follow Ryokan, then this is what to go after: not an imitation of Ryokan, but the discovery of one's authentic voice, true to what one hears. This quest for authenticity must bring us back to the vow, because in order to achieve this fidelity, it takes devotion, work, attention, commitment, and love. It would take all of this to discover the hidden Ryokan, but in that process, the one we would truly uncover would be the Self.

Awakening and Wisdom

True, all the seasons have moonlit nights,
But here's the best night to see the moon.
The hills never so aloft, the streams never so clear,
In the infinite blue of autumn sky flies a disk of light.
Neither light nor gloom is graced with a life of its own.
The moon and the earth are one, and myself one with them.
The boundless sky above, and autumn chill on my skin,
I stroll about low hills, leaning upon my priceless cane.
Quiet night has held firm the flitting dust of the world.
The bright moon alone pours streams of rays all about me.
I mind it not if another like-minded is also admiring it,
Or if the moon deigns to look on others as well as on me.
Each year as autumn comes, the moon will shine as before,
And the world will watch it, will face it, till eternity.
Sermons at Mount Ryozen, lectures in the Vale of Sokei,
Were teachings so precious, the audience needed the moon.
My meditation under the moon lasts till the ripest night.
The stream has hushed its cry, dew lies thick everywhere.
Who, among the moon-viewers tonight, will have the prize?
Who will reflect the purest moon in the lake of his mind?
Surely you all know of that riverside moon-viewing of long ago,
When Fugan alone, the rest lagging, ran beyond the flesh,
And of Yakkyo who, moon-inspired, cracked a laugh on a hilltop?
Their reputation rose high, when the feats were reported,
But over a thousand years intervene between now and then.
People have watched for naught the vicissitudes of the moon.
I am, nonetheless, swayed in my thoughts by the ancients.
Tonight, I keep a bright vigil, my robes soaked in tears.

Awakening and Wisdom

What are we to take from the life of Ryokan who did not become a teacher in the usual sense? He did not create a monastery or a temple. He did not preach. He did not create a schedule for Zazen and invite the townsfolk to join him. He did not take students apart from one young man who died in the plague. This student's death made him so disconsolate that he vowed he would not take another student. The grief was too great. He did not write long Dharma articles seeking to have them published. He did not teach in the typical way that Zen masters, as we know them today, or even in Ryokan's time, tend to teach. In a way he was a secret teacher and it was rare for him to come out of hiding.

Shakyamuni Buddha did not preach until he was urged to do so by those who witnessed his startling change of demeanor. The impetus to teach publicly is a rather strange phenomenon, filled with pitfalls and challenges one could never conceive of that follow one's first spoken word. Once we begin, the first sentence falls into the next and the next. There is no end, just the piling on of one idea and thought after another. Even if no one listens, the ship has been launched. The word leads to people gathering, a place to stay, rules for community, the need for food. There is no end. Human activity, like the gathering of honey for bees or the roaming of ants, is inevitable.

By avoiding the first teaching, Ryokan, the glorious fool, never put the matrix of temple organization and institution into operation. He had had his taste of running a temple when he left Entsuji and he was not prepared to take on more. He did not have the impetus even to build much of a lean-to on his own, until someone felt sorry enough for him and offered him Gogo-an which was already 100 years old, weather weary, and a home to small rodents. Yet Ryokan was a great teacher whose influence is felt worldwide and although it would be almost impossible for most of us to live in the same way today, the fact that he was eccentric and unconventional gives us cause to examine the possibilities that might be available for Zen Buddhist teachers today. If we don't build and manage zendos and temples, can there be a presence of practice, a useful change and influence in society, and a way of practice that makes sense in today's climate? Are there alternative ways and expressions of Dharma and can we open to teachers while honoring and following the integrity of *Okesa*, the holy robe?

Dharma Transmission is an awesome and pure moment that includes great responsibility. Yet no Zen master gives Dharma Transmission with the sense that the new priest will go forward and build vast empires or even a simple Zen center. There can be no expectation except the pure face-to-face immersion in the stream of Dharma, soaking in the dance of the lineage and not knowing where the current will go. There is a mystical trust that the new priest who has already undergone many years of practice, discipline, and training will carry the Dharma lineage forward. Many teachers who feel the inspiration and influence of the power of the Transmission aspire to build or create a center as a gift to their own teachers whose incredible gift actually cannot be repaid. No matter what the new priest does, the Dharma and the transmission of *Okesa* are larger than anything that can be imagined. They are beyond measure.

My own Dharma Transmission Ceremony took place in the heat of summer at Ryokan-do, in the room where Ryokan lived at Entsuji. As I mentioned, the building is extant and the musty old tatami mats fill the atmosphere with a sense of time and history. It is a sacred space endowed with spirit. It was midnight when the ceremony began and I was led by candlelight to the red-draped room where this profound and intimate transmission took place, the implanting of Dharma responsibility from teacher to student. The ceremony actually takes a week and I had been making my bows to the ancestors, 108 bows three times a day. My thighs were so badly swollen that I could not sleep on my side or stomach and had to rest only on my back. But the bowing was a mercy to my grief. My mother had died while I was enroute from Olympia to Japan for the ceremony. I had been one of her caregivers during the six months of her final illness. A few days before she became comatose, I told her I would be leaving for Japan on June 26th for the Transmission Ceremony, which had been planned a long time in advance and would have been very difficult to postpone. It would be one of the most important moments in my life. I thought about Dogen Zenji reminding himself of the focus on the Dharma and making the decision to leave for China when his teacher was dying. I thought of Ryokan in training at Entsuji and absent at the time of his mother's death. Yet the look of anguish on my own mother's face when I told her I would be leaving is a difficult memory still. In better times she would have been proud and celebratory, but her illness removed any appreciation of the step I was taking. She had placed great importance on her children and it seemed as if her life was being erased. Two other siblings had said their goodbyes weeks earlier, and two were still there at the bedside.

Two hours after my mother died, my daughter, the eldest of the grandchildren, took a disastrous fall at her workplace when she tumbled off a chair and she was undergoing surgery to replace the bones in both her wrists because the bones inversely telescoped as she braced her fall to the floor. This was so much turmoil on one day. When I learned of these events after arriving in Japan, I determined I would stay there and finish the Dharma Transmission. Ryokan at Entsuji when his mother died knew he had made his choice to be a monk and would follow the vow no matter what. In my case, it was not as stark for me since I would return to Olympia in a week to be there for my mother's funeral and then to help my daughter while she had both arms in unbendable casts and was unable to do anything at all for herself. Thus I entered the mystery of Dharma Transmission, the great beauty of vow, clear about my choice, but filled with the complexity of grief and family need, and Olympia Zen Center already forming its own circle of twists and complications that any community undergoes.

What is a person to do after the years of training, concentration, and discipline, only then then to be "let go" as it were, put out in the stream, dropped like a seed from the tree and left to sprout. What ground, what expression is right and good? Of all the living koans that confront us, right livelihood is by far one of the most difficult. In the culture of the Americas, the receiving of *Okesa* does not relieve one of the problems of food, clothing, and shelter. There is typically no family temple to take over and no easy means of support. Many new priests, without necessarily wanting to, experience poverty and the simplicity that comes with the vow and the non-attachment to goods. The most obvious way to make one's way in the world is to create a Sangha that will generate a circle of practice and support. We may have come to think that this is the only means of going forward because so many have gone this way, but truly there is endless potential to work and do good in the world. The appearance of *Okesa* creates its own life. *Okesa*, the Great Robe of Liberation, finds its own pathway; the road starts out and has a direction that the new priest follows. It isn't the other way around. The new priest simply says yes and *Okesa* leads the way, opening one gate after another, the innumerable Dharma gates that will use the best talents and deepest inner strengths of that new priest. We simply have to stay open to all possibilities.

Zen Buddhism is new enough in the Americas that we have hardly had time to establish a few centers before opening to engaged Buddhism. The condition of society, nevertheless, calls for a response. While it is right for some to remain in the monastery holding the deep fire of practice, it is also right for others to take on social services and be present and practical in answer to the institutional perpetuation of suffering in our society. The problem of making a deeply Zen Buddhist response to modern social dilemmas faces several challenges. People have to be cautioned against individualism and putting their own stamp on social programs. We have to beware of insisting on particular answers to world problems. There is a fine line between allowing people to work out their issues and really helping to relieve suffering. We don't have all the answers.

At the same time that we want to help and to have a sense of community, the present situation calls for us to organize and even institutionalize in ways that can be most effective toward change in this context.

Ryokan's way of teaching was remote from organizational modes and yet he and his teachings have become global. Why is this? Is it because he stands outside the institution? Or is it the supreme quality of his virtue that endures? Most of us can understand Ryokan's youthful decisions in response to the Dharma and his 800 kilometer walk across Japan in the footsteps of his teacher, Kokusen Roshi. We can fathom his twelve or thirteen years in practice at Entsuji; we can even imagine his five years of wandering, making the best of it here and there and stopping at various temples as he went. What seems formidable is the more than thirty years during which he returned to Niigata, faced homelessness and hunger, moved into the tiny space of Gogo-an, and remained faithful to his vows to live as a begging monk in the Dharma for the whole of his life. All this took place while his body aged, his intestines weakened, and the seasons dished out extremes of heat, humidity, biting insects in summer, and drifting snows, ice, and wind in winter. Most of us would run for cover into the arms of family, friends, work, and community.

Ryokan's vow raises thoughts about how we can continue to practice with vitality while in the midst of the comforts of America in the 21st century. It presses us to probe the integrity of our own vows and our ability to express constancy in practice as we honor the commitment to practice the precepts. It asks at what depth we wish to live and what meaning our vow has if we are so fickle that we can lay aside the Dharma on a whim. What drives us? What can we say is the core of our being? What is our vow? What is the impetus to live? Is there anything at all in the guts? What is our worth in practice?

Ryokan's choice to live as he did awes us, but in some ways, he had no other possibility because the Japanese system is such that once a young person makes a choice, she may not change her mind. Today's system and the one that developed through history is simply a continuation of a long, cultural attitude toward vocation. In the teen years, a child must choose the life she or he will lead. Most follow the family's craft and take on the business that they will eventually inherit. Others enter a life committed to a company. The direction for this was decided in high school, when students had a small window of a few years to get into a college. If they are lucky enough to pass the exams to get in, they must then choose their major field of study, and they may not change it once they commit to it. Even if they learn to dislike the subject and discover they do not have a facility for it, they are locked into finishing the course they have chosen.

On the one hand, the Japanese system seems heartless and cruel, forcing someone to stick with a choice they make at an age when they are ill equipped with experience and knowledge to choose a wise, lifelong direction. On the other hand, it awakens the ability to learn through devotion and long care, to learn to love the life we have chosen rather than choosing a life we think we love. Obviously, these could come together for some people, but most of us are lacking in youthful insight and we flop around for years wondering what we should do with our lives and what we should study. When we get tired of something, we are all too easily inclined to lay it aside and dream up different circumstances for ourselves.

This is not to say that we shouldn't be open to ways to extricate ourselves from impossible or extremely painful situations. After all, Ryokan is one who left his temple after he was given the responsibility for it when his teacher died. We look at the part of his life in which he lived out this tremendous commitment and yet he lived with the knowledge that he had walked away from the temple that his teacher entrusted to him. And this was not his first rejection of responsibility. He had also rejected the expectation that he would succeed in his father's footsteps as head of Izumozaki, the town where he lived. Some of his poems reflect his pain and regret, and yet he had neither the organizational capacity nor the political acumen to negotiate leadership as a mayor or as a master in a training temple in a fairly volatile atmosphere. It is wisdom to step aside even though one may feel regret.

A Japanese film, *Woman in the Dunes*, shows the dilemma of commitment, devotion, and the life we find ourselves in. A woman has been captured by a community and forced to live hidden in a makeshift hut in the bottom of a sand pit at the edge of the ocean. There she must work every day to remove the sand that drifts in from the wind and storms in order to avoid being completely buried and to be served the food and water the community provides for her to survive. A man who is out hunting butterflies is also kidnapped and thrown into the pit with the woman where he must choose to help remove the sand, or live a miserable existence of anger and complaint, and not receive enough food and water for two people. Ultimately, the man chooses to help and along the way he learns to love the woman with whom he shares this miserable existence. When she becomes pregnant and requires medical help, she is hauled out of the pit in a harness and he is left alone to continue the work. Over time, he discovers the ability to convert seawater into drinking water and he is fully transformed and liberated. He discovers happiness through devotion to the work that he is doing and is freed of the need to escape.

The film is a powerful metaphor for the notion of freedom and commitment, the hidden and the revealed, the dilemma of life and what it takes to survive. We have fewer freedoms than we suppose. In America we have come to believe that we can do whatever we want to do but this is not really so. Someone owns almost all the land where there is water and we can no longer set ourselves down on a plot of land to claim on a homestead. Even if we could do this, the amount of work involved to raise enough food to eat is more than most of us are capable of. People of privilege imagine they can go to any school and study any subject. How is it once you have a relationship, a family, and a responsibility to support the lives of other people? You can succeed only if you start hauling buckets of sand each day, one by one. You keep going until someone says you have hauled enough. Freedom seems to be in the ability to manage our commitments and to sustain older commitments with care when we decide to take on a new one. Happiness is found in the practice of devotion surrounding our work. As with the man in the sandpit, apart from situations of abuse, it is about not looking to escape the life we have but embracing the work we are doing.

Ryokan's single life as a way in the Dharma is a stumbling point for many partnered people. Because Ryokan chose practice as his partner, he could find his way in the world in whatever appeared before him. To live unattached is about the most complete and free possibility for Ryokan. Yet Ryokan never supposes that others should take his route. In fact, Ryokan discourages others from becoming his students essentially because he cannot be followed. He is not prepared for what it would take to bring a monk through training to full blossoming as a functioning priest. He lives outside the institution. Had he ordained someone, what then? Would the two have lived together in Gogo-an? Would the town have supported two hermits? Are you any longer a hermit if you live in company? Is Ryokan a functioning priest in the typical sense?

While Ryokan is singular and solitary in his way, he is not alone nor does he set up individualistic motivations. He lives in a culture that supports mendicancy and the hermitic life, both of which must have community support in order for the hermit to survive. Without this cultural commitment, Ryokan could not have managed, since he needed the material support of the townspeople and he needed their lifestyle to balance his way. The hermit must be accepted by the society in order to remain stable himself. He is not a freak; he represents the solitary body in Awakening. He manifests the completion of vow in its most intense form. He gives the society an opportunity to air its own complex structures. By right of his solitary nature, he gives others the opportunity to dream, not that they should run away from their own responsibilities. His existence lets others know there are alternatives to their own life circumstances. Just as Ryokan had the alternative to live in a more comfortable situation, members of the larger community too had the alternative to live in a less structured way. Having an alternative is a sign of health. Without alternatives, we become crushed by our own circumstances. Someone who commits to something has the alternative to choose something else, but they choose a particular way. This is why commitment or vow is such a treasure. The person chooses to be constant to a particular way because it is true for their lives, and then she continually chooses it, not just once, but again and again.

Awakening is at the heart of Ryokan's choices and the activity of his life. What is this question of enlightenment, awakening, realization that we can barely speak about? It is not something we can even communicate. But there is a quality in Ryokan's life that we can relate to in a nonverbal way. We can intuit him and sense there is something particular in his life that is worthy of the deepest consideration. The poem that begins this chapter comes closest, so far as I can tell, to pointing toward an experience that Ryokan had that places him in company with those who have gone before him, the enlightened teaching masters.

There does not seem to be an experience from the time of Ryokan's training at Entsuji that we can point to as a kensho, an opening, a defining moment of realization. As a matter of fact, his time at Entsuji was lonely and difficult. He gravely missed his family and the environment, culture and dialect of Niigata. The slang of Okayama is considerably altered from the Northern dialect and is not always easy to understand even for Japanese speakers. So he was an outsider to the tight social contracts that are made between monks in training who find roots, connections, and trust through their shared knowledge of the local speech. And, since Ryokan was deeply favored and loved by his master, Kokusen Roshi, he would have had difficulty with his brother monks who may have felt jealous about his closeness to the teacher. He begins a poem:

> Under the roof of the Entsuji temple, I often complained
> Of my utter solitude, my isolation from others around me.

He goes on to say how hard he worked to be a good monk and that eventually he "left the temple at my own whim."

We know from the few poems he wrote while at Entsuji that he had differences of opinion about how some things should be handled. For instance, monks have to find some freedom from the tremendous stress of training. For this, they will occasionally sneak out and have a hideout or hidden meeting place where they can relax and let loose. In the case of Entsuji, monks would climb to the top of the nearby mountain and sit together on a huge rock beneath the stars. They would get some sake or beer, have a drink together, and laugh, tell jokes, and let off steam. Then the next day they would go back at it and continue the hard work of keeping a training temple intact and functional.

One year when one of the senior monks declared that there would be no more sake, Ryokan wrote a poem decrying the proclamation and pointing out his disagreement with the new stipulation:

> *In protest to the priest Shakuan*
> *Against his notice of prohibition*
> *At Entsuji*
> Seven times have I known frost in the seven years of tramping.
> I now find my former hourglass lifeless, its water nearly dry.
> Who will have mercy now upon the thirsty souls under the roof?
> After my pious bow, I yearn for the old days prohibition-free.

After all, the monks worked exceedingly hard and the times when they could take such a pause in the discipline were rare. Because they were able to relax, they could be faithful to the discipline. Without any notion that they could get away sometimes, the atmosphere would become rather glum. If a cord is stretched too tight, it can more easily snap. Ryokan would be well aware of this for even though he was an outsider, he would certainly have been included in the parties and he would have enjoyed them. He deeply enjoyed social exchange.

At Entsuji, Ryokan was introduced to *Shobogenzo*, The Treasury of the True Dharma Eye, the great spiritual text by Eihei Dogen Zenji. Master Kokusen had been able to acquire a copy of the text, a rarity at the time, and he engaged his monks in the study of it. This examination was important in Ryokan's spiritual development. Dogen's depth of vow apparent in all of his work had a resonating effect upon Ryokan and made a mark on his priesthood. Although ultimately Ryokan's life would take an opposite expression from Dogen's monastic direction, the stamp of his vow on his life choices is clear. In this vow Ryokan is unswerving.

I want to point out this important matter in Ryokan's life, for I have to wonder if a conversion moment occurred, not in the bold sense of a transfiguration, but a *kensho* of some sort that directed and convinced him of his true daemon such that he could sustain himself in the difficult times that lay ahead. He was about to enter a solitary path against the institution and outside of any familial comfort in a relentlessly extreme climate, and continue on this path year after year after year. He would have to endure hunger and cold, loneliness and poverty, all the while maintaining himself as a priest. Who was watching? Who would have known or even cared if he had come down the mountain and chosen the conventional comforts of life? He certainly wasn't taking up this life to make a name for the future. He had abandoned other commitments. Why does he stand supreme in the fulfillment of this vow?

Ryokan had a lifelong engagement with insomnia. I can't say how many of his poems are middle of the night experiences. There are physical reasons for insomnia, but nighttime is also a spiritual time. From a physical standpoint, when we are too cold or too hungry, we can't settle down. The body will not give in to relaxation. Ryokan was known to nap in the afternoons when it was warm and he would have some food in his stomach after begging. He went many nights without any food at all, particularly if the snow was too deep and he couldn't get down the mountain. Sometimes he just didn't get much in his bowl. If he became ill, then he would be up the mountain for several days until he was able to trundle to town or someone would notice they hadn't seen him for a while and climb the mountain to check on him.

But the spiritual and artistic aspect of nighttime is in his bones. As a boy he sat up reading at night when he could sneak into the garden and find a lighted torch, and then he would be too tired to wake up for school. His father scolded him for this bad habit, but nighttime was the poet's natural setting. In darkness his imagination roamed free and in darkness he could listen to nature and allow his mind to invite poems. Poetry was one of Ryokan's forms of prayer, not petitionary prayer, but the natural prayer of silence and listening when he might sense Buddha Nature. The sounds of the night were a trigger for Ryokan to feel the resonance of the voice of the Dharma and what better time is there for this than in darkness when the eyes are beyond duality? Dogen Zenji wrote about a Chinese man named Shisen who wrote this poem about his experience in nature:

> The valley stream's rippling is indeed the eloquent tongue of Buddha:
> The mountain's contour is not other than that of the body of Buddha.
> With the coming of night, I heard the eighty-four thousand songs,
> But with the rising of the sun, how am I ever to offer them to you?

The eighty-four thousand songs refer both to the uncountable number of atoms in the body and to the many possible illuminations of Amida Buddha, the Buddha of Immeasurable Light. Dogen writes further:

> If you yourself do not prize fame or gain, body or mind, then
> the valley streams and mountains will, in turn, be unstinting
> in revealing to you That Which Is. Whether the voice of valley
> streams and the contour of mountains manifest for you the
> eighty-four thousand songs or not is, simply, what comes in the
> darkness of night. (*Shobogenzo, Keisei Sanshoku*)

Ryokan was able to demonstrate and manifest the true voice of the Dharma and he became the valley stream and the mountain and the true form of Buddha Nature.

It is in part because of this unusual and deep choice he made that I decry the emphasis on anecdotes to relate the accounts of his life. Surely there are sweet stories, but these give a limited picture of who this human being was. Too often, such stories tend to celebrate the one who is doing the telling rather than the true person of Ryokan. Come and stay a week in Gogo-an in the winter and see if the stories tell us anything of his mettle and fortitude, or if instead they hide our own inability to meet him on the ground of his being. How few in history have succeeded in such a holy endurance.

Without any historical record of Ryokan's having had a great awakening moment, we can point to his whole life as a slow blossoming into wisdom that began with an exceptional childhood of devotion to learning and education. As Dogen points out, we are already enlightened: the important point is to recognize this and live it fully and faithfully. Ryokan seems to have grasped this from an early age as he demonstrated in his youth the qualities and virtues that would be fundamental not only for his survival but for the bright illumination of Dharma throughout his life.

Path of Aging

As I cast my eyes about me, to learn how men live on earth,
I see them all busy trying to satisfy their hungry desires,
And lagging far behind what they strive so hard to possess,
They fret, mourn, and torture themselves into deep despair.
Be they ever so lucky as to seize the prize in their palms,
How long, let me ask them, could they hold it as their own?
For every blissful pleasure they seek to win in this world,
Ten times they must rack themselves with the pangs of hell.
Ah, how can they find peace by trading anguish for anguish,
To stay forever caught in the tangles which bind them fast?
To use a simile, they are like the apes on a moonlit night
That in their mad appetite to grab the silver disk of moon,
Shedding its bright beams, halfway across a running stream,
Leap one after another into the fathomless whirlpool below.
Alas, I cannot but take pity on the proud men of the world,
For they are doomed to an endless struggle, robbed of rest.
Tears run down my face in spite of myself, as I sit alone,
And muse on man's wretched state over and over in the dark.

Path of Aging

Even the most restless among us evolve toward quietude in the later years of life. Many aging people become invisible to the people around them. Perhaps it takes some a long time to settle into acceptance and peaceable expression, while others are dragged slowly by time, resisting the aging process all the way. Ryokan was not soothed by the thought of advancing years:

> It must have been so, I think
> Always in the past,
> While doubtless it is so now,
> And so it shall be
> For numberless years to come.
> Then of all evils
> The worst that can fall to us
> Is no other than creeping age.
> How obligingly
> They come seeking after me.
> Hidden far away,
> Deep inside a grassy house,
> I can not escape the years.

Age comes without our consent and as something we cannot evade. Decoys and deceptions are powerless against time. Having taken advantage of being human, we discover ourselves slipping toward the end of the movie, or the dream we haven't quite sorted out. Just at the point in life when we get comfortable and begin to accept ourselves, the signs of time appear without warning. Skin sags, teeth wear down, the bladder becomes more demanding. All this occurs before our very eyes and we see it with some level of disbelief. Oh no, not I, such things do not happen to my body.

All you others get these problems, but not I. Enough evidence begins to convince, we catch a glance of the old body in the mirror, and the skin appears to be melting like icing on a cake. We at last admit what Ryokan writes, "I can not escape the years." From the inexorable movement of time there is nowhere to hide.

Ryokan has a heart-wrenching poem about his developing incapacities and his uneasiness with being so alone on the mountain. Since the poem reveals that he has moved down the mountain from Gogo-an to the Otogo shrine, both on Mount Kugami, we know he is advancing in years. He moved to the Otogo shrine when he could no longer manage the climb and the distance to Gogo-an.

> Mount Kugami,
> Some steps up its precipice,
> In the holy shade,
> Close to the Otogo shrine,
> I live by myself,
> Each morning and each evening,
> Up the rocky way
> Climbing with a heavy burden
> To gather firewood,
> Or down the steep valley way
> To draw fresh water.
> Day to day, for countless days,
> Thus I have managed,
> Till at length in recent years
> A sickness holds me,
> And tortures me with the fear
> That I might perish,
> Friendless like cicada shells,
> But few days ahead;
> And that I might be laid down,
> A rotten thing beneath a rock.

Even if one dies alone, no one wants to think that her or his body won't be properly cared for in death. Such is the mind in aging as we wonder what the final day looks like. If we step out of the bathtub and slip, who will find us? No one wants the ignominy of being forgotten in death even though we ourselves won't know of it. We may have many friends but not a daily companion to check on us. This was Ryokan's problem.

He came down the mountain after a time when it was clear he could no longer negotiate the steep, slippery trail to carry food back and take care of himself in the very primitive situation of his hut, Gogo-an, and then later at the Otogo shrine. He had damaged his intestines by eating far too much spoiled food with grubs, worms, and maggots in his eating pot. He suffered from dysentery. Even the people who took care of him couldn't continue as they too were getting old and could no longer run up and down the mountain to see after him when he was sick. In winter the snow was deep, the ice was treacherous, and in that part of Japan the cold penetrated with a terrible insistence. Like many of us who are faced with how to care for our aging parents or relatives, the people of Izumozaki must have convinced Ryokan that moving down the mountain was the sensible thing to do. Ryokan was never one to worry about "being sensible," but the reality of his declining body became obvious even to him and he actually had very little choice. It was a sad day when he left his precious Mount Kugami for the fate of "creeping age." He was nearly speechless with disbelief.

He must have dawdled over everything on that final leaving, worrying over the plants growing beside the hut and giving a final goodbye to the trees, the same grand old elegant pine and maple trees that stand there today. People came to help him, of course, to bring his meager belongings down the mountain, but the idea that his precious Gogo-an would be abandoned was painful for him to realize. Similar to a journey to a convalescent home, Ryokan's transfer to the Otogo shrine and then later to the Kimura house in the town burned his heart deeply. Now, all the life choices he had made were welling up in him and he had to realize that the hermit's life may be rich and free until the moment arrives when one cannot take care of oneself. What are the choices then? We either go off to die, or we accept the arrangements and the good will of others. Such is the painful dilemma of the elderly.

The grief of age is apparent in Ryokan's later poems. For example,

> Have I, really,
> Any friend who will help me
> To forget my age?
> I wondered alone, the night
> I left my cane by mistake.

And,

Had I been aware
That the years were after me,
Upon the highway
I would have put a fast gate
To lock them away from here.

The adjustments Ryokan had to make while living in a tiny little teahouse at the back of the Kimura family home were difficult. He no longer had the freedom and privacy to organize his own day. If people came to visit him there was always the family watching over his activities. Too, he had far less space than he had had in the already tiny hut of Gogo-an. It is hard to imagine how he could have downsized further. He was uncomfortable to say the least and he wrote to a friend saying that he expected to move to another place when spring came. But he never did.

We look at the aging Ryokan and ask about the aging Zen practitioner in today's practice. Are we not faced with what to do about our aging priests? Are we not faced with similar dilemmas about how to care for their lives and in what surroundings? Are the priests not equal to Ryokan in their resistance to time's withering on the body? Active Zen practice has its physical demands which serve in the long run to benefit the aging process because of its great physical activity—maintenance of posture in Zazen, bowing to the floor in ceremonies, continual bows in other daily activities, the practice of art, work in the kitchen, mopping floors, gardening, raking, carrying trays, laughter and exchange with people in the Sangha. The spectrum of the monk's life in the monastery helps to keep the body and the mind fit. Nevertheless, the body and mind change and resist the suppleness of a full bow to the floor, the knees become more vocal than the throat as they creek and moan in their repetitive bending, the breath used for melodious chanting becomes short, the voice clouds with morning phlegm, the muscles droop, and Zen practice becomes ever more challenging. There is continual adjustment to what the body can actually do and there is a readjustment to the elegance of Zen that has been learned and practiced and enjoyed through repetition in the sheer pleasure of the forms. Meanwhile, young monks flit past in their swishing robes, displaying their preciseness and grace of form as they bypass the elders in the hallways, and outdistancing them in the long grueling schedules of retreat. None of this is problematic except to the aging ego. The difficulty comes though in the aging priest's evolving loss of ability to continue to practice without creating further suffering by harming the body. If the practice is too hard, the priest may feel increasingly disfunctional or left behind. The community must make accommodations.

I began monastic training at age 54. I was agile enough, menopause was rearing its hot-headedness, and it took far more physical and mental energy than before for me to do what the young men could do fairly easily. I tired faster than I imagined possible. If I could have a half hour to rest in the middle of the day, I could make it through the continuing hard work of the afternoon and the evening. Without a short rest, my body just gave out. I asked for this small consideration and Godo Roshi, the training master, agreed. Anything that was granted to me was also granted to the other monks. As soon as we finished lunch, I and the other monks could go and rest for 30 minutes. This lasted only a week, and then the system reverted to its old, regular style, and the lunch cleanup dragged out the full hour and quickly the bell rang for outdoor work and we were expected to respond. Sometimes I snuck out of the kitchen early out of desperation and exhaustion. In my case, exhaustion was a medical issue and not just self-indulgence.

In the system where I trained, everyone worked together at everything. Everyone set the table, everyone hovered while the *tenzo* cooked, and everyone washed the dishes and dried them together. Assignments were made for the practice positions, that is, those positions related to the meditation hall, the Dharma Hall, or the ringing of various bells for ceremonies. Otherwise, we were in it together and no one was left out. If you retreated to your room when it was time for the *tenzo* to prepare dinner, a knock came at the door and you were expected to appear and participate. While the *tenzo* cooked, you prepared various dishes or condiments, set the table, or washed up the pots as they were used. You did not stand around; you did something. It was competitive participation. You had to hop into some activity and look busy. You had to look busy.

I liked to wash dishes because then I didn't have to compete. Few monks wanted the dishwashing job. But after awhile, monks would negotiate me out of the way so that I was forced to do other things and not stay in the comfortable position of dishwasher. They felt similarly, I'm sure. Everyone had to be doing something all the time, so we were challenged to figure out what would be useful. Naturally, my organized American mind thought that this arrangement and organization was foolish. Why not allow some monks to study during this period and have only the number of people you really needed to prepare the meal in the kitchen? I told this to our head monk. He just laughed and said, "Ha! This is training."

193

Well, I was an upper middle-aged, menopausal woman who had raised three children, put herself through college and graduate school, and had a career directing non-profit programs. The young monks were 18, 20, or 22 years old and some of them had never washed a dish in their lives and they needed this kind of discipline. They had been allowed to grow up without any responsibility for the kitchen. In the Japanese system of child rearing boys do not enter the kitchen and sometimes it is also the case in American homes that do not teach equality in children's training. Boys are not shown real life and consequently they look around for someone to take care of them and they grow up believing that they are superior to this kind of work. Many young monks would eventually marry and never have to wash another dish thereafter; at least for a time in training they had gotten their hands in soapy dishwater and they couldn't hide from kitchen work.

There was plenty of hide and seek in training too: dodging in and out of jobs, handing jobs over to less senior monks, trying to escape from some of the assignments. Many of the young monks were terrified of ghosts and tried to avoid jobs that took them into dark areas of the temple. If they couldn't avoid it, they often asked a friend to accompany them. At Shoboji there were plenty of ghosts. There was a legend that a young girl had died on the temple grounds and each night she wandered the halls weeping in search of her parents. The belief was that not only her shadow could be seen, but also her sobs could be heard. No one wanted to do the night duty of rining the bell for closing rounds at the end of the day because to do so you had to walk through the darkness of the Dharma Hall to get to the *han* near the zendo where this ghost resided. It was pretty scary in the dark and sometimes the monks would run as quickly as possible just to cross this dark distance.

One night when I was particularly down in spirit, very exhausted, and desperate to speak English, I decided to use the telephone to talk to a friend. We had to have permission to do this because we had to stay one hundred days without leaving the grounds, and somehow, the telephone technically was not leaving the grounds, yet it represented a connection to the outside world. I knew other monks had secretly used the phone, but I had not done so. I didn't want to ask permission because it wasn't urgent; it was more that I was deeply lonely and felt isolated in language deprivation. This breaking of the rules was probably more healthy than a blind adherence to regulations. If you keep yourself too strict, you might begin to believe that you are more important than you actually are. I had explored numerous dark secret passageways at Shoboji and knew my way through them in ways the young monks didn't because they were afraid of the dark. Young and old have different kinds of fears. Whereas as an older person I would be frightened to dive off a cliff into a deep lake, the young men in training were afraid of the dark and of ghosts. Age became a kind of toy for me and I could play with the boys concerning the simple fears that they ran from.

It was in this unilluminated, mysterious, hidden section of the temple where a copy of the secret *Shobogenzo* written by Dogen Zenji in the 1200's was discovered resting on a shelf in the darkness. This was a version of the text that had heretofore gone unpublished and unexamined by contemporary scholars. A dim electric bulb hanging from an old wire revealed shelves of old Buddhist texts that rose up the wall as high as twenty-five feet. It was impossible to read the titles in the blackness of the passageway and texts could lie there unseen for centuries. The heavy dust on them showed they had gone untouched for as long as that, it seemed. I used this passageway for quick access to parts of the temple while the other young monks would not dare go here for fear that something unseen would leap out at them. Through this route I could pass across through much of the temple without encountering anyone. It saved my old, aching feet when walking in the thin, unsupported sandals that we were required to wear.

Gathering up my coins, I made my way barefoot to the public phone in the hallway near the main entrance. Lyn was the one person who could lift me out of this morass. Lyn was a colleague at the women's college, and perhaps the funniest person I've ever known. Laughter with her was deep and crazy and refreshing. I dialed her number and she answered and came to the rescue. I told her she had two minutes to cure me, to save me from this terrible abyss of being an old lady adrift in a sea of young squirts who couldn't understand me and were wearing me down. Within seconds I was laughing and just the joy of hearing her and speaking English helped me know the world outside was continuing, and life was thriving in a sympathetic language. But I couldn't laugh loudly or the monks who were having tea in a nearby room would hear me through the thin walls. I gulped and stifled the laughter, yet in a moment, a door opened as someone investigated the sounds and I had to hang up. But I couldn't be caught. I felt too old to endure the shame and petty discipline that would come from exposure for having made a phone call that would bring me balance. A monk moved furtively down the dark passageway away from the light at the doorway, looking for the unusual noise. Perhaps an animal had gotten in through an open door. I ducked behind a pillar and my shadow just caught a piece of the light. "Who is there?" "Who is there?" he kept calling. As he approached, I moved around the pillar and again my shadow must have made the slightest motion. Suddenly the monk became fearful and almost seemed to weep from fear as his voice trembled and he turned and rushed back to the light, racing inside to close the door behind him. For my part, I was lifted into further silent laughter as I rushed into the darkness and along the secret passageways back to my room where I could be found in case anyone came looking. My amusement at the young monk and thoughts of Lyn's remarks took me over the hump. Yes, the undeclared and actual game of hide-and-seek played out continually and was not always related to age. Yet as an older person and as one who stood apart from the culture, I was perhaps more equipped for being surreptitious, at playing with the minds and the system. It saved me from thinking I might be holy.

My novitiate at the training monastery made it possible for other older monks to enter training. After all, if this mere woman in her fifties could survive, why not older men! Thus, at the point when I was leaving, the temple had accepted one older priest and was planning to accept others. The temples needed trained priests to run them. It was to me a remarkable development of this Japanese training temple that it allowed for older people to complete the body of training which we hold as sacred, even though it may not be ultimately as edifying to some as they would want it to be. Nevertheless it throws trainees into a deeper understanding of the breadth of practice, creates a genuine respect for those who spend many years in training temples, and gives a confidence to practice that one may have longed for over the course of many years.

This deepening was visible in a ceremony I attended a few years ago at my teacher's mountain temple. The series of ceremonies included a Shuso Hossen Ceremony, or a Shuso (Head Monk) Ceremony in which the Head Monk must demonstrate an understanding of the Dharma by answering questions posed by other monks or lay practitioners. The Shuso in question at this ceremony was 75 years old, and his teacher and Zen Master was his son.

Whether a Shuso ever becomes a head of temple doesn't matter. What was important in this case was that the man was given the ritual opportunity to fulfill his heart's wish. It was one of the more beautiful moments I have seen. As the Shuso completed the ceremony, he was required to bow to all the teachers who were present. At last, his final bow was to his teacher, his son. At that moment, he totally lost it and began to sob while deep in his bow to the floor. He was overcome with a sense of completion, relief, and gratitude pouring out of him. Everyone felt this and everyone present began to sob with tremendous tears of thanksgiving at this unusual relationship and the beauty of this new old monk, Ryushin.

Ryushin went on to practice at Entsuji, helping Niho Roshi in the demanding work of keeping the temple running smoothly. As I mentioned, hundreds of pilgrims come through Entsuji temple every day and this requires that the temple be maintained and the pilgrims served in their visits. It is demanding, exhausting work. Mrs. Kimiko Niho, Roshi's wife, serves as a manager, keeping Niho Roshi on his schedule and seeing to the smooth operation of activities. Obaachan, Niho Roshi's mother, is the spirit who shares the work and serves as the matriarchal figurehead of the traditional family. When grandchildren are born, the grandparents do fifty-percent of the childrearing, taking on a huge physical load of the work. Naturally, the grandparents are proud of their children's offspring, but physically it takes its toll on the body. The joy of taking care of the children compensates for this, but the elder grandparents do not simply sit around all day drinking tea. The little ones arrive about midmorning and may be in the grandparents' care until they go home for dinner, so all day the elders are running after the toddlers. I was awed at the happy grace with which the grandparents, Niho Roshi and Mrs. Niho, received the children, knowing how exhausted they would become as such days wore on. Their other activities and responsibilities were not put aside. The temple still had to be run, cleaned, polished; the visitors taken care of; ceremonies prepared; food cooked, dishes cleaned, tea served; clothing washed, dried, ironed. There was simply no rest in the day and no one begrudged the work, no one spoke with annoyed words. They had come to their advanced age without the bitterness than can destroy the beauty of the matured soul.

But what will become of the old monks when they can no longer take care of themselves? Who will take care of them? Many in America have given up careers other than their vocations to be priests and to mentor at Dharma centers. They have not been contributing to retirement systems except at the bigger temples where even then the aging populations weigh on the fragile economy. Like Ryokan, full dependence and reliance upon the Dharma is called for throughout the whole of life and not just when we are young and vital, floating like clouds and able to take to the open road. Aging is part of being on the open road called life and the growing incapacities of the aging make the dependence on Dharma all the more heroic and beautiful.

I have no answers to all of these questions as I myself age and realize that my future demise gets closer by the moment. I have no sense of distance, of the time ahead of me to expand the temple or make renovations; it is all right here in the present, in the now. My ability to sit for long retreats has diminished because my body won't cooperate in remaining in one position for very long; the pain is too great and injury occurs more easily. It no longer seems right or necessary to bear pain in meditation, as even the work I do in stillness has shifted.

There is no doubt about the breadth of the mind in the aging process, provided there is no disease. Aging is the opportunity to do our homework through the natural review process that takes place. We remember events with intense clarity and have a chance to see our history in a new light, settling ourselves and accepting the lifetime we have been given. If we sort things out well, we can find new freedom in the later years, if they come to us. We can release ourselves from emotional encumbrances, settle into rapprochement with the gaffes of our terrible humanness, and just become exactly who we are. Ryokan objected to the advance of time on his tired bones. After all, he needed his body to navigate the mountain and to beg for food, as he had no idea what he would do otherwise to survive.

> Beside a slow fire,
> I stretched out my weary legs,
> And lay on my back,
> All the time feeling the chill
> That pierced into my stomach.

We can feel his slow decline as his lifestyle takes its toll. As though he had never before seen an elderly person, and as though it couldn't happen to him, and almost out of innocence he writes,

> Why does sick old age alone
> Creep on me, and stay with me?

He would grieve the passage of time and his fragility in it, the ephemeral world forever in the forefront of his awareness. This is a Buddhist teaching, that everything continually changes and that all things shall pass away. Without the transit of time being, there is no life activity. At the same time, it is part of our suffering that we get old and die and that we see others do the same. This dreamy life will come to an end. Our youth must give way to youth in others.

Before or after
Hardly matters in my view.
Sooner or later
We must abandon the world
Hollow like cicada shells.

Like all of us, Ryokan stumbled upon his own history and relived it in his thoughts, feeling the sentiment of lost moments that were dear to him. He lived the fate of aging to look back to see where he had been, to remember others and miss their passing, knowing he might be next in line.

Wholly unawares
I was thrown to the bottom
Of abysmal tears,
Seated, facing an old book,
Reading about bygone days.

But then, an amazing, fortunate, and blessed meeting came to him several years before his death. He seemed to stop sorrowing over his plight and he moved into an even deeper softness that captured his heart, as he was able to bear up under the difficult circumstances of his spare living space. It was an unexpected, treasured gift that would throw light and hope on his old age.

Teishin and Women

False delusion and true enlightenment sustain each other.
Evident causes and secret reasons so merge, they are one.
From morning to dusk, I read in silence my wordless text
And, until dawn, I give myself to thoughtless meditation.
Spring warblers whistle to me from wind-inspired willows.
Dogs bark at me, as in alarm, far from a moonlit village.
No laws can define the great surge of emotion filling me.
How can I bequeath to posterity the heart so overwhelmed?

You point with your finger to denote the moon in the sky.
But the finger is blind unless the moon is shining there.
What relation do you see between the moon and the finger?
Are they two separate objects, or one and the same thing?
This metaphorical question is asked as a handy expedient
To inspire the beginners wrapped in the fog of ignorance.
One who has learned to look into mystery beyond metaphor
Knows that neither the moon nor the finger exists at all.

Teishin and Women

It was the year 1827 and Ryokan received this poem from Teishin, a beautiful nun whom he had recently met:

Having met you thus
For the first time in my life,
I still cannot help
Thinking it but a sweet dream
Lasting yet in my dark heart.

Ryokan's heart leapt for joy. He was 69 years old, scrawny, with dark, weather-beaten, leathery skin sagging on his bones. He was still not sick enough to die, but death was peering around the corner. He had been forced to move down from the mountain to the town where he had been offered a place to stay. The place was unimaginably small and he felt his life cramped and ordered in ways he had not felt at Gogo-an or at the Otogo shrine. Too old to live on his own, he was now contained and sedentary.

Unexpectedly, Teishin, 29 years old, with a shaved head, and shy and delicate in her nun's robe, must have seemed as clear and pure as the morning star. She had asked to meet him, making inquiries of the Kimura family where Ryokan had moved in 1826 to the small tea hut in the back of their house. Teishin had taken Tendai sect monastic vows following the death of her husband. She came from a comfortable *samurai* family, married a country doctor and had been widowed at a young age. Teishin had learned about Ryokan and had admired his poetry and calligraphy. Her temple was within a reasonable traveling distance to where Ryokan lived and she frequently traveled to see him in the succeeding years.

Their meeting was the lighting of a deep fire that grew between them. For the old man, it must have been a tender, warm sweetness after the challenge of life on Mount Kugami, the struggle to keep his health, the loneliness, the uncertainty of daily life, and the surrender of his independence by right of being cared for by the Kimura Family. By this time he had gathered the nickname "Crow" because after living nearly entirely out of doors for 35 years his skin shone with the glow of blackbirds in sunshine.

Ryokan sent Teishin this response to their encounter:

> In the dreamy world,
> Dreaming, we talk about dreams.
> Thus we seldom know
> Which is, and is not, dreaming
> Let us, then, dream as we must.

Love poems between Ryokan and Teishin were exchanged in the next five years up until Ryokan's death. Their love poems stand among the most beautiful in the library of world literature.

We can imagine the warmth and joy in this relationship. An old man suddenly became engaged in an association that encompassed a high level of romance with a profound spiritual dimension. Teishin was not Ryokan's student, so they were free to approach the tender language of love. Yet Teishin saw in Ryokan a master teacher at least forty years her senior and a seasoned poet who spoke to her own creative nature. She came into his life like a precious jewel, an unimagined gift that one could not even hope to receive. Perhaps the immediacy of the magnetism surprised them both as they were taken into a sudden elation at their first meeting. An intense happiness came over both of them. Whatever intimacies may have occurred between them in their succeeding meetings, they realized Buddha Nature in one another and stood on the ground of complete dignity. Yet they were surely discreet in their meetings, for Ryokan must have cared for Teishin's reputation as a woman and a nun. Their meetings were held in privacy and the true intimacy of their relationship was honored in secrecy until Ryokan died. They held one another in a settled spiritual nobility that could not be shaken.

Teishin wrote:

> Face to face with you
> I would sit for countless days
> And for endless years
> Silent like the cloudless moon
> I admire with you this night.

Ryokan answered:
>Changeless if you are,
>Steadfast in our sacred faith;
>Long as a creeper,
>Endlessly, for days and months,
>We shall sit down side by side.

The relationship deepened until during one meeting they exchanged vows late at night:

>Seated side by side
>In front of our First Teacher
>Upon Mount Ryozen,
>We vowed our pledge together.
>Let us keep it though we die.

Once when Ryokan was visiting a nearby town, Teishin learned of his presence there and went to meet him. On this occasion they exchanged poems.

Teishin wrote:
>When a father crow
>Sets out from his forest home,
>Aiming for a town,
>Will he e'er leave behind him
>His soft-feathered baby crow?

Ryokan replied:
>I'm not unprepared
>To carry out your sweet wish,
>But what can you do,
>If someone, watching us both,
>Should surmise we are sinners?

We all owe everything of this to Teishin. She published the collection of love poems under the title *Dewdrops on a Lotus Leaf*. In this collection she wrote an account of Ryokan's death, giving to all of us here now in this century an intimate and human view of his final moments, his innermost heart and mind. Teishin lived to be 75 years old and during all the years after his death, she devotedly collected the poems of Ryokan, gathering all that had been written and forgotten in various households around the area.

She made it possible for us to touch Ryokan today. Without her devotion, we would not know his work.

Not only Ryokan's relationship to Teishin and the love poems, but also other poems give us insight into Ryokan's open attitude toward women. He was a man ahead of his time. There are anecdotal stories about women in the surrounding villages and his poems reveal tender concern for his mother and sisters. There is an openness in his poetry that invites women in the twenty-first century to stand with him and honor his ideals about equality, reverence and respect for all beings.

Women liked Ryokan. He was the strange eccentric who lived up on the mountain and wandered into town every few days. He played with the children and developed a concern for the welfare of their families and for everyone in the whole community. In spite of his eccentricity, he was part of the scenery and fabric of the town. He was accepted by women and cared for by them, and they knew up close the rough, worn, cracked texture of his begging bowl. It was they who put rice and gruel regularly into it when they had enough to spare. The townswomen also supplied him with cloth and underclothes.

If you live in Japan, you discover that whatever anyone may think of you, you are still included in the welfare of the nation. If you live in a village, some fellow villager will remember you and help you out. The women did not dote on Ryokan, yet they did not abandon him when he was most needy or sick. Everyone knew that his diet was meager and that his gut was ailing from having eaten too many grubs and maggots and too much spoiled food. He had a good relationship with the quiet, unassuming, unnamed women of the town and with Kokujoji temple, which oversaw Gogo-an and which was within a stone's throw of his mountain retreat.

During the month of August, the Japanese celebrate the Obon festival. For several days, candles are lighted outside the houses to invite the spirits of recent dead ancestors back into the home for a visit. Buddhist priests make prayer and alms rounds through the homes during this season. The festival culminates in a *matsuri*, a local street celebration, in which there is folk dancing, drumming, and a parade. People dress in *yukatas*, light weight, flowery summer kimonos. Women wear flowers in their hair and dance in wide circles around the drummers. This summer *matsuri* festival was a favorite for Ryokan. He loved to dance and he was known to appear in women's clothing so that he could join in the festival.

Buddhist priests were not permitted to dance in public. The folk dances were quite harmless, nothing like our contemporary unbridled heavy metal frenzies or mosh pits. Nevertheless, priests would not participate—except Ryokan. Ryokan borrowed the longest *yukata*, summer kimono, he could find, a scarf for his head, a flower to tuck into the scarf, and a pair of *waraji*, laced up straw sandals. He would apply some lipstick and rouge and enter the circle of dancers with everyone pretending that they did not recognize this new arrival in the town. Ryokan carried off the role in deepest sincerity and seriousness and fully believed that he had executed a master disguise. Or at least he managed to allow people to believe that about him. Out he went with the dancers, head and shoulders above them, singing as he went, keeping the perfect rhythms of the dances,

The townsfolk played along and in succeeding days, they told Ryokan all about the festival as if he hadn't been there. How sorry they were that because he was a priest he couldn't enjoy the dancing and singing! They recounted the marvelous footwork of the mysterious tall woman dressed in her beautiful *yukata* with flowing sleeves. How delicate her makeup was and how poised and elegantly she moved. Ryokan listened, enraptured, taking it all in without the slightest giveaway smile.

Hearing this kind of story, it is easy for a contemporary woman to feel a fondness for Ryokan. His ease in the culture and the environment of his community opens the way for participation in his life. He does not hold his priesthood as a shield against women for fear that the sight of a woman will corrupt him or tempt him into a sexual tryst. He does not have to hold women at arms' length. Ryokan does not arch his back, proclaiming doctrines of celibacy that imply a fortification against sin and fire. He is a man for all people, continually natural and comfortable in his own spirituality. The idea of women as problematic to his own purity doesn't occur to him, which makes him more pure and complete in his life choice.

There is an orchestrated manner of exchange between men and women in Japan. Perhaps an awareness of patriarchy arises, because one of the reasons this form is possible is because women serve men and this maintains a kind of peace between the sexes. Japan runs smoothly because women keep it going. We rarely see women take or receive credit for their work. In the Japanese culture women have been bred toward shyness and humility, and temple women, in particular, maintain their support of daily life while moving together and supporting one another in the background. The entire temple system would die without the service of women. In the contemporary world, many temples are closing for a variety of reasons, one of which is the difficulty of finding women willing to partner with a priest and to give their lives to such hard labor.

If you refuse to follow the correct behavior, there are penalties to be paid. Some young priests seemed to think I shouldn't have been in the monastery in the first place.

During priest training at the monastery, I found myself in numerous situations in which I was clearly shunned because I was a woman. This shunning came from the younger men, the ones who were clustered in their training groups and who would have been castigated by their male peers had they shown me any favor. Older monks were more understanding and willing to see me succeed. They helped and supported me, unlike one monk who entered the monastery three days after I did. We received seniority according to the date we entered and so I was senior to him. During the entry period, we sat a regimen of concentrated meditation to demonstrate our serious intention to engage in rigorous practice and our willingness to give ourselves over to the training master. Entering monks were placed in a room for meditation that would continue from morning to night interrupted ony by meals and the freedom to go to the toilet. The rest of the time, we sat silently in meditation.

When the meal times drew near, a bell rang and we got up, went to the toilet, and prepared the room for the food trays. This particular monk was openly and deliberately hostile to me. He refused to assist me in any way, refused to pass me food at the table, refused to allow his tray to pass through my hands, and in essence, behaved as though I did not exist. In his eyes, I was an untouchable, an invisible entity. This hostility continued throughout training and he never relented, nor was he properly disciplined for his behavior. It was I who received scolding for challenging him. He chastised any of the other monks to whom he was senior for speaking to me. When the hostile monk was not around, some of the others interacted, but the fact of my being a woman posed tremendous difficulties that added to the challenge of training in a new culture.

Many times I thought of quitting, but it was always more painful to think of walking out than it was to continue. For the first time in my life, I created a calendar and crossed out each day with a determined "X" the way prisoners are seen to do in old movies. In my own culture I had some voice even if I weren't listened to as a woman. At least I had language and expression. In this situation I could not argue or challenge; I could only accept. This was not a true acceptance, but rather a putting up with the circumstances for the duration of my sojourn. Why this monk was never reprimanded I would never know. Perhaps his father held some important position. I had seen this man literally kick a cat out of his way, surely injuring the animal, and nothing was said about his behavior. I never understood why. This experience taught me that the monastery is full of human beings, totally imperfect, often acting out their personal issues on the community, causing distress and difficulty. Those same human beings are also full of goodness, doing kind acts for one another, suffering with their inadequacies, looking to others for assistance, and providing help in myriad ways. What learned is that I was and am one of those humans who was and is doing her best in challenging circumstances where there is no perfect outcome and no magic wand to make everything right. A monk, priest, or nun is someone who becomes spiritually visible and vulnerable and stands as a mirror to society where the examining light shines on them more brightly than on others. In America, the tiniest loss of virtue can be condemnatory. In Japan, the humanness of clergy is far more tolerated and accepted. The Japanese do not blame their priests for being human; in America we expect perfection, especially from women.

Western women concerned with gender issues find the service of Japanese women hard to accept. It isn't so much that Western women need recognition; what smarts is that women will be expected to fulfill only certain roles. A Western woman can serve tea and coffee for only a short period of time. She will soon realize that she has moved from the practice of virtue into an object of service with the sole purpose of pleasing men. Somewhere in this transaction and certainly in the realization, virtue cannot survive. She can only teach by withdrawing or challenging. If she continues, she compromises herself because she is participating in and encouraging the continuation of sexual objectification. If she challenges, she is disrupting the ancient system of privilege that Japanese people, both men and women, perpetuate as a matter of course. Examples abound.

During Sesshin at a famous temple with the Zazenkai from Entsuji, we were engaged in a midmorning work period during which we washed the floors on our hands and knees, men and women working side by side to clean the temple, equally soaked with sweat in the summer heat. Following this it was time for a break, to rest and have tea. We had all been up since 4:30 a.m. The men all flopped onto the floor to await tea service from the women while the women were called into the kitchen to dry and put away huge mounds of dishes from the breakfast meal. This took the entire time of the rest break until the bell rang and we hustled to get to the next activity.

Another time I was travelling to Niho Roshi's mountain temple along with four men from the Zazenkai. We worked around the grounds, then hiked over to the rural home of a temple member. Our appearance forced these poor mountain people, so bedraggled from working in the field, to suddenly display their hospitality, as this was a surprise visit. The woman, well into her 80s, was sent off to put together tea service with cakes and fruit and whatever she could find in the kitchen. We all sat down and when I saw this hunched woman shuffle with swollen feet and ankles into the kitchen I immediately got up to help her. She was very grateful and we put together trays of food and tea such that they made her husband proud of sharing what they had. Later, Niho Roshi thanked me for getting up to help. He took it as a gender matter. To him, I was finally coming around to find my place as a woman in the Japanese culture. For me, there was no gender involved. Anyone who had two eyes could see how exhausted this woman was and how now after toiling all day in the field she was having to serve these sedentary lumps of men who sat flat on their behinds and allowed her to exhaust herself even further without their lifting a finger to help. Later, one of the men told me that Japanese men feel it is women's joy to serve them. Privilege certainly creates its own blindness.

I shouldn't imply that these situations occur only in Japan. In America, the problems are more subtle and inbred so that we don't always see them as the underbelly of various problems that crop up in our interactions and in our communities. Very often, when in the Sangha we are struggling with gender issues, a man will remind us that in the true practice of Buddhist virtue, there is no such thing as gender. We are all above gender in Buddha Mind. Well, yes this is so. The implication is then that the woman who brings it up is less virtuous for having pointed out a problem in the relative world. But, of course, this is the matter of privilege, that someone who holds privilege doesn't have to deal with the manifestations of it. It is profoundly lacking in virtue to allow privilege to rear its ugly head at the expense of any human being. If the problem exists, it is because of the one who holds privilege and not the other way around. The problem belongs to the one on the dominant, privileged side. The problem of racial discrimination resides with privileged whites; that of gender discrimination lies with privileged men; that of discrimination against the disabled rests with privileged able people; that of age discrimination is an issue for those who are younger. Those in the groups discriminated against participate in the discrimination if they support a privileged person who gives them a certain level of privilege in a quid pro quo transaction.

Nevertheless, the presence of many women leaders in Zen practice in America is changing the face of Zen and how women are able to participate in the Zen community. The recognition of the presence of women through Zen history is being realized through the scholarship and research of devoted women writers such as Paula Kane Robinson Arai, Miriam Levering, Rita Gross, Nancy Falk, Sandy Boucher, Myo-on Grace Schireson, Susan Murcott, and Lenore Friedman, to name just a few. And in Japan, Kito Shunko, and Shundo Aoyama are among the courageous ones who stood up and challenged the Soto Japanese system, demanding equality for women. For centuries we have behaved as though there were only men in the lineages while research has shown this assumption to be completely untrue. We have identified the names of our matriarchs and now use them to complete the ancestry and to give them full voice in the development of practice and the transmission of the Dharma.

Mahapajapati, the Mother of Buddhism, comes to mind. Her name Maha means "great" and Pajapati means "one who leads a great assembly." At her birth it was foreseen that she would become a great leader and thus we see her name fulfilled in the woman who raised the Buddha child from his birth after the death of his natural mother, and in her leadership of the monastic order of women. In my experience, Mahapajapati is not featured in the Japanese Buddhist culture, where women are silently serving in the background. There, she presents a problematic role model. Mahapajapati ultimately becomes fully enlightened, leaves home, stands in protest before the Buddha himself, attracts hundreds and hundreds of women to stand with her and to join the monastic order, and in essence helps to bring about a complete change in the social structure. She becomes a mother on a grand social scale, nurturing the torn emotional outcasts, the prostitutes, the forgotten, the abandoned widows, and those who generally had no place else to go. She takes them all in and helps them find meaning and life in the Four Noble Truths. With her leadership, women had a place beyond marriage and a way to stand against the struggle of oppression. Discrimination would continue; yet still it was a profound beginning and Mahapajapati courageously fought for equality until her death.

When the Buddha returned to his home ground, Mahapajapati, who had carefully raised him as a child, counseled him, tended his needs, taught him about human relationships, and stood quietly in the role of parent through every upset, was herself awakened on hearing his teaching. How spiritually ready Mahapajapati must have been to so immediately recognize awakening. She paid homage to the Buddha, whose teachings brought her own awakening and yet she stood fully confident in the light of her leadership and understanding because she challenged him again and again in his cultural limitations.

In many ways, she remains the wise parent whose view is sometimes culturally wider and more far reaching than the Buddha's and who must remain patient until the child grows into understanding. Mahapajapati sees through privilege in ways that Shakyamuni Buddha does not and is willing to act upon change and to bring about equality. She is the first activist and the miracles that took place after her death were equal to those that took place following the Buddha's cremation.

There is something about Ryokan's stepping out of the realm of privilege which makes him an ally of women. He has gone beyond the dependency that men in the life of privilege develop and expect. Ryokan could fully enter a life of equality which people of the robe are expected to embody, and which ideally we would all advance toward. Ryokan continued in this stance even after he went beyond the wall. He never set himself up in a situation in which he created dependence through privilege. This practice is his clear teaching about equality for our time.

As Americans, we gaze at the Japanese culture as if white male privilege were non- existent in America and that as Americans we are far more advanced in our liberation of women than any other culture. Nothing could be further from reality. We simply permit privilege to persist in different ways in our different culture. The subtle behaviors of privilege take root in our interactions when we are not alert. Allan Johnson in his book *The Gender Knot* writes, "Sexism isn't simply about individual enlightenment; it isn't a personality problem or a bad habit. Sexism is rooted in a social reality that underpins male privilege and gender oppression" (123).

The forms of practice are meant to take us far beyond issues of oppression, but at the same time, these forms of practice allow us to see oppression and the activities, attitudes, beliefs, and actions that perpetuate as they lie hidden in the culture. Practice helps us to be able to critique the very culture that creates oppression, to foster the courage to confront it and bring it into the light, and to develop the insight and skillful means to bring about lasting and meaningful change.

It remains to be seen how we will go forward in Zen practice in America with clear open dialogue concerning gender oppression and a practice toward equality. The same discussion must be opened around racism, sexual orientation, age discrimination, disability, ethnic origins, and the systems of privilege that give rise to maintaining oppression. Johnson writes in *Privilege, Power, and Difference*:

> "The trouble is produced by a world organized in ways that
> encourage people to *use* difference (gender or race) to include

or exclude, reward or punish, credit or discredit, elevate or oppress, value or devalue, leave alone or harass...To have privilege is to participate in a system that confers advantage and dominance at the expense of other people." (19, 39)

If Buddhism is to live up to its spiritual teachings, then it must challenge the culture in which it takes root. Women too must give up their hold on privilege and be willing to admit their part in maintaining it. Teishin, in gathering Ryokan's poems and bringing them to publication, did not stand back and defer to his work. She included her own poetry in the publication, standing as equal to the great poet and priest himself. Of course, Ryokan's body of work surpassed Teishin's and took up appropriate residence in Zen and world literature. Yet we owe Teishin profound gratitude for her sincere devotion and labors.

A figure such as Ryokan can throw a flashlight on the sticky web of rigidity and small behavior. We can grasp Ryokan's response to our own small mindedness and thereby let it fall away into kindness and open acceptance of all beings and creatures in a more highly developed equality. When each one is practicing at the highest possible level, we have the means to face our own ignorance in ways that bring about transformation. Ryokan has the capacity to include everyone in the breadth of his robes, gathering them all into himself where he may hold them in supplication in the midst of their suffering.

The poems between Ryokan and Teishin expressed an enduring love, a deep sense of life and experience, and an appreciation of one another and the teachings of the Buddha. The language between them was the intimate language of lovers and yet Teishin unashamedly opens this intimacy to the world. Why should they not have expressed the profound delight in the life of the Self and Other? In this, she stands in equality open to the whole world and at the same time on a platform with Ryokan. She does the exquisite work of delivering their relationship to world literature. She doesn't just publish Ryokan's poems by standing back and remaining hidden; she comes through the gate into the light and stands as equal to Ryokan in her collection *Dewdrops on a Lotus Leaf.* And this relationship was a culminating point in Ryokan's life for it showed his complete humanity and humanness, his vulnerability, and his strength of feeling in the face of love. Through these poems we hear the voices of two souls afire with the beauty of life, and at a time for Ryokan when he was making his own passage through old age and his life was beginning to ebb.

A Darkening Time

Maple leaves scatter
At one moment gleaming bright,
Darkened at the next.

A Darkening Time

Ryokan's death poem is said not to be his own work, but he loved it and loved the maple leaves, the loveliest in Japan, and he fully lived the nature of the ephemeral implicit in the poem. He had lived a life of choice and he well knew he would one day die. He owned very little, his robe and bowl, of course, along with a few pieces of clothing, a sleeping blanket, a brush, ink, and paper. He also had a food jar where he kept extra rice and food that he couldn't eat immediately. He would collect it in the jar where it stayed with the maggots and other insects that climbed through it, and he would move them out of the way when he wished to eat. After so many years of living nearly out of doors, he was not put off by the presence of insects and animals. He had a highly developed sense of the natural life around him and thus had no need to discriminate.

The diet that Ryokan kept solely from begging likely contributed to the deterioration of his stomach and intestines. On the other hand, he lived a good long life considering the lifespan of the people at that time and the poverty and extremes of weather he lived in. We know from his poems about the struggles with diarrhea, which also caused weakness:

> Upon the dark night,
> When will the dawn come to smile?
> Upon the dark night,
> If the pied dawn starts to smile,
> A woman will come
> And wash my foul garments clean.
> Tossing many times
> I fouled my shirts and my pants,
> Aching through the entire night.

He expresses gratitude to the women who came up the mountain in the mornings to clean his body and wash his soiled clothing when he was too sick to move. This admission of his condition brings us right to the heart of Ryokan, for when do we hear poets talk about such a private matter? It is a stunning admission to allow us into this scene and gives more insight into exactly what this sometimes-idealized life was actually like. Of course, Ryokan never wrote any poem with the intent to publish it. Nevertheless, we feel the strength of his commitment to remain on the mountain given the pain of his physical difficulty, although at the time he had nowhere else to go. We witness the surrender of dignity to his human circumstances and sense the actuality of the body in the aging and dying process.

The townsfolk took responsibility for Ryokan and refused to abandon him in his life choice. His entire life had been a cooperative event between himself as a hermit and the townsfolk as the ones to maintain awareness of his existence. Unless the culture supports the religious ideal of the solitary monk, the monk cannot survive. If someone simply flees into the mountains without acknowledgement of the community, then it is not a spiritual act; it is simply isolationism and setting oneself apart from people for some kind of personal satisfaction. The true hermit is acknowledged and supported by the surrounding community so that the community participates in the life of the hermit. The hermit gives the community the opportunity to demonstrate respect and generosity. The hermit shows gratitude though prayer and good works and in this shows that he or she is not separate from society. If this mutuality is not the dynamic, the hermit faces the danger of the development of an inflated ego, abject loneliness, distancing, and mental aberration. For these reasons, huts are often placed on the outskirts of monasteries so that monks can be looked after while they experience the beauty of solitude. The solitary life is not a totally isolated and separate life.

Such mutuality was surely the case with Gogo-an and the Otogo shrine where Ryokan also spent some years. The adjoining temple oversaw the huts so everyone was aware that someone was nearby in case of need. Except in monasteries, our American culture does not seem to support the life of the hermit. Our sense of individualism says that we are all on our own and we should each be responsible for ourselves. Generally as a society, we don't want to be put out or to take on long-term inconveniences. But this is not true of Japanese society and its homogenous nature; it is far more inclusive, or at least it was in the time of Ryokan. Western influence on all global cultures has seen an erosion in the basic rhythm and structure of all societies, for individualism, technology, globalism, greed, have torn at their fabric.

Nevertheless, Ryokan's final years with the joy of Teishin in his life seemed happy. He did not like that his living space was so cramped. It was not larger than a moon-viewing house with a little space to sleep. He also had less privacy, with people stopping in constantly to tell him how to take care of himself and to talk away the time. He wasn't used to that much social activity and it wore on him. He told someone he hoped to find another place to move to, but it didn't happen.

The last time I visited in that area, the moon-viewing house was gone from the back of the Kimura residence. I don't know why it had disappeared, but I had witnessed it once on an earlier visit some years before during the winter. I stayed in Niigata and took the local train to Izumozaki, about an hour's ride. The train was packed with commuters and school children. Along the way it began to sleet in a terrible cold, wet downpour. I had no umbrella and no hood on my jacket to protect me from this extreme weather, but I did wear a winter cap. I wondered how it would be hiking up the mountain in this weather and decided it would help me feel how it might have been for Ryokan, out in the cold and wet. I doubted there would be a place to buy a cheap umbrella often sold at the corner convenience shops. As the train went along, it began to empty until I was the only one left in the train car. And there was an umbrella left on the seat across the aisle. It was a beautiful, wide, magnificent grey umbrella with a curved wooden handle and an automatic open button, a gift from the gods. Whether someone actually forgot it or saw that I didn't have one and left it for me, I shall never know, but it was there for me to pick up and use and it was truly a day for a wide umbrella. I took it as a sign or a piece of magic.

I hiked up the mountain to Gogo-an and passed by Kokujoji temple on my way. The wet sleet had turned to a soft snowfall of fat, wet flakes. I approached, having had to climb onto a huge drift of packed snow until I stood high above the temple door. As I went by, the temple master stood in the doorway looking up at me just ten feet away as if I were Mary Poppins in flight, a crazy person hiking in this weather, and a foreigner to boot. We said good morning and I continued the climb up the hill to Gogo-an. There is an ascent through a wooded grove of cedar and then a descent onto a small plateau where Gogo-an rests. Balls of snow dotted the boughs of cedar and the smell of wet, cold woods permeated the air. Except for the sound of falling snow and the crunch of my own footsteps, the forest lay silent. Steam rose from my breath.

Only a few old footprints of hikers from the days before showed any signs of life. The doors of Gogo-an stood open as they always are so pilgrims can easily pray at the sacred site. Leaves and debris had blown in and had scattered around the floor and altar, so I didn't hesitate to take off my boots and enter. I cleaned away the debris, dusting the altar and the statues with a clean handkerchief from my bag. Then I chanted the *Hannya Shingyo*, the Heart Sutra, with the heat from my breath rising over the statue of Ryokan. It was desperately cold and I felt intensely happy to be alone in the home of this spiritual friend. For a long time, I sat in the atmosphere listening to the drip and stir of the forest, a sudden release of a snow pack from the top of a tree, a bird calling in the distance.

I thought long and hard about Ryokan's life and the ruggedness of his choice to remain a priest in the hardship of his circumstances. It stings the heart if we stay only with the hardship. It thrills the soul to touch his embrace of freedom and dignity as a prince of Buddha's teachings. He made his choice and allowed his life to unfold, letting happen what would happen. Friends came to his aid and made this temporary existence at Gogo-an possible. And so he stayed in his solitary palace of kindness and simplicity working out his spiritual path, which transcended the comforts that were available to him. Uncle Ryokan would have been welcome in the village where he would be offered a warm bath and regular meals. But going down the mountain permanently, oh the worldly entanglements! He had given up that life and embraced the wandering clouds, free in his mountain retreat.

> Adrift as a cloud,
> I have naught to hold me back,
> For I am a priest.
> With my heart void of desires,
> I must leave all to the winds.

The approach of other pilgrims pulled me away from my reverie. It had been a few hours of quiet, and I quickly moved out of the hut, as no one should set foot inside this precious shrine even though there are no signs forbidding it. It is simply an unwritten Japanese assumption that one would not step into a sacred place uninvited. Newcomers to the scene would feel I had intruded on their encounter and intimacy with Ryokan. My being inside would have violated their sensibilities. Nevertheless, I felt a secret happiness and couldn't express the gratitude for the experience of this quiet encounter with the Master.

The same route back past Kokujoji seemed the most sensible way to return although there is now a brightly painted suspension bridge across a ravine to get to the Otogo shrine. There would be another day, another time for that. I found a teahouse with a telephone where I called for a taxi to take me to the station. I was chilled to the very bone. There were only two afternoon trains and I thought I would catch the earlier one given the cold and rain. A woman driver came to pick me up and asked if I had ever been to the Kimura Residence where you must make an appointment to see their personal collection of Ryokan memorabilia. No, I hadn't been there, so she offered to take me and I agreed to get the later train. She took me around to the back of the Kimura Residence. It was here that I saw the teahouse where Ryokan lived his final years until he died. She slid the wood door slightly open and pulled back the curtain and I burst into spontaneous, hard sobbing tears. The poor woman didn't know what to do, but I was overcome by the smallness of the space and the fact that I was standing in such proximity to this intimate abode where Ryokan and Teishin had met and Ryokan had died. There was the enormity of his life, known and celebrated all around the world, suctioned into this place as though all his essence were siphoned into a single tatami where he lay dying. There was an awesome humbleness to the space. All of his life rolled backward for me, then hurled again into open space and sky.

Like much of Japan, on first glance there is nothing extraordinary about one place as compared to another. We are simply told that some historic event took place here, or someone of importance stood in this place. It isn't that the place looks different from any other place. What happens is that the event comes to life and the residue of the profound nature of life activity swells inside us. It is as if ghosts are in place reenacting the meaning- laden event as an offering to the myth of the people. It is nearly an alternative universe of the past that gives value to the present and says to the living, "Do not forget." It is the Confucian Heaven of ancestors visiting the living and bestowing blessings upon them, provided the ancestors are well remembered and honored.

When I finally contained myself, the driver brought me inside the Kimura home, a dark and musty clutter, filled with things and collections of tidbits over time. Mr. and Mrs. Kimura huddled in a warm room filled with well-worn furniture and cushions which was closed off from the rest of the house. If the Kimuras were in their 70's they would have been born in the 1920's. This made them the second generation after Ryokan, the grandchildren of the original Kimuras who were there when Ryokan had lived and died. Because the Kimuras inherited many Ryokan artifacts, they have assumed responsibility for being open to researchers and people who have an interest in Ryokan. One can only enter their house by appointment. Because interest in Ryokan has continued, at this point they have passed on many of the artifacts to the nearby Ryokan Museum, a newly built cultural site.

Soon I was offered a cup of tea and I explained that I was from Entsuji temple in Tamashima, Ryokan's training temple. The elderly husband and wife were a bit skeptical about my authenticity so they produced a brush, ink and paper and asked me to paint something. I took up the brush and immediately painted a picture. Mr. Kimura took it and handed it to his wife, "Hmmm. That's Ryokan," he said. It seemed to satisfy. With that he got up and went into the next room and came back with a box. He opened it and took out a small ball and placed it in my hand. He explained it was a ball that Teishin had given to Ryokan, about the size of a hacky sack ball but not as soft. What a beautiful thing, delicately wound with twine so that a pattern of flowers appeared with a blue background. Tears ran down my face.

We talked a little more and then I was invited to chant at the home altar in the interior room. The altar was old and musty yet a small flower stood upon it like a shaft of light in the dark of winter. Here they kindled the memory of the old Kimuras and made offerings to the spirits. A small bell with old wrapping on its striker sat to the right. I rang the bell and began to chant. What a joy to intone *Hannya Shingyo* and to dedicate it to gratitude to the Kimuras and the memory of Ryokan and Teishin. As I was wearing a medal of *Kannon Bosatsu* with an inscription from Entsuji, I took it off and left it on the altar as a gift and proof that I was truly connected there. No doubt they found it later on. Soon the driver took me to the station to be on time for the last train. Still clutching the umbrella, I boarded and rode back to the connection to Niigata. The train filled with passengers as it progressed toward Niigata and the little towns of Ryokan Country fell into the distance. Of course I left the umbrella on the train. It had been on loan and I felt certain it would find its way back to its owner. Oddly, however, no one reminded me to pick up my forgotten umbrella when I got off the train. I felt as if it were invisible or a blessing that had appeared via Buddha's hand or Ryokan's bowl as a sign of my pilgrimage of remembrance.

There is a small anecdote about Ryokan's death that has deep resonance and some basis in truth. Soto monks when they are traveling wear a kind of backpack, ancient in style, but adequate to carry what they need. The whole backpack is only ten by twelve by three inches in size. It carries a change of underwear, clean socks, personal care supplies, and a razor for shaving the head. Strapped onto the outside are the *Oryoki* bowls, the monk's eating bowls. Thus it is a contained unit and has all they need for practice when they arrive at the next temple. But there is one more item in the backpack. The monks are required to carry money with them to cover the cost of their death expenses and funerals. In the event that they die along the route, it would be impermissible to cause someone else the financial burden of one's own death. So, death money is placed in an envelope and tucked into the backpack.

It is said that upon Ryokan's death, a stash of gold coins was found tucked into a bag in his monk's belongings. I feel rather certain that Ryokan would have followed the Soto Zen monk's rules for traveling with death money. It's also conceivable that his father gave him these coins when he first started out on his journey with Kokusen Roshi. Ryokan received novice ordination just before the party left Izumozaki and he would have been required to carry the death money for the walk to Tamashima and Entsuji. It was simply the custom. Even in today's world, it was a requirement that I carry it. No one would have known whether I had it or not, but it was the ancient custom and so it continues to be practiced.

Considering Ryokan's simplicity, his naiveté, and in some ways his simple practicality, he would have kept the gold coins for his death money regardless of his occasionally empty larder. How could he have shown up at the market with gold coins? How could he say, "Oh yes, this is my death money I'm spending for groceries." He simply would not release those gold coins until they were released by his death. I am inclined to believe this story because it sounds quite plausible and Ryokan's character seems to verify it.

Ryokan and Teishin continued to meet on occasions when they could, but gradually Ryokan's health deteriorated and he refused to see any visitors. At last he sent a poem to Teishin, for he must have sensed his own demise:

> Come at once to me,
> As soon as spring is with us.
> Here at my cottage,
> I long to meet you once more,
> Though for a twinkle of time.

By the end of that year, Ryokan's health worsened and he simply grew weaker and weaker. A friend wrote to Teishin telling her it was urgent that she visit Ryokan, as it was clear that he had very little time to live. She came immediately but found him sitting up and talkative. Nevertheless, she decided to stay and nurse him, even though it was evident the end was nearing as he again fell into a state of collapse.

Teishin held him and comforted him as he grew weaker, giving him sips of water as he was able to swallow and keeping him warm with hot coals in a metal container which was wrapped in a towel and placed near his back and feet. She again pledged herself to him, promising to be faithful, knowing full well life is ephemeral. The tears were plentiful and unrestrained and Ryokan mumbled softly, struggling to find strength to speak his heart. He was enclosed in love and tenderness in his final moments.

Ryokan died on January 6 on a cold day of falling snow. Word went out quickly that he had died and two days later a funeral was held and a gravesite prepared at Ryusinji temple in Shimazaki very close to the teahouse behind the Kimura home. Many townspeople came from far and wide and tramped through the snow to pay honor to this holy man whom they had had the good fortune to live with and to know. A great emptiness came over the area as Ryokan was suddenly gone from them, his *Kakurenbo* finished, his footsteps and singing with the children silenced, his easy laughter and the chink of his begging stick hushed from their neighborhoods. At the same time, a tranquil light came over the region, as if an eternal lamp had been turned on at the gate, opening the way for all who would follow to understand the nature of spiritual freedom, revealing the natural play of hiddenness and discovery in its deepest spiritual and mythic sense, and preparing a way for realization along the circuitous and mysterious path to wisdom.

Coda

Coda

In the entryway where we gather following morning Zazen at Olympia Zen Center, we form a circle that includes the statue of Ryokan as he stands among us, a practicing monk holding his begging bowl. In this symbolic way, he holds out his begging bowl as an act of giving. He seems to be saying, "Here, please take the teachings of the Buddha from the abundance of this bowl of Emptiness." We receive his wisdom-voice as we stand in the circle in our ongoing confabulations, which invariably fall into observation and comment about our environmental and political climate which we are all concerned about and for which we have no answers. For a long time we have thought our exchanges to be a source of gloom as we skated from Zazen into the complex problems of our time: our stunning global challenges, political intrigues, and local disorders. I have come to think differently about this tendency toward despondency and how preciously important it is for us to continue to chew on the state of our planet, our union, our town, even when we cannot bring answers to the dilemmas facing us. These discussions reveal how much we care about our world.

Ryokan is not just standing silently in the circle, he is present to our concerns because he has lived through parallel times and because we keep his teachings current in our discussions at this time in history. Our lives are made better by this because we receive the wisdom of his teachings that tell us to be alive to what is happening around us and to have the courage to challenge what we can in our society. He was concerned about the condition of the environment, the state of politics, economics, health, child development, the community, literature, poetry, philosophy, education, aesthetics, and art. As citizens of the world, it is our duty to inform ourselves and to seek wise answers to the crises of our times. Ryokan serves to bring a virtuous tone to all these considerations.

Among the most important virtues Ryokan teaches, given the conditions we live in, is persistence or constancy. We can also call this "vow."

You might choose other virtues, but in this fickle land of ours with our inability to look to the needs of the distant future and the incapacity to make sacrifices for the welfare of our descendants, I say nothing could be more urgent than for those who would call themselves Zen practitioners to sustain the practice of Zazen. To engage in the practice of Zazen as an overall life practice. We have generally become a nation of spiritual window shoppers, unable to settle into an authentic focus for looking into ourselves honestly and straightforwardly. We have become superficial in our exchanges by handing our souls to the lure of images and technology. We have lost the balance that comes with commitment to daily practice. We misunderstand compassion and misinterpret empathy as a standard for ethical behavior.

Wholehearted Zazen—as a community equalizer, a force for transformation, a practice to temper hubris, arrogance and ego, an act to awaken the heart of mercy, a standard for maintaining the Precepts, a practice for growth in wisdom, an agency for understanding the mind and its tendencies, a way to calm greed, anger and ignorance, a vehicle for peace- keeping, an exercise in consistent daily living, an influence against delusion, an answer to address suffering—this is what we do and persistently practice. It is in essence what Ryokan taught. We take him then as our spiritual friend who encourages us in our commitment to a Way that has been given us by the "Ancient sages who left their works behind, not to let us know about themselves, but to help us understand our own stamp." This is the ancient sage Ryokan's importance to us at Olympia Zen Center, to Buddhism, and to the world.

Appendices

Chronology

1754	Ryokan's parents marry
1758	Ryokan is born in Izumozaki, and named Eizo
1760	His sister Murako is born
1762	His brother Yasunori is born
1769	His sister Takako is born
1770	His brother Encho is born
1773	His brother Kaoru is born
1777	His sister Mikako is born
1779	Studied with Genjo Haryo at Koshoji temple in Amaze and meets Kokusen Roshi, takes novice priest vows, and goes with Kokusen Roshi to Entsuji in Tamashima
1783	Ryokan's mother dies
1786	Ryokan's father retires; his brother Yasunori takes over the township responsibilities
1791	Kokusen Roshi dies
1791 to 1796	Ryokan leaves Entsuji and wanders, whereabouts uncertain
1792	Ryokan's father goes to Kyoto
1795	Ryokan's father commits suicide
1796	Ryokan goes to Kyoto for his father's memorial and then returns to his birthplace
1796 to 1804	Ryokan lives at various places including Gogo-an, Mitsuzoin temple, and Saiseiji temple
1798	Teishin is born
1804	Ryokan receives permission to stay permanently at Gogo-an on Mount Kugami
1816	Ryokan leaves Gogo-an and moves down the mountain to the Otogo shrine, closer to the village
1826	Ryokan leaves the Otogo shrine and moves to a small hut at the Kimura residence
1827	Ryokan meets the nun Teishin
1830	Ryokan is taken ill
1831	Ryokan dies on January 6

Following the Way of Ryokan

Daily Home Practice and Ceremony in Honor of Ryokan

To follow in the Way of Ryokan is to live daily life with an awareness of the Buddha's teachings, Dogen Zenji's teachings, and the natural inclination to want to make the world a better place. The Buddha's teachings show us to do as little harm as possible; to recognize suffering and how we contribute to suffering; to alleviate suffering by living well; to understand and take responsibility for the consequences of our actions; to realize the ephemeral nature of life. Dogen Zenji models a pathway of spiritual training in Zen for insight into Zazen practice, devotional expression, and recognition of the importance of Awakening. If we wish to live well in the world, not just amble along through life without any examination of our being, then we engage in the effort to find meaning in our lives. In order to do this, we have to find a way to balance our own interiority with empathic recognition of others. Without this balance, we can become invested in our own needs and performance while forgetting there are others in the animal, vegetable, and mineral world. Or we can become so outwardly directed, perhaps even to the point of interfering, as to fail to see our own shortcomings. We must ask: for whom do we practice? We have the paradox of the self in the world, focusing inwardly in order to manifest outwardly. The inward look is the outward view. Ultimately we practice for others as our inward polishing manifests itself as good action in our activities.

At Olympia Zen Center, the life of Ryokan has a deep influence on us. We pay homage to Ryokan and to his life, finding this balance in continual daily practice. We follow his Way, which helps us remember to be as a Buddha in daily life through the expression of kindness, simplicity, compassion, equality, and the expression of art. His life reminds us to avoid haughtiness, accumulation of unnecessary goods, hoarding of riches, and living in fear. He enjoins us to keep our sleeves wide and to hold the entire universe in our arms.

In living the virtues of Ryokan, we join in the community of the Order of Ryokan, committing ourselves to:

Remain constant to Zazen
Live modestly with goods and belongings
Live in awareness of the environment and its fragility
Practice kindness

Maintain creative practice and activity in the arts
Be faithful to solitude
Propagate peace in the world and the surrounding communities
Remain in active communication with other members of the Order

Each morning we begin the day with Zazen, meditation in silence as the sun rises. We follow this with Morning Service during which we include chanting of one of the poems in the Song of Ryokan, which is a series of poems philosophical in nature that have been selected from the translation by Nobuyuki Yuasa. Ryokan never preached, he only wrote poems that show us his mind of doctrinal thought rendered in the classic Chinese poetic style. Ryokan also loved Hannya Shingyo, The Heart Sutra, and his childlike calligraphic style displayed in tile above the entrance to the sanctuary of the Dharma Hall at Entsuji, reflects the simplicity and beauty of the Sutra itself and we feel it in a new way, without guile or pretension—just as it is and speaks to us.

People who live alone or in family or community may conduct a simple Morning Ceremony each day to fill their homes with the sound of the Dharma and lift the spirit of the indwelling place and all the surroundings. Particularly if we live alone, it is best to chant out loud to allow the throat to open and confirm ourselves in practice and in our own living space. Such a simple ceremony gives hope to the world and strengthens the spirit when we actually allow the music to penetrate the walls. Since The Heart Sutra should be chanted in every place of practice each day and, since each of our homes is a place of practice, we can begin with the Heart Sutra and follow with the Metta Sutta and a verse from Song of Ryokan.

I believe in a day of rest and silence every week. Living a Day of Reflection is a holy way to restore life. Such a day lifts us out of the banal, gives us a time in which we honor life and limb, when we offer our non-activity as a gesture, a moment to look and listen to our surroundings and our own interior longing. Thus, in the Song of Ryokan, there are only six poems. The seventh day is the Day of Reflection.

A dedication, recited following the chanting of the sutras, can be adapted to fit your surroundings or personal life. One should change it to fit the situation. For instance, perhaps you are concerned about family or loved ones. Perhaps you know someone who is dying and you wish to remember that person in ceremony. Their names can be recited to bring healing from one's own heart into the situation.

Ceremony to Honor Ryokan

Heart of Great Perfect Wisdom Sutra

Avalokiteshvara Bodhisattva, when deeply practicing Prajna Paramita, clearly saw that all five aggregates are Empty and thus relieved all suffering. Shariputra, form does not differ from Emptiness, Emptiness does not differ from form. Form itself is Emptiness, Emptiness itself form. Sensations, perceptions, formations, and consciousness are also like this. Shariputra, all Dharmas are marked by Emptiness; they neither arise nor cease, are neither defiled nor pure, neither increase nor decrease. Therefore, given Emptiness, there is no form, no sensation, no perception, no formation, no consciousness; no eyes, no ears, no nose, no tongue, no body, no mind; no sight, no sound, no smell, no taste, no touch, no object of mind; no realm of sight...no realm of mind-consciousness. There is neither ignorance nor extinction of ignorance...neither old age and death, nor extinction of old age and death; no suffering, no cause, no cessation, no path; no knowledge, and no attainment. With nothing to attain, a Bodhisattva relies on Prajna Paramita and thus the mind is without hindrance. Without hindrance, there is no fear. Far beyond all inverted views, one realizes nirvana. All Buddhas of past, present, and future rely on Prajna Paramita and thereby attain unsurpassed, complete, perfect enlightenment. Therefore, know the Prajna Paramita as the great miraculous mantra, the great bright mantra, the supreme mantra, the incomparable mantra, which removes all suffering and is true, not false. Therefore we proclaim the Prajna Paramita mantra, the mantra that says: "Gate, Gate, Paragate, Parasamgate! Bodhi! Svaha!"

Metta Sutta—Lovingkindness Sutra

This is what should be accomplished by the one who is wise
Who seeks the good and has obtained peace.
Let one be strenuous, upright and sincere,
without pride, easily contented and joyous.
Let one not be submerged by the things of the world.
Let one not take upon one's self the burden of riches.
Let one's senses be controlled.
Let one be wise but not puffed up.
And let one not desire great possessions even for one's family.
Let one do nothing that is mean or that the wise would reprove.
May all beings be happy.
May they be joyous and live in safety—all living beings
whether weak or strong, in high or middle
or low realms of existence, small or great,
visible or invisible, near or far, born or to be born.
May all beings be happy.
Let no one deceive another nor despise any being in any state.
Let none by anger or hatred wish harm to another,
even as a mother at the risk of her life
watches over and protects her only child.
So with a boundless mind should one cherish all living things
Suffusing love over the entire world.
Above, below and all around without limit.
So let one cultivate an infinite goodwill toward the whole world.
Standing or walking, sitting or lying down,
during all one's waking hours,
let one practice the way with gratitude,
not holding to fixed views,
Endowed with insight, freed from sense appetites.
One who achieves the way
will be freed from the duality of birth and death.

Song Of Ryokan

I

Early, on August the first,
I set out to beg in a city.
Silver clouds sail with me.
Golden winds ring my bells.
At dawn I see the thousand gates and doors thrown open.
At noon I feed my eyes with cool bamboo and basho tree.
East or west, I will not pass a single house unvisited,
Not even the slimy haunts of drunkards and fishmongers.
Straight glances of honest eyes break a pile of swords.
Strides of steady feet scorn the heat of boiling water.
Long ago the Prince of Pure Eating preached how to beg,
And the Beggar of Beggars truly acted out his teaching.
Since then it is two thousand, seven hundred years and more.
Yet am I no less a faithful pupil of the First Teacher.
Therefore I beg, a bowl in my hands, a gown on my back.
Have you not read or heard
Of that noble one of high repute, who solemnly decreed,
Equal in eating, equal under the divine law we must be.
Look out, everyone lest you should run loose unawares.
Who stands secure against the lapse of countless years?

II

Words come sweeping out of your mouth, when your lips move,
Your arms are slow to act, be you anxious to use them well.
You often try to cover up with your ready-to-flow speeches
What your lazy arms have not quite succeeded in performing.
The harder you try to polish, the more you spoil your work.
The more words you pour out, the greater evils you provoke.
Let us not commit such folly as to flood the fire with oil,
To cool it down for a moment, knowing it will soon explode.

Do not drive after this or that thing in your mad pursuit.
Lock up your lips in deep reticence to do your daily work.
Never fill your mouth till hunger revolts in your stomach,
Nor rattle your teeth until you are fully awake and aware.
Ever since I learned what I know about the life of Hakuyu,
I have some means at least to sustain myself in the world.
Master your breath, so you may be tense with inner spirit.
No ills, then, can break into your heart from the outside.

III

True, all the seasons have moonlit nights,
But here's the best night to see the moon.
The hills never so aloft, the streams never so clear,
In the infinite blue of autumn sky flies a disk of light.
Neither light nor gloom is graced with a life of its own.
The moon and the earth are one, and myself one with them.
The boundless sky above, and autumn chill on my skin,
I stroll about low hills, leaning upon my priceless cane.
Quiet night has held firm the flitting dust of the world.
The bright moon alone pours streams of rays all about me.
I mind it not if another like-minded is also admiring it,
Or if the moon deigns to look on others as well as on me.
Each year as autumn comes, the moon will shine as before,
And the world will watch it, will face it, till eternity.
Sermons at Mount Ryozen, lectures in the Vale of Sokei,
Were teachings so precious, the audience needed the moon.
My meditation under the moon lasts till the ripest night.
The stream has hushed its cry, dew lies thick everywhere.
Who, among the moon-viewers tonight, will have the prize?
Who will reflect the purest moon in the lake of his mind?
Surely you all know of that riverside moon viewing of long ago,
When Fugan alone, the rest lagging, ran beyond the flesh,
And of Yakkyo who, moon-inspired, cracked a laugh on a hilltop?
Their reputation rose high, when the feats were reported,
But over a thousand years intervene between now and then.
People have watched for naught the vicissitudes of the moon.
I am, nonetheless, swayed in my thoughts by the ancients.
Tonight, I keep a bright vigil, my robes soaked in tears.

IV

It once grew in the heavenly country far away in the west,
No one knows how many years since its coming to the world.
Its white petals are wrapped in a profusion of shiny dews.
Its rare-green leaves spread everywhere in the round lake.
Chaste is its scent wafted over the fence by a quiet wind.
Arrestingly calm, its whole poise as it rises above water.
The sun has already hid itself behind the hills before me
But I cannot move a step for the charm of the lotus plant.

Now I sing the glory of the bamboo trees around my house.
Several thousands stand together, forming a placid shade.
Young shoots run wild, blocking the roads here and there.
Old branches stretch all the way, cutting across the sky.
Frosty winters have armed them with a spiritual strength.
Rising mists wrap them with the veil of profound mystery.
In their healthy beauty they even rank with pine and oak,
Although they do not vie in grandeur with peach and plum.
Their trunks are upright and their knots are far between.
Their hearts are void of stuffing and their roots sturdy.
Bamboo trees, I admire you for your honesty and strength.
Be my friends, and stand about my retreat until eternity.

V

Ancient sages left their works behind, not to let us know
About themselves, but to help us understand our own stamp.
Had we wisdom deep enough to know ourselves, single-handed,
No benefits would result from the works of ancient saints.
A wise person learns the mystery of existence in a flash
And climbs in a leap beyond the world of hollow phenomena,
Whereas a foolish person holds willfully to facts and details.,
To drown in subtle differences of words and lines,
And being envious of others in their supreme achievements,
Wastes the mind night and day in efforts to exceed.
Truth, if you cleave to it as truth, turns into falsehood.
Falsehood, when you see it as such, becomes at once truth.
Truth and falsehood are the mated edges of a double sword.
None alive can separate with certainty one from the other.
Alas, too many people drift with the skiff to fathom the sea.
From time immemorial they are causes of endless deception.
Sweet saintliness is to be sought as a work of your heart.
The rightful path lies not amid things of constant change.
This plainest truth must be implanted time and time again,
Lest you should fall a witless victim to deceiving voices.
If you turn your shafts northward, hoping to travel south,
Alas, how can you ever arrive at your desired destination?

VI

In its innocence, the heart is like water pure and bright.
Boundless, it presents itself to the sight of its beholder.
Should a proud desire rise, however, to disturb its peace,
Millions of wicked thoughts and pictures will bog it down.
If you take these fancies to be real enough to engage you,
You will be led farther and farther away from tranquility.
How sore it is to see a person crazed about earthly thoughts,
A heart bound closely by the cords of the ten temptations.
To hear the words of truth, you must wash your ears clean.
You will not, otherwise, stand true to what you will hear.
You will ask what it is I mean by washing your ears clean.
It means to rid yourself of all you have heard beforehand.
If only one word of your previous learning remains within,
You will fail to embrace the words when they come to you.
Resembling what you know, a plain lie may seem acceptable,
And a simple truth, strange to your ears, may sound false.
How often, alas, we have our judgments made in our hearts,
When truth lies outside, in a place beyond our conception.
Let us not commit such folly as to steep a stone in water,
To hide it for a moment knowing it will show in due time.

Dedication

Our words ring out through space beyond the stars, their virtue and compassion echo back from all the many beings. We dedicate our reciting of Heart of Great Perfect Wisdom Sutra, Metta Sutta, and Song of Ryokan to:

The Ancient Seven Buddhas and all teachers, past, present, and future.

And for the enlightenment of bushes and grasses and the many beings of the world, for the renewal of Buddha mind in fields and forests, homes and streets, throughout the world, in grateful thanks to all our many guides along the ancient way, and in particular gratitude to all,

(Here, if you wish, you can recite the names of personal family members, friends, or those whom you wish to reach out to or to send healing or protection, or those who have died.)

whose practice has reflected the light of the morning star shining forth in perfect harmony.

All Buddhas throughout space and time,
All beings, bodhisattvas, mahasattvas,
Wisdom beyond wisdom.
The Maha Prajna Paramita.

Credits

Frontispiece: Gogo-an in snow at Olympia Zen Center. Photo: Eido Frances Carney, hereafter EFC

Page 1: On the grounds at Olympia Zen Center. Photo: EFC

Page 11: A portion of the main gate at Entusji temple. Photo: EFC

Page 29: Vast Cliff Torii Gate built by Randal Johnson, with Gogo-an in the distance at Olympia Zen Center. Photo: EFC

Page 45: Bamboo grove at Shorinji temple. Photo: Fletcher Ward, hereafter FW

Page 61: Statue of Ryokan near his gravesite at Shimazaki. Photo: FW

Page 81: View of Gogo-an on Mount Kugami, Japan. Photo: FW

Page 97: Ryokan's authentic begging bowl from the Ryokan Memorial Hall in Izumozaki. Photo: FW

Page 113: Stained glass window at the Ryokan Memorial Hall depicting some of the various bouncing balls that Ryokan played with. The craft of making these balls from wound yarn is a specialty of the people from Ryokan Country. Photo: FW

Page 125: From inside Gogo-an at Olympia Zen Center. Photo: EFC

Page 139: "Katsu" by Shoen Tokunaga Sensei. "Katsu" is a kind of declarative shout by a Zen master to cut through delusion and express this very moment as Awakened.

Page 151: Calligraphy and painting of Ryokan by Niho Tetsumei Roshi. The poem says: "I played with village children this long spring day, till gloom buried us at length."

Page 163: Woodcut of Ryokan by Shigeomi Ogura. A large print of the woodcut hangs in the residence at Olympia Zen Center.

Page 177: Calligraphy by Ryokan which says, "Above the Heavens, Great Wind." Ryokan came upon a child who was crying because her kite had broken. Ryokan fixed the kite for her then wrote the calligraphy on the kite and helped her send it aloft. "Above the Heavens, Great Wind" is said to have become Ryokan's life motto.

Page 193: Statue of Ryokan and Teishin at the Museum in Shimazaki. Photo: FW

Page 209: Painting of an Enso, a Zen circle, by EFC.

Page 221: Statue of Ryokan as a young monk in training outside the Zendo at Entsuji temple in Tamashima. Photo: FW

Page 225: Gogo-an at Olympia Zen Center. Photo by EFC.

Works Used In This Writing

All poems are by Ryokan unless otherwise noted and are translated by Nobuyuki Yuasa.

"Art of Begging," chapter seven, was previously published in two different versions as: "Zen and the Art of Begging: Practicing Takuhatsu in America." *Tricycle Magazine*, Fall, 1998, and translated into Japanese in *The Journal of Ryokan* by the Ryokan Society of Japan, 2000.

"At the Beatification of Mother Teresa." Vatican, Oct 13, 2003. CatholicWorldNews.com

Bays, Jan Chozen. *Jizo Bodhisattva, Modern Healing and Traditional Buddhist Practice*. Boston: Tuttle, 2002. 211.

Eihei Dogen. *Shobogenzo*. Trans. Hubert Nearman. Mt. Shasta: Shasta Abbey Press, 2007.

Johnson, Allan G. *Privilege, Power and Difference*. New Jersey: McGraw-Hill, 2005.

Johnson, Allan G. *The Gender Knot*. Philadelphia: Temple University Press, 2005.

Katagiri, Dainin. *Returning to Silence*. Boston: Shambhala, 1988. 172.

Rowell, Andy. "Remember Saro-Wiwa." SpinWatch.org. March, 17, 2005.

Ryokan. *Great Fool, Zen Master Ryokan*. Trans. Ryuichi Abe and Peter Haskel. Honolulu: University of Hawaii Press, 1996.

Ryokan. *The Zen Poems of Ryokan*. Trans. Nobuyuki Yuasa. Princeton: Princeton University Press, 1981.

Author Biography

Eido Frances Carney is the founder and guiding teacher of Olympia Zen Center in Olympia, Washington. She received Dharma Transmission from Niho Tetsumei Roshi of Entsuji temple in Kurashiki, Japan, after training at Shoboji temple in Iwate Prefecture. As Entsuji is Ryokan's training temple, the lineage takes a particular interest in and promotes the teachings of Ryokan. Eido taught as adjunct faculty in Humanities at South Puget Sound Community College for ten years and is former president of the national Soto Zen Buddhist Association. She is a published poet and exhibited painter. She is editor of *Receiving the Marrow: Teachings on Dogen by Soto Zen Women Priests*, published in 2012.

Translator Biography

Nobuyuki Yuasa retired as professor of English at Hiroshima University in 1995 and then taught at Baiko Women's University in Shimonoseki until his second retirement. He is an eminent translator of haiku poetry and literature. Among his many publications are *The Zen Poems of Ryokan*; the Basho Penguin Classic *Narrow Road to the Deep North and Other Travel Sketches*; and *The Year of My Life: A Translation of Issa's Oragu Haru*. He is a recipient of the Translators' Association of Japan Prize for his work on the poetry of John Donne. He lives in Tokyo and writes poetry.